CHRISTIANITY AND INCEST

THE AUTHORS

Annie Imbens-Fransen is founder of the foundation for Pastoral Care for Women, which provides pastoral counseling for psychologically, physically, and sexually abused women. She also trains counselors, ministers, priests and teachers. She is a member of the European Society of Women in Theological Research and author of such books as *Thecla and the Church* (1984), *It's better (not) to talk about it* (1987), *Hold not thy peace, my brother* (1991). Her new book *God in women's lives* is scheduled for publication in 1992. She was raised a Catholic and later studied theology at the Theological Institute of Tilburg. Gardening is her greatest joy.

Ineke Jonker-de Putter is a therapist-counselor specialising in sexual abuse of children. She is author of *Incest, een Stem en een Aanklacht* (1988) and *Als je kind misbruikt is* (1992). She was raised a Protestant and later studied history and cultural anthropology at the University of Leiden.

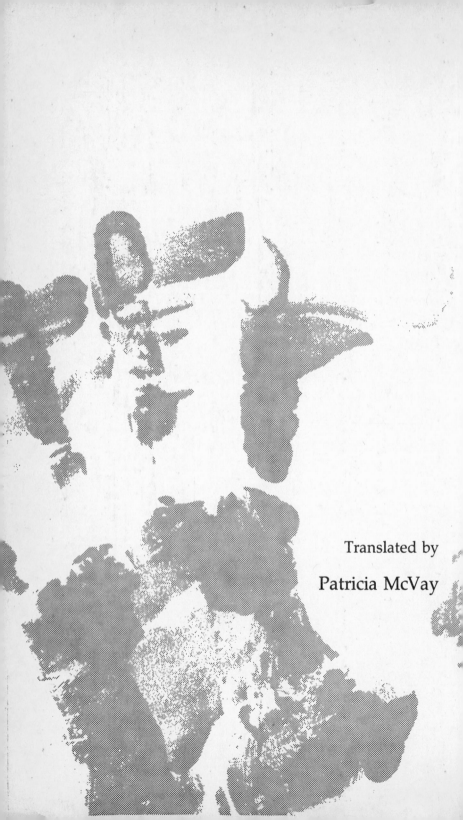

Translated by

Patricia McVay

CHRISTIANITY

AND

INCEST

Annie Imbens

and

Ineke Jonker

BURNS & OATES

First published in Great Britain 1992
Burns & Oates
Wellwood, North Farm Road,
Tunbridge Wells, Kent TN2 3DR

This book is a translation of *Godsdienst en incest: De
Horstink i.s.m. de Vereniging tegen Seksuele
Kindermishandeling binnen het Gezin* by Annie Imbens and
Ineke Jonker. Copyright © 1985 J. E. L. Imbens-Fransen
and C. K. Jonker-de Putter. Dutch edition originally
published by De Horstink, Postbus 400, 3800 AK
Amersfoort in cooperation with the Association against
Child Sexual Abuse within the Family. Third Dutch
edition 1991 published by Uitgeverij An Dekker,
Overtoom 270, 1054 JB Amsterdam.

English translation copyright © 1991 Foundation for
Pastoral Care for Women (Stichting Vrouw en
Pastoraat), Eindhoven.

The English translation of this book was funded by a
grant from the Prince Bernhard Trust to the Foundation
for Pastoral Care for Women.

Interior design: McCormick Creative

ISBN: 0 86012 198-4

Composition by Genesis Typesetting, Rochester, Kent
Printed in Finland by Werner Soderstrom Oy

"My father had very 'Christian' ideas about women. He thought women should be submissive, obedient, servile."

From chapter 1

Contents

Foreword

Until recently, child sexual abuse within the family seemed nonexistent. Since November 1981, however, abused women and girls in the Netherlands have been breaking the taboo on speaking out on incest. By going public, they have made incest visible: one by one, myths have been dismantled. In doing so, these women have raised serious questions about male codes and behavioral systems. In their view, incest is essentially structural and relational sexual violence committed by men against girls.

This book contributes to our insight by exposing one of the conditions under which the abuse of girls has been able to occur for hundreds of years. This study shows that religion can be a factor that is conducive to incest and compounds trauma. This insight is essential to every individual who is in some way involved with children or the church.

Many women who have been raised as Christians, whether they were sexually abused as children or not, will recognize themselves in this book. It examines extreme, personal experiences of oppression and denial, clearly showing how the patriarchal view and experience of Christianity work. The authors show that church authorities occupy a crucial position with regard to child sexual abuse in two ways: as the protector of male codes and as the perpetuator of the traditional family mentality. Incestuous acts in Christian families put this family mentality, in which the male is regarded as the authority inside as well as outside the family, in a disturbing perspective. Everything that falls outside the male code or structure means punishment, damnation, guilt, and negation for the girl. Biblical passages offer many boys and men the opportunity first to enfeeble the girl, then to rape her, and finally to force her into silence.

Sexual exploitation is supposedly part of human 'nature'. Church ideology appeals to these "natural" characteristics and images that are stimulated by girls and boys from a young age, and thus perpetuates a religious legitimacy of incest. The authors rightly question these views, which many hold to be self-evident.

Sexual abuse of girls can be prevented only by exposing the causes so that they are visible to everyone. For this reason, all of us must summon the courage to recognize how Christian texts are interpreted and used: one gender is expected to subject itself to the authority (the will) of the other; men determine how women should be, and women derive their right to exist from men. This ideology is not only oppressive to women who have experienced incest but also to all women. The authors show how closely related this ideology is to the reigning church and secular "old-boy" mentality that direct the abusers' thinking and acts. This study clearly shows how sexual abuse is the direct result of the imbalance of gender power. Age difference is a less decisive factor than the difference in gender.

If those who commit incest act *im*morally, then church authorities react *a*morally when they pass judgment on or withhold compassion from these abused children. Their sympathy frequently consists in denying and/or minimizing the child's feelings and experiences. This denial can be rooted in insecurity, originating from a lack of adequate information about incestuous abuse: "There's no such thing as traumatic incest". The sensitivity of these authorities, through either their own denial or powerlessness, thus offers as few guarantees as their religious reliability when it comes to understanding abused girls and women.

The analyses of the interviews are conducted with great care and respect, toward the women interviewed and churches in general. The authors demonstrate an unfailing and flawless sense of the injustice done to women through the influences of religious ideologies and upbringing. They leave it to the reader to form her or his own judgement.

Ineke Jonker and Annie Imbens demonstrate their respect for the women interviewed in their repeated appeal to the "positive energy or strength" in each of these women. More than ever before, norms and values propagated by the church are sadly outdated and visibly intolerant to women. The women interviewed in this study no longer allow these norms to be forced upon them. Their message to society is that the limit of power lies in the respect for personal integrity and physical inviolability of men as well as women. They rediscover their strength from within. They learn to believe in themselves first. The authority of the patriarchal god is crumbling.

M. J. Nottet and M. Punter
The Association against Child Sexual Abuse within the Family

In the last twenty years, women in our society have been speaking out more frequently on the subject of their sexuality. This has had a wide-ranging impact on society. Scholarship has also been affected. Current research on the behavior and experiences of men and women differs from the research that was planned and conducted before 1960, and the research results are different as well. Psychologists, doctors, and other caring services professionals have had to retrain themselves in this area. Jurisprudence in this area has also been deeply influenced. The most significant effect, however, is that more and more women have become aware of their right to their own sexuality—and to their own expression of that sexuality.

As a result, a group of women in our society has become more deeply aware of the crime that has been committed against them: Those women for whom the family was not a safe harbor but a school of hard knocks, robbing them of their carefree childhood, their assertiveness, their right to their own body and sexuality, and their right to stand up for themselves.

This book shows every aspect of incest in chilling detail: how these women had to function as adults while they were still children, had to shoulder the guilt feelings for others, and be responsible for the sexuality of men in their families or immediate surroundings who should have been protecting *them*. But more important, this study examines how incest relates to views on male and female roles within the traditional family in our society as well as its correlation to how religion was experienced and practiced in these families.

For these incest survivors, the prevailing views on women in our Christian churches have deepened their despair and guilt rather than providing the safe shelter that these people need in their craving for security and acceptance.

Moreover a good deal of tension has often existed between what the Christian churches teach and experiencing one's own sexuality. As a result, the general humanity of Christian faith has been greatly sacrificed; women are regarded more as the bearers of evil than as human beings with full rights to a Christian life.

Women trying to solve this dilemma can find new perspectives in this book: a new existence as a whole human being with self-esteem as a woman and as a person. It also gives a new perspective to men who have been responsible for conducting an incestuous relationship. In this book, they can understand the reasons that prevent them from shifting this responsibility onto the shoulders of these young children—their daughters, sisters, grandchildren, nieces—whom they have made their accomplices. (It is obvious that these men were not comfortable with sexuality either, but that is the subject for another book.) As a group and as individuals, they have always been more capable of serving their own interests (and often still are) than those of their victims.

I feel very good about this book, about the strong women who speak out in it. I hope their voices will be heard.

Dr Gerda van Dijk
Sexologist, Women's Clinic, University Hospital of Leiden

Children are gullible because they are trusting, and they easily accept stories about the real world as "the truth." This also applies to religious stories and Bible passages, and to the images of good and evil that they contain. Therefore, it is only logical that this should apply to the stories and justifications that some children are told about the sexual abuse they experience within their family.

Yet, this is a very confusing and extremely damaging experience for girls: On the one hand, the reality of incest, and, on the other, the daily admonition that sexuality or "unchastity" is bad and sinful, and that women are at fault because they are temptresses and have loose morals. There is so much fear, guilt and isolation involved that incest can affect girls who experience it in childhood for the rest of their lives.

This book is about these experiences, about the confusion they cause. The study is an initial—and to my knowledge unique—attempt to examine and chart the effect of a religious upbringing on incest survivors' experiences, the impact of those experiences, and their attempts to work through them. The authors have not attempted to determine whether or not incest occurs more frequently in religious families than in other families. Nor has an attempt been made to conduct a representative survey. The study was intended to show how a religious upbringing can affect a traumatic experience such as sexual abuse within the family. The authors show this through interviews with women who were willing to break their silence about their incest experiences. They broke two taboos: first, the taboo on speaking out about incest, and second, the taboo on speaking out about religious traumas. This last taboo is a modern-day phenomenon: In much of Western society today, people are either passive Christians, or they shrug their shoulders when it comes to religion. Discussion of religious traumas outside the church is highly unusual.

Research is not really the right word for this exploratory study of nineteen women. This study is more than that. It's an indictment of sexism in the church, of the images of womanhood—subservient, sinful, and powerless—in the Bible, and of a sadistic god who lets children drift helplessly in their desolation and requires them to forgive their tormenters. It is also an indictment of the fathers, brothers, grandfathers, and uncles who, with a prayerbook or collection plate in one hand, molest their daughters, sisters, granddaughters, and nieces with the other. The authors have conducted this study from a power-dynamics perspective. They view the sexual abuse of girls within families as the ultimate consequence of what they term the "patriarchal mentality" and "patriarchal relationships" in Christianity. They also analyze the authoritarian relationships in the families of these women in the same terms. In this analysis, mothers who have offered their daughters no protection or support are not always completely absolved of blame.

This book has been written with great commitment—sometimes with bitterness and rage about the lies and torment within the family, the religious traumas these women have undergone, and women's place in the church; sometimes, too, with hope and anticipation of a possible liberation in experiencing faith. This may seem a little strange to someone without a religious upbringing: it is as if the authors do not want to break with their faith, as if they do not want to live without the illusion of a "liberating religion," as if there must be a Father, a good Father or Mother, who takes care of us in our imagination. But for someone with a religious background, this book is a first, unpleasant confrontation with a huge pile of "dirty linen," a terrible suffering long silenced. I hope that this confrontation with these experiences of humiliation, torment, and misrepresentation is not so painful for the reader that she or he will prefer to repress or shrug such experiences off; it is tempting to do so by minimizing their seriousness or, for example,

by disqualifying the authors as bearers of this painful news. From
the interviews, we can see just how crucial talking about the
influence of a religious upbringing is to working through traumatic
childhood experiences. The authors conclude with helpful advice
to priests and ministers, and in my view to other caring services
professionals outside the church, on helping women deal with
these issues.

Nel Draijer
Clinical Psychologist

Authors' Prefaces

Since I began talking about my own sexual abuse with other abused women from the Association against Child Sexual Abuse within the Family in 1982, it has gradually become clearer to me that I am not only tormented about the abuse itself, but also about my religious feelings, which were violated in a brutal and systematic way. For years, my mother's father, who was also my rapist, regularly told me that women are unclean, evil, sinners, sly, and devious creatures who are constantly trying to rob men of their strength. These "lessons" were illustrated with stories from the Bible: Potiphar's wife, Isaac's wife, Samson's wife, not to mention Eve. Even Rachel deceived God and Jacob with the image of an idol god under her unclean saddle. Jesus had a collection of whores thronged around him. When women were not evil, they were described as weak, crying, stupid, or unbelieving. Sin, impurity, and weakness were the characteristics of their gender. The passage about the great whore Babylon (Revelation 17) echoed inside me, on and on. The city of Babylon, which is the enemy of Israel, is compared to a woman with whom the kings of the earth have committed fornication. She is called the mother of harlots and abominations of the earth. In these sentences from the last book of the Bible, hatred and contempt toward women reaches its climax. As a young girl, I was confused by the discrepancies between these words and the story of King David when he was old and lying on his deathbed. His servants searched for a young girl, a virgin, to warm his cold body and to lie with him. In this way, they hoped that he could stay alive a little longer (1 Kings 1). This girl was ruthlessly trained to be a whore of the same class as the whore Babylon, but the prostitute of only one king instead of many. Nothing is written of this child's feelings. In her best-case scenario, the servants deluded her into believing that this was a great honor, so that she was left with no way out of her revulsion and humiliation. Did King David not have enough (slave) women? Because the king is never reproached for what happened, male Christians have been able to justify themselves by using this precedent. They are free to accuse women of being the great

xiv

temptresses, likening them to the whore Babylon, the mother of harlots, because that comparison is part of the Word of God. Thus the Christian male has the authority of the Bible to support him when justifying his behavior toward women. Because of its inconsistencies, this ideology is an effective weapon in the hands of a powerful person. If theologians believe that humanity is inclined toward evil, why do they provide men and themselves with this book, which is accorded divine authority, although it is full of atrocity for women?

When I confronted theologians with these discrepancies, I was told that these stories were not meant that way, that the Bible had been explained incorrectly to me, or that I had taken the passages out of context. I should interpret them differently from the way they appeared in the Bible or were explained from the pulpit. I kept asking myself why God's Word requires such a complicated explanation, when Jesus himself said that children can understand it. Is that perhaps the idea—to confuse children so that big boys and men can do with them what they choose? I became aware that the church can never be held responsible for all the pain it has caused. In practice, the Bible has been used to keep women and girls under men's collective thumb: In theory, this was never the intention, but concepts such as forgiveness, loving one's neighbor, sacrifice, and martyrdom require deep ethical thought on a theological level. Children who have experienced incest have profited very little from this deep ethical thought. They sense acutely that someone who continues to humiliate and torment them, despite their tears and protests, does so deliberately. In my opinion, such a person does not have to be forgiven. Someone of good faith does everything possible to compensate for the damage he or she has done. A person is then free to forgive.

During this study, my question evolved into a demand, an indictment of so much theologically legitimated violence. In addition to the stories of the women interviewed in this study, I have conducted conversations in the last two years with over sixty women and children in my capacity as the provincial ombudswoman for the association. Many of these women and children came from religious backgrounds. Other women were not offended in their religious feelings, but were repressed by a secular ideology of servitude and self-sacrifice to men. The dominant group in society created the conditions enabling the sexual abuse of children and did not permit these children to express their feelings about what had happened to them. Because I was able to share my anger with other women and men, I was able to find room for myself. I no longer feel any aggression toward the church and its powerful men.

Ineke Jonker
Historian

Looking back on my experiences during this study, I realize that it took me a long time to work through my response to the first incest story that Joan told me three years ago. Through the conversations I have had with her in the past years, I was enabled to listen to and work through new stories. During these interviews, I was repeatedly shocked by the methods these male family members used to sexually abuse and to silence girls. The variations were endless. In the course of a conversation, one of the women would sometimes mention in passing that Father had also abused all of the other sisters in the family. It gradually began to sink in that sexual abuse does occur in each and every milieu: in Christian families but also in anti-religious families; in low-income as well as in high-income families. The way these girls were abused was repulsive. I often needed several days after an interview in order to work through what I had heard. I realized that the primary taboo is on talking about incest, not on committing it. The impact of a religious upbringing is much broader and much more serious than I had previously presumed. Their Christian upbringing made these girls easy prey. Offenders used Bible passages or church-authorized texts in order to be able to abuse girls and to keep them quiet about it. Mothers were powerless to do anything about it. They were subservient to their husbands in everything, as was and and still is requested of women marrying in Christian churches.

The most astounding realization is that these girls in Christian families have had experiences comparable to those undergone by people in concentration camps. The offenders were decent, well-functioning adults in the community, sometimes with highly respected professions. With the exception of one, all of the women interviewed have turned their backs on the church. The majority of the offenders, however, are still involved in the church. Half of them still occupy an official church position.

I am pleased to have been able to work on this study and to see its publication. The therapeutic effects of the interviews and follow-up sessions enabled me to maintain my commitment to the project. Making these experiences visible is an important step in the process of liberating women from their subservient position in the church and in society. Through listening to these women's gripping stories and watching how they wrestle with these experiences, I feel that I have been strengthened in my struggle against the patriarchal experience of Christianity. Moreover, I feel that this has confirmed me in my hope and my search for a way of keeping the faith that will liberate both men and women.

Annie Imbens
Theologian

We wish to thank:
— the women we interviewed for making their stories available to us, and for their assistance in the form of advice and critical questions;
— priests, ministers, professionals in the health and welfare sectors, police, and judicial authorities for their interest and stimulating questions;
— families and friends for their supportive and critical contributions;
— the Ministry of Welfare, Public Health, and Culture for funding the material costs of the study;
— the Committee on Projects in the Netherlands for providing initial funding to organize pastoral care.

The Authors

Preface to the English Edition *Christianity and Incest* would never have appeared in English, nor would it have had a third printing in the Netherlands, had it not been for the repeated encouragement of so many who believed in the book's importance to women. These responses enabled me to generate the energy and perseverance needed to effect publication of the English and new Dutch editions.

Sixty applications to domestic and foreign funding organizations, both religious and nonreligious, had to be made in order to secure funding for the English translation alone. Repeated attempts to explain the importance of this book for women were made to national and international religious organizations; despite my efforts and those of many of the people mentioned below, not one request for even partial funding was honored by a religious organization. In the end, the long quest to fund the English translation met with success just when every possibility seemed exhausted. It was the Prince Bernhard Trust, a nonreligious cultural funding organization, that finally provided the necessary funding.

During this long process, I was often reminded of Virginia Woolf's words on trying to set up a women's college (written in 1928), "That was the way it was done presumably sixty years ago, and it was a prodigious effort, and a great deal of time was spent on it. And it was only after a long struggle and with the utmost difficulty that they got thirty thousand pounds together." This still seems to be the case in 1991 (yet again sixty odd years later) as far as issues of importance to women are concerned.

The energy needed to generate this "prodigious effort" was provided first and foremost by the encouraging responses of incest survivors themselves. They said that they recognized themselves in this book and that it helped them to gain some insight into the problems resulting from their incest experiences and their Christian upbringing. It provided the impulse they needed to go into therapy, to enter into a dialogue with priests and ministers, and to confront these various counselors with their problems resulting from their religious upbringing and with sexism in the church today. The book helped these women to break the conspiracy of silence within their families and to confront the offenders with the damage they had done. They also took the book with them to doctors, ministers, priests, and "caring services professionals" (meaning all those who come in contact with incest survivors in a caring/helping capacity: counsellors, therapists, self-help groups, social workers, police, teachers, and so on). They advised these people to read the book, saying, "Would you please read this book? It says what I'm trying to say."

Many women from Christian backgrounds who had not experienced incest also gave encouraging responses. A number of these women had serious problems resulting from their religious upbringing and requested counseling to help them work through

those problems. Others recognized many details from their
upbringing and supplemented these with their own stories. All of
these women responded in the same way: "I never experienced
incest, but I certainly recognize a lot of my own upbringing in this
book." Through these responses, these women reconfirmed what I
had written in the introduction, "We see the sexual abuse of girls
within the family as the ultimate consequence of patriarchal
thinking, of patriarchal theology, and of the patriarchial experience
of Christianity. What these women have to say is therefore familiar
to many women and girls from a Christian background. However,
their extreme experiences enable them to put into words the
humiliation and denial of all women in Christian churches."

Women who are incest survivors as well as those who are not
said that it is nearly impossible to discuss their problems with their
Christian upbringing and Christian theology with the local (almost
exclusively male) ministers, priests, or counselors, therapists,
teachers, or social workers.

Despite slogans such as "Justice, Peace, and Integrity of
Creation" and the World Council of Churches' "Ecumenical
Decade of Churches in Solidarity with Women," and despite much
urging by women, churches in the Netherlands do not see the
need to take policy measures to bring about professional
counseling for women with religious problems by women trained
in this field. Many caring professionals and their organizations or
agencies do not see it as their responsibility to offer help where
religious problems are concerned. This is why it is difficult for
women to find good counseling to help them work through their
religious problems in combination with incest. This is the reason I
decided in 1986 to establish the Foundation for Pastoral Care for
Women. This foundation is partially and temporarily funded by
the City of Eindhoven in the Netherlands.

In addition to the encouragement from Christian women and
incest survivors who recognized themselves in this book, a good
deal of encouragement was provided by both women and men:
They gave suggestions; requested advice; provided names and
addresses of funding sources, publishers, and interested parties;
wrote letters of recommendation; and contacted publishers and
funding sources. The first of these was Georgie McLean of the
Women's Counseling Center in Eindhoven. There were the
women from the European Society of Women in Theological

Research, including: Professor Emeritus Catharina Halkes and Professor Mary Grey (both of the Catholic University of Nijmegen); Sarah Jane Boss (Anglican Seminary "St. Stephen's House," Oxford, England); Dagny Kaul (Institut Systematisk Teologi of Oslo, Norway); and Margaret Collier-Bendelow (theologian, France).

Others who offered their encouragement and assistance were: Gertie Bögels (neurologist and psychoanalyst, Nijmegen); Professor Etty Mulder (Faculty of Music, Catholic University of Nijmegen); Freek De Leeuw (Eindhoven city Deputy Mayor and Alderman of Education, Social Affairs and Health); Jan Van De Kamp (city of Eindhoven Public Health Services, and member of the Healthy Cities Project of the World Health Organization); Els Tiemeyer (Educational Institute for Health and Public Welfare, Eindhoven); Dr. Frans Lohman (Senior Clinical Psychologist, England); Sheila A. Redmond (Faculty of Theology, University of Ottawa, Canada).

There were the American women, including: Elisabeth Schüssler Fiorenza (author and Professor at Divinity School, Harvard University, Cambridge); Reverend Marie M. Fortune (author and Executive Director, Center for the Prevention of Sexual and Domestic Violence, Seattle); Rosemary Radford Ruether (author and Professor at Harvard University, Cambridge and Yale University); and Isabel Carter Heyward (author and Professor at Episcopal Divinity School, Cambridge).

There were many more who, often at the request of others, offered their assistance in order to secure publication of the third Dutch edition and the English edition.

I would also like to thank An Dekker, publisher in the Netherlands, for her efforts in securing publication in English, as well as Fortress Press for agreeing to publish *Christianity and Incest* in the United States.

I would like to express my gratitude to the Prince Bernhard Trust (Prins Bernhard Fonds, Cultuurfonds voor Nederland) and the members of its Advisory Board for recognizing the importance of *Christianity and Incest* to women when many religious (and other) funding organizations were unwilling to do so, and for providing full funding for its translation into English.

In addition to thanking all of those mentioned above and those whose names have not been mentioned, I would especially like to express my gratitude to the translator, Patricia McVay. She has translated this book with great commitment and expertise, with much patience and care; I wish to thank her, too, for her extensive efforts to make the English translation and publication of this book possible.

Annie Imbens

Translator's Notes

Except where otherwise indicated, the Bible translation used in translating *Christianity and Incest* into English is the Authorized (King James) Version.[1] The King James Version best meets the criteria used in selecting the Bible version for this translation. The first of these criteria was that the language of the English Bible should approximate that of the Bibles that were read during childhood in the churches and families of the incest survivors interviewed in this book. Like the King James Version, these Bibles use(d) the Dutch equivalents of thou, thee, thy, thine, and other archaic language, contributing to the mystique and power (as this language is only half understood by children) of the Word of God. This criterion eliminates modern versions such as the New Revised Standard Version (1989), the Revised Standard Version (Old Testament 1952, New Testament 1946 and 1971), and The Jerusalem Bible (1966–1968). Another criterion was that the English language Bible reflect the collective European cultural heritage of which the Netherlands is a part; here, again, the English King James Version is therefore preferred over versions such as the American Standard Version (1901) or the Revised Standard Version, both American versions of the English Revised Version (1881–1885). The final criterion was the Bible version's usage and availability: How long has the Bible version been in use? How widely has it been used? Has it been widely available? Here, too, the Protestant King James Version must be preferred over other versions such as the English Revised Version and Catholic translations (including the Douay Version for reasons of general use and availability involving the Index Librorum Prohibitorum and the Catholic Church's traditional discouragement of Bible reading by the laity, which are too lengthy to explore here). As the

---

1. *The Authorized (King James) Version of the Holy Bible* (London: Trinitarian Bible Society, 1611). Other translations consulted include: The Rev. John Brown, *The Holy Bible with Analysis, Explanatory Notes, Evangelical Reflections, Etc.* (East Lothian, Scotland: Brightly and Childs, 1813); *The Jerusalem Bible* (New York: Doubleday, 1971); *New Revised Standard Version Bible* (New York: Oxford University Press, 1989); and *The Revised Standard Version of the Holy Bible* (New York: Collins, 1971).

Preface to the Revised Standard Version states: "The King James Version (1611) had to compete with the Geneva Bible (1560) in popular use; but in the end it prevailed, and for more than two and a half centuries no other authorized translation of the Bible into English was made. The King James Version became the 'Authorized Version' of the English-speaking peoples".

I am indebted to each of those who contributed to this translation by providing assistance in her or his particular field of expertise; to the Prince Bernhard Trust for funding the translation; and to Annie Imbens for her tireless support in the neverending search for the right word.

Patricia McVay

Introduction: Giving Voice to Family Secrets

THIS STUDY WAS INITIATED by Ineke Jonker of the Association against Child Sexual Abuse within the Family in the Netherlands. In August of 1983, she issued an invitation to feminist theologians to join her in examining the theological aspects of sexual abuse experienced within the family, and in formulating questions on this subject directed at Christian churches.

Searching for Answers The aim of the study is to formulate questions directed at Christian churches, so that their teachings may offer a liberating perspective to women and children as well as men. We decided not to include these aspects in the study: Does child sexual abuse occur more frequently in Christian milieus than in other milieus? Does child sexual abuse occur more frequently in dogmatic Christian milieus than in moderate or liberal Christian milieus? A sociological and quantitative study is needed to examine these questions. The results of such a study would not provide material suitable to the objective of this study: to call on Christian churches to provide a liturgy and an approach to Christianity aimed at liberating women and children. Moreover, we must realize that, until very recently, the Dutch population was predominantly Christian.

In this study we have concentrated solely on sexually abused girls. The number of registered cases involving sexually abused boys is currently rising. During a conversation, one of these boys indicated that he recognized his own Christian experience in the statements the women in this book have made on God and forgiveness. We hope that, as a result of this study, others will be motivated to conduct a similar study with sexually abused men.

We searched for answers to two questions: 1 How can the sexual abuse of girls occur in Christian families? and 2 What is the impact of the religious upbringing in the family, in school and in the church on these sexually abused girls? We expected our findings to provide us with the necessary material to approach the churches.

As far as we have been able to ascertain, this study is the first attempt to acquire insight into the relationship between religion and incest; it must be seen as an exploratory study of the subject matter.

We believe that women who have been sexually abused in childhood are the obvious persons to answer our questions. We allowed only women over twenty to take part in this study. We did not want to allow children to participate because we did not know the potential effects of the study on the participants. Therefore, it is incorrect to conclude from this study that traumas no longer occur as a result of a religious upbringing and sexual abuse. Sexual abuse of girls still occurs with alarming frequency. Estimates in the Netherlands are between 5 percent and 15 percent for girls and about 1 percent for boys.[1]

---

1. N. Draijer, "Seksuele Kontakten tussen Kinderen en volwassenen of ouderen" [Sexual Contacts between Children and Adults or Elders], in *Seksueel geweld en heteroseksualiteit: Ontwikkelingen in onderzoek sinds 1968* [Sexual Violence and Heterosexuality: Research Developments since 1968] (The Hague: Ministry for Social Affairs and Employment, 1984).

In 1988, the results were published of a "national study on the magnitude, nature, family backgrounds, and emotional, psychological, and psychosomatic impact" of the sexual abuse of girls by relatives, in N. Draijer, *Seksueel misbruik van meisjes door verwanten: Een landelijk onderzoek naar de omvang, de aard, de gezinsachtergronden, de emotionele betekenis en de psychische en psychosomatische gevolgen* [Sexual Abuse of Girls by Relatives: A National Study of the Magnitude, Nature, Family Backgrounds, and Emotional, Psychological, and Psychosomatic Impact] (The Hague: Ministerie van Sociale Zaken en Werkgelegenheid, Ministry for Social Affairs and Employment, 1988). This representative study in which 1,054 women between twenty and forty years of age were interviewed yielded these findings:

* One hundred sixty four women (15.6 percent) experienced sexual abuse by a relative (father, stepfather, foster father, brother, uncle, grandfather, or cousin) prior to their sixteenth birthdays. This is one in six or seven women of those interviewed in the study. Nearly half of these (one in fifteen women) experienced a serious and traumatizing form of sexual abuse.
* Seventy four women (7 percent of the total number of women interviewed and 45.1 percent of the incest survivors) were sexually abused by more than one person prior to their sixteenth birthdays.
* Three hundred fifty eight women (34 percent) were sexually abused within the family or by someone outside the family prior to their sixteenth birthdays.

Religious upbringing, as described in this book, will remain relevant as long as the patriarchal experience of Christianity is still considered "traditional" or "normal" by many churches.

We have no desire to seek answers to Ineke Jonker's questions from behind a desk through an examination of literature and theories. We want to show, through actual life stories, the impact a religious upbringing has on women who were sexually abused during childhood, and how this upbringing and abuse have influenced their later lives. These women's stories serve as the basis for the study and are used to illustrate the analyses and theories we want to formulate. The interviews we conducted were partially structured and partially open in order to allow the women to use their own words in relating their experiences. In order to achieve this combination, we drew up an interview guide with reference points. In this way, the interviews were given a certain amount of structure and we were able to ensure that all of the aspects we considered important were examined. We hope that these stories are so abundantly clear that the churches, which are the ultimate objective in this study, will take to heart the questions posed in the Epilogue and closely examine the issues at hand.

Incest Defined The full title of the study reads: *Study of the correlation between a religious upbringing and the sexual abuse of girls within Christian (extended) families.* Because this title is too long for the title of a book, it has been shortened to *Christianity and Incest.* When we use the word incest, we are not referring to voluntary contact between adult family members (blood relatives) or sexual relations between children in a(n) (extended) family which occur with mutual consent. We use the word "incest" to refer to sexual abuse of children within the (extended) family. The term "sexual

Regarding statistics on violence against women in the United States today, the Reverend Marie Fortune, Executive Director, Center for the Prevention of Sexual and Domestic Violence, Seattle, has observed ("Did You Know That . . ." [pamphlet]) the following:

* One in six women is raped in her lifetime
* One in two women is battered within her family
* One in three female children is sexually abused before reaching eighteen years of age
* One in seven women is raped by her husband

abuse within the (extended) family" refers to sexual contacts initiated by adults (father, stepfather, uncle, grandfather, a friend of the family, older brother), in which the wishes and feelings of the child with whom the acts are committed are not taken into account.

One of the myths surrounding incest is that the children themselves want it and provoke it, because they long for sexual contact with adults. We have observed, however, that the sexual contacts adults initiate with children have a confusing and destructive effect on children. Children do have a need for warmth and tenderness. Adults who fulfill this need and progress to sexual contact, however, exceed the boundary between tenderness and sexuality for their own needs and at their own initiative. They have the power or the authority over children to force sexuality on them. In sexual abuse, the issue is the power inequality between the initiator and the one who is abused. The power discrepancy is based on the differences in power between men and women (gender power), and due to age. These are expressed in the differences in verbal ability, differences in the ability to pose sanctions, and differences in physical and psychological power.

The verbal abilities of the initiator differ from those of the abused child because the words of fathers and older brothers, for example, carry more weight than the words of girls. Moreover, a child cannot express what she feels and experiences in words as well as an adult can.

The ability to pose sanctions between the initiator and the abused child differs, because the older person has more room to apply sanctions (punishment and reward) than the child.

In sexual abuse situations, physical and psychological power also differs. The initiator can make the child submit to sexuality by using force or threatening to use force. He can put the child under psychological pressure by constantly badgering the child or by giving her extra attention in exchange for sexuality. Even when adults do not use all of these methods explicitly, the child still knows that the adult or older person is ultimately the one who determines what will happen.

Religion and Abuse   From this study of women who have survived incest, we can conclude that, through their religious upbringing, they were made easy prey to sexual abuse in the (extended) family. Moreover, their religious upbringing caused them problems in working through their experiences. During this study, we gained insight into the factors that foster incest and that block or stimulate one in working through past incest experiences. This has enabled us to formulate questions for the churches, and advice for priests, ministers, and other pastoral counselors as well as caring professionals providing counseling for incest survivors.

The incest survivors we interviewed were young girls when they were exposed to the influences of their religious upbringing. The influence of church teachings, school lessons, conversations and, most importantly, rules at home were legitimated by religion. We know from experience that adult Christians, ministers, priests, caring professionals respond to these stories in different ways. One response is to absorb these stories and to feel what they are saying. Another is to read them from acquired standpoints, namely the knowledge and insight of contemporary Christians and theologians. Examples of these responses are: "Their interpretation of the word 'forgiveness' is wrong"; "That's not the right way to look at God"; "It's funny they should feel guilty about that"; "Those statements and biblical stories have to be read in context". Readers who react in this way are not hearing what these women have to say because they are missing a crucial point: the actual way in which these teachings and passages affect people, and especially children. Children do not consider that a certain teaching might have been written in another context and was meant for use in a different situation from the one in which they find themselves. Readers who respond this way are also ignoring the way in which priests, ministers, and other officials in the many different churches preach. When these incest survivors were children, modern theological and exegetic insights were not incorporated into teachings from the pulpit, and that is frequently the case today as well. The statements made by these incest survivors cannot be dismissed as products of a child's imagination that were caused by the confusing situation in which she lived, or as the naive stories of grown women who should know better. The women we interviewed talked about their Christian upbringing in the context of their repression and suffering resulting from their extreme experiences. We see the sexual abuse of girls within the family as the ultimate consequence of patriarchal thinking, of patriarchal theology, and of the patriarchal experience of Christianity. What these women have to say is therefore familiar to many women and girls from a Christian background. However, their extreme experiences enable them to put into words the humiliation and denial of all women in Christian churches. The plea of women to Christian churches to put an end to sexism within and outside the church, is reinforced by the words of Christian incest survivors.

Authorship   This book was written in close collaboration. Due to our different experiences and insights, each of us had her own questions with regard to this study: Ineke Jonker from her own experience with incest, her Dutch Reformed background, and her history and cultural anthropology studies; Annie Imbens from her Catholic upbringing and her theology studies. We each proposed questions to the other, formulated hypotheses, posed new questions, supplemented each other and in this way arrived at theories we had both developed. Ineke Jonker wrote about incest and its social aspects. Annie Imbens wrote the sections of the book dealing with the religious aspects of sexual abuse. We are both responsible for the total content of the book, but each of us bears a separate and final responsibility for the chapters she wrote. The questions for the churches in the Epilogue were written by both of us. Each of us conducted interviews with the incest survivors. As to those published in this book in their entirety, the interviews with Ellen, Nell, Susan, and Ingrid were conducted by Ineke Jonker and those with Joan, Anne, Margaret, Carol, Mary Beth, and Amy were conducted by Annie Imbens. Chapters 2, 3, and 4 were written by Ineke Jonker; the introduction and chapters 5, 6, 7 and 8 were written by Annie Imbens.

Reporting the Interviews   In August 1983, *Woman and the Word* published an article written by Ineke Jonker of the Association against Child Sexual Abuse within the Family.[2] The article gave a brief description of the association and its goals:
The group of women who came from all over the country in 1982 to talk about their personal experiences with sexual abuse within the

2. *Vrouw en Woord* [Woman and the Word] no. 4 (1983): 6–9. *Woman and the Word* is an information bulletin published by the Committee on Women in the Church and Society, the Netherlands National Council of Churches.

family has now grown to an association which has been in contact
with over 500 women (in October 1984, 1700 women and children,
both girls and boys).[3] *For many of us this was the first time we had had*
an opportunity to talk with other women with the same experience. The
group was very supportive and as a result we all felt less isolated in our
experiences. We want to go on in our struggle to work through our own
feelings to help other women work through theirs and to try to prevent this
from happening to other girls in the future. In addition to our own incest
support groups individual counseling, and our book The Sentence for
Silence is Life, *we provide support for women when they file complaints*
against their offenders and we provide educational information to police,
doctors, and other caring professionals.

The article went on to say that in incest support groups and
sessions with caring professionals, survivors are continually
confronted with the question: Why is it that a relatively high
number of children who are sexually abused by men within the
family come from very strict religious families? At that time, no one
had yet been able to find a satisfactory answer to this question.
People always got hung up on concepts such as "strict beliefs in
authority" and the "patriarchal system," in which the woman is
subservient to the man. This raised the following questions: Is that
all that can to be said? Does the Bible not also have a liberating
message? Does that message not apply to women and girls? The
article said that this issue needed to be examined more closely,
including a critical examination of the marriage liturgy, for
example. Do words in these services perhaps prompt a man to use
the girls in his (extended) family for his own sexual desires? Can
one's faith in the self-sacrificing subservience of the Virgin Mary be
a factor? If sex is sinful and is permitted solely for the purpose of
procreation, is the wife viewed solely as the ideal mother? Must the

---

3. In 1985, the number of incest cases being reported nationally (in the
Netherlands) grew so rapidly that the Association against Child Sexual Abuse
within the Family was compelled to expand its services. Association branches were
started in every province as well as many of the large cities. At the same time, incest
case registration overflowed into other long-established services that were
well-funded by the national health service and the government, such as child
protection agencies, mental health and medical services, social services, and so on.
Reports of new cases are now received by one or more services, including the
association; it currently receives some government funding which supports a staff
of four and the self-help counseling services of sixty volunteers.

daughter satisfy the man's need for tenderness? The girl's resistance or his own fear of betrayal often leads the man to use violence or blackmail. Do the strict norms of the Bible not forbid this?

The article suggested that these questions could best be laid before the church. In the assumption that women working in the field of feminist theology are more familiar with such issues than the incest survivors struggling to deal with these questions, the idea of first asking feminist theologians for their advice was born. The questions directed to these theologians were: How can we best formulate our questions? Do you have any leads that can help us draw them up? What are your own feelings on this issue? What are your views on the nuclear family, which churches still hold in high regard as the cornerstone of society? The child is unprotected against the whim of its parents: The father can vent all of his lust on the child and the mother all of her frustrations. Are Christian women willing to discuss this problem with us?

This was followed by a declaration of trust in feminist theologians: When we know we have the support of our sisters in field of feminist theology, the next step—approaching the church authorities—will be that much easier.

The article then continued with the stories of five women who had been sexually abused during their childhood in Christian families by their father, stepfather, or grandfather. It concluded with an appeal: We are seeking feminist theologians to examine with these women the theological aspects of their experiences and to formulate questions for the churches. Interested theologians are requested to write to the editors of Woman and the Word. Several students and feminist theologians responded to this invitation. Annekee Schilthuis-Stokvis (editorial staff member of Woman and the Word) organized the first meeting between the women of the Association against Child Sexual Abuse within the Family and the women who responded to the article.

Investigation Formed During this meeting, the women decided to use interviews in order to gain more insight into the impact of religion on the sexual abuse of girls in Christian families.

The interviews were conducted in two phases. The first phase consisted of looking for the right questions and reference points for our interview guide, and attempting to establish the right balance between the two main aspects of the interviews: the research aspects, and therapeutic value for the women interviewed. During the second phase, we worked with the interview guide we had developed. By that time, we had gained some experience in the impact of these interviews and some knowledge of how to deal with that impact.

Methods Used During the first meeting, we agreed to the methods to be used in the study. We would draw up an interview guide, which would be used to conduct the pilot interviews. The women interviewed would be asked to critique the content of the interview guide and the interviewing method. Our progress would depend on the results of the pilot interviews.

Before these interviews took place, the Ecumenical Broadcasting Foundation for the Netherlands (IKON) approached us.[4] They were preparing a radio program on child sexual abuse within the family to be broadcast on November 13th, 1983 and wanted to examine the impact of religion as well. After some deliberation and an intensive preliminary meeting with IKON, in which we emphasized that our study had just begun, we decided to participate in the broadcast. We were aware that our only bases for doing so were our ideas, a number of conversations with women who were survivors of incest, and our feminist views on Christianity. However, we felt it was important to call attention to the religious aspect of child sexual abuse. We also explained our plan to conduct the study and to broadcast an appeal to women of various backgrounds to participate in the study by agreeing to an interview.

Nine women responded to the broadcast. They were between twenty-five and fifty-seven years of age. They came from large cities and small villages all over the country. The milieus in which they grew up were Dutch Reformed and Catholic. Three had been abused by their fathers, five by a brother and one by an uncle. In preparing for the radio broadcast, we had conducted telephone interviews with a Dutch Reformed and a Catholic woman (Ellen and Joan). We asked them two questions, which we consider the

---

4. IKON, Interkerkelijke Omroep Nederland, is a relatively progressive Christian television and radio network in the Netherlands. — Trans.

start of the study: (1) What was the impact of your religious background on your incest experience? and (2) Why did you have to allow it to happen to you and what prevented you from breaking your silence?

By phrasing the questions in this way, the women themselves were able to indicate which religious aspects had influenced their incest experience. This led to these reference points:

— the religious situation of the (extended) family;
— the views on mothers and motherhood in the family and in the church;
— the views on women in the family, school, and church;
— marriage instruction;
— problems with the image of God as the Father;
— the place of prayer and the Bible in the family;
— the views of the family, school, church, and the woman's own views on women in biblical stories ;
— church teachings and Bible interpretations that were experienced as oppressive or inspiring;
— trust in people;
— dealing with feelings.

We included these aspects in the first interview guide with a checklist of reference points and supplemented them with other aspects we considered important. We taped the initial interviews conducted with this guide and made transcripts of the interviews. This enabled us critically to examine the interview method a second time. In keeping with our agreement with the participants, the tapes were then erased. Each participant received a copy of the transcript and was asked to provide us with her comments.

We redrafted the interview guide and checklist to incorporate the critique of both the interviewers and the women interviewed. Among these criticisms were that the questions were often too theological and did not sufficiently correspond to how these women had experienced their incest. The women also felt that the questions were not open enough. The women from a Protestant background had particular difficulty answering the questions about sexuality. Their answer was usually that such things were not discussed at home. These women did know what their parents forbade, although they could not say how they had arrived at these ideas. From school and from church sermons, Catholic women knew that sexuality was unchaste and that it was steeped in sin. But it was not discussed in their homes, either. We recognized this situation from our own backgrounds and tried to examine how we had acquired information about sexuality at home. We remembered that we had been warned about various things. We had also been told about the shame classmates had brought on their families because they had to get married. The following questions were prompted by these memories: "What was the reaction when someone had to get married? What were you warned against? Why?" These questions worked well in the subsequent interviews.

The remainder of the redrafted interview guide primarily included reference points for ourselves, aspects to be covered during the interviews that we could ask the participants to talk about if they did not introduce that particular subject themselves. After conducting ten interviews, we decided to sort out and analyze the available material. We wanted to use this as a basis to decide how to proceed, what more we wanted to do, and how we could ultimately pose our questions to the churches. After analyzing and discussing the completed interviews, we drew up a work plan and a new, definitive interview guide which we used to conduct the remaining nine interviews (see Appendix). This final draft of the interview guide worked very well. All of the women we interviewed reacted positively.

When the nineteen interviews were completed, they were completely transcribed and sent to the participants. The transcripts were then shortened. These shortened interviews were submitted for each woman's approval prior to publication. Due to the limitations of this book, however, only ten of the interviews have been included.

Assessing the Therapeutic Value By *therapeutic value* of the interviews, we mean the liberating effect of being permitted to talk about that which has never been put into words before: the painful aspects of the incest experience; the act of sorting out this confusing experience and the consequences involved; and the ways the participants learn to go on living with their traumatic experiences. For some of the participants, this was the first time they had talked about their incest experience, although they may have been in and out of psychiatric institutions or in therapy for years. Most of them had also never talked about the religious traumas they had undergone: "That's one thing you simply can't talk to them about" (Margaret).[5]

We discovered the therapeutic effect of the interviews during the first two telephone interviews. Joan kept telling us what her father (the offender) thought and felt. She found it difficult to say what she herself thought about guilt and about various Bible passages. When we pointed this out to her, she said, "That means that I'm still not free of my father. I see now how much influence he still has over me." She told us that the questions made her aware of the repressed aspects of her incest experience. Because of this, we thought it was important to close the interview by offering the participant the opportunity to become aware of her own sources of strength and of her own capabilities to go on living with her painful experience. This is how our concluding question came about: "Where do you get your courage and strength to break the taboo on incest or to go on with your life?" Both of these women said that, through the questions asked during the interview, they had acquired more insight into their experiences and into the impact of religion on those experiences. This is why they also asked us to type out the transcripts for them. Because we were aware that we had reopened a lot of old wounds during the interviews, we called again after a few days to ask how things were going. Ellen and Joan both said that they had been thinking a lot about the interview. For each of them, the interview had deepened her insight into her experience, its consequences, and the various options open to her for working through it. With the therapist she was already seeing, Joan was working on her discovery that her father still had so much influence on her. Both accepted our offer to talk further about the religious aspects of their incest experiences.

These first interviews clearly showed us that there were two sides to the study: the research side and the therapeutic side. We began the study in order to acquire more insight into the relation between religious upbringing and sexual abuse. In the first two interviews, we became aware of the effects of the interview on the participant. We decided to conclude subsequent interviews by offering the participant a follow-up interview. In these follow-up sessions, the participant was able to indicate the effect our

---

5. All names have been changed and, as necessary, situations modified to protect the privacy of the individuals described.

interview had had on her. Anne told us that, after reading the transcript of the interview, she was better able to answer the questions because it had brought long-forgotten events to the surface. We had several follow-up sessions with Anne, which finally enabled her to go to her parents to talk about her incest experience with her (by that time deceased) brother. The method we used in the follow-up interviews and in counseling women who did not participate in the study is discussed in chapters 4 and 8. We should like to share some of the reactions of the participants with respect to the therapeutic impact of the interviews.

One woman later told us that, after the interview, she was working on learning to believe in herself. Another said that the interview served to bring order to the chaos in her mind, which had caused the past and the present to keep flowing together. Through the interview and the follow-up sessions, the past lost much of its threatening character, and she was again able to see the present in the right perspective.

Ingrid found it liberating to be permitted to tell her life story to someone who only listened carefully and posed a question now and then. As a result, much about her personal history and her way of overcoming it became clearer to her. Charlotte thought we asked the right questions. "Those questions are never asked by people who are supposed to be counseling you; they're questions we don't really want to hear. But those are the questions that help you work through it."

Incest Survivors' Data   Of the nineteen women we inter-viewed, we approached three to participate in the study. Nine women contacted us in response to the IKON radio broadcast and seven women came to us through the Association against Child Sexual Abuse within the Family or via therapists. One of the participants (Carol) had an anti-religious upbringing. Her father wanted nothing to do with religion. She wanted to participate in the study, because she believed that the same ideas and images about women and men prevail in progressive leftist milieus as in religious milieus. Through the interview, she wanted to gain more insight into the relation between her leftist upbringing and her incest experience.

In order to protect the privacy of the participants and their families, all personal information and circumstances about these women and their families that could identify them have been separated from the actual interviews and listed below. The names of the participants have been changed for the same reason.

Age When the interviews were conducted, the ages of the participants were between twenty-five and fifty-seven. The years of birth are: 1927, 1928, 1934, 1940, 1946, 1947 (2 times), 1948, 1949, 1952 (2 times), 1953 (2 times), 1954 (2 times), 1955, 1956, 1957, and 1958.

Place of Birth Five women interviewed were born in a city, two of these in a large city. Fourteen were born in a small town or village. Two of the participants were born abroad. They are located in the provinces of Drente (2 times), Overijssel (2 times), Gelderland (2 times), Utrecht (1 time), North Holland (2 times), South Holland (4 times), North Brabant (3 times) and Limburgh (1 time).

Religion Eight women grew up in Catholic families and six in one of the Dutch Reformed churches.[6] In these families, both parents were members of the same church. In one family, the parents were members of different Dutch Reformed churches. In the other families the mothers and fathers respectively, were: Dutch Reformed/non-religious, Free Evangelist/Dutch Reformed, Dutch Reformed/anti-religious, and Catholic/non-religious.

Of the Catholics, most (seven) women were required to go to church every day. The Catholic school kept attendance records. There was a good deal of prayer in these Catholic homes, in the evening and before and after meals. Prayer was more frequent in May and October, the traditional months in which Mary is honored. When the children could not sleep, they were told to say Hail Marys until they fell asleep. Three of the women interviewed told us that various members of their families had taken religious vows. In four families, one of the sons (brothers of the survivors)

---

6. For the purposes of this translation, the term "Dutch Reformed Churches" and its shorter version "Dutch Reformed" refer to all of the churches belonging to the Reformed Churches in the Netherlands as well as those belonging to the Netherlands Reformed Churches. Even though all of these chuches are basically Calvinist Protestant in character, their individual beliefs and practices vary; descriptive terms, such as "orthodox" and "strict," are used in order to give some indication of the nature of the beliefs and practices of a particular church in which a girl was brought up. — Trans.

had attended the seminary; one of them was an offender. One father is a former monk—and an offender. Most of the offenders are still involved in the church. Several of them still have positions of authority in their church. With the exception of one, all of the women we interviewed with a Catholic upbringing have turned their back on the church.

The Protestant families attended church every Sunday. The fathers are particularly interested or involved in the church. One father is a minister (offender), one a sexton (offender); one grandfather (offender) reads the Bible aloud quite often. He chooses the passages himself and gives sermons on them. This survivor has been left with the impression that all women in the Bible are seductive and sinful. Most of the Protestant women we interviewed said that they were no longer involved in the church; the offenders, however, usually are. Several of them still hold positions in the church. Several of the participants told of a grandmother or aunt whose faith was a liberating force. Two grandmothers read aloud from the children's Bible, although father had forbidden it. One father (orthodox Dutch Reformed) thought this was frivolous, like special services for children. Another father (anti-religious) did not want religious matters discussed in that way.

The children of the Catholic families attended only Catholic schools from kindergarten up to and including high school; institutions of higher education were primarily Catholic. Protestant children attended Christian schools when possible. (The anti-religious father went to great lengths to enroll his children in non-Christian schools.) The clubs and associations to which the children of religious families belonged were primarily church-oriented. They participated in choirs, catechism classes, and gymnastic clubs. Carol (who had an anti-religious upbringing) was only allowed to go to the meetings of her father's political party. She refers to the milieu she grew up in as "dogmatic leftist." Many of the mothers did not belong to clubs or associations, because family circumstances did not permit it. Several were active outside the home in church and club activities, and burdened the incest survivor with numerous household tasks. On the surface, most of these were model families. Some were always willing to help someone less fortunate. In six of these families, it was evident to the outside world that something was wrong, because the father drank. One pastor said that he could understand why the father drank, "with a wife like that." This woman was the one who did all of the church work, which her husband neglected, and for which he was paid. This was the case of two incest survivors' mothers.

Other Family Information   The size of the family varied from two to thirteen children. The number of children per family was: 2 (2 times), 3, 4 (3 times), 5 (2 times), 6, 7 (2 times), 8, 10 (2 times), 11 (3 times), 12, and 13. Eight of the women we interviewed knew that they were unwanted. Most of them were conceived before their parents married. One of the participants told us that this caused a lot of argument in both families at the time.

Prior to their marriages, the mothers had paying jobs as household help, in nursing, teaching, offices, factories, or in the family business. After they were married, most of them were exclusively homemakers. Two held paying jobs outside the home for a time. Several worked in the family business out of their home or on their farm.

The offenders can be categorized as follows: unskilled workers (5 times, 3 in technical professions, 1 in the theater, 1 in a bank); skilled workers (5 times, 2 in technical professions, 2 in construction, 1 in the postal, telephone and telegraph company); and farmers (2 families had farms: in one, the mother worked the farm alone with her son while the father sometimes had a paid job outside the home. The other family had a large farm and both the father and the mother had grown up on farms. Father came from a large family and took over his father-in-law's farm because there was not enough work to support everyone on his own family's farm). The professions of the other fathers were: male nurse, small businessman, social worker, civil servant (upper echelon), the director of a large educational institution, and a minister. Ten women interviewed were sexually abused by their fathers. Their fathers were unskilled workers (3 times), skilled workers (5 times), minister, and the director of an educational institution. The professions of the other offenders (grandfather and uncle) were doctor and successful businessman. The brothers who sexually abused their sisters later worked as: unskilled worker, skilled worker (2 times), trained farmer on a large farm, artist, real estate agent, and in the upper echelons of nursing, education, city management, and a technical profession.

In most of the families, no distinction was made between boys and girls as far as education was concerned. Four of the participants said that Father or Mother believed that girls should have a good education. Four said that there was a definite distinction between boys and girls. In these families, the girls were not allowed to attend a regular high school but, largely at their fathers' insistence, were made to attend a high school that specialized in homemaking so they would be better equipped to help their mothers with their large families.

Fifteen of the nineteen women were asked to indicate which political parties their families voted for; which radio and television programs they listened to and watched; and which newspapers and magazines they read. This information has been categorized by religion.

In the Catholic families, both parents voted for the Catholic populist party (KVP) and later, when it joined with other parties, the Christian Democrats (CDA). One of the participants suspected, however, that her father voted for the Labor Party (PvdA), which was forbidden in Catholic circles at the time.

In the Protestant families, the parents voted for strict religious parties: Dutch Reformed Political Alliance (GPV) and Dutch Reformed Political Party (SGP); for moderate religious parties: Christian Historical Union (CHU) and Anti-Revolutionary Party (ARP); and for a nondenominational moderate left party: the Democrats of 1966. The parents who earlier voted for the moderate religious parties (CHU and ARP) now vote for the Christian Democrats, with the exception of one mother who now votes for the Radial Political Party (PPR).

During the childhood of the woman who was raised in an anti-religious milieu, the parents were supporters of the small Pacifist Socialist Party (PSP). The father is now a member of the Labor Party.[7]

The Catholic families listened to and watched the Catholic Broadcasting Organization (KRO, Katholieke Radio Omroep, a Catholic-affiliated network) and two nondenominational net-

---

7. The actual party names and literal translations would be as follows: KVP, Katholieke Volks Partij or Catholic People's Party; CDA, Christen Democratisch Appel: Christian Democratic Appeal; PvdA, Partij van de Arbeid or Labor Party; GPV, Gereformeerd Politiek Verbond or Dutch Reformed Political Alliance, and, SGP, Staatkundig Gereformeerde Partij or Dutch Reformed Political Party (both fundamentalist parties); CHU, Christelijk Historische Unie or Christian Historical

works, the Independent Netherlands Radio and Television Broadcasting Network (AVRO) and the TROS Broadcasting Organization. The father who probably voted Labor sometimes listened to a program on the Labor-affiliated station ("Morgenrood" broadcast by the VARA Broadcasting Organization). One mother immediately turned this off, as Catholics were forbidden to listen to it. One of the women told us that at her house, it was still forbidden to watch a certain avant garde network (the VPRO Broadcasting Organization). Two women said that they listened to the Labor-affiliated station family program on Sundays ("Ome Keesje" on the VARA network). "It was exciting because we knew it wasn't allowed. We did it anyway, because we knew the whole town was doing it." One participant said that the radio was always on at her house but nobody paid any attention to what station it was on. Two of the women said that their families watched a lot of news and documentaries. One family watched a lot of films on a German network.[8]

The Protestant families mainly listened to and watched the Dutch Christian Broadcasting Association (NCRV) and the more recently established Evangelical Broadcasting Corporation (EO)[9]. Programs mentioned were: "The Minister," church services,

---

Union; ARP, Anti-Revolutionare Partij or Anti-Revolutionary Party; and Democraten '66 or The Democrats of 1966.

The Christian Democrats were formed through a merger of CHU and ARP with KVP. The PPR, Politieke Partij Radicalen or Radical Political Party, is a small Roman Catholic socialist splinter party that broke away during the Christian Democrat merger. The PSP, Pacifistisch Socialistish Partji or Pacifist Socialist Party, is a small pacifist party. — Trans.

---

8. Until the recent appearance of commercial radio and television in the Netherlands, the public broadcasting system was composed solely of separate networks funded partially by the government and by religiously, philosophically affiliated and deliberately nondenominational organizations. Also one nonaffiliated network was funded solely by the government. In addition to paying a flat fee to the government for radio and television privileges, proceeds from which were then distributed among the various networks, any person over eighteen years of age could pay yearly dues to become a member of the organization of his or her choice, which also included a subscription to the organization's own program guide. The broadcasting time allocated to each organization's network was based on its membership size. This system is still in operation, although it is undergoing increasing competition from commercial broadcasting networks. — Trans.

---

9. The KRO, Katolieke Radio Omroep, is a Catholic-affiliated network.

The NCRV is a moderate Protestant network; EO is a fundamentalist network comparable to some religious programming in the U.S. — Trans.

gospel singers, Jewish cantors, "Test Your Wings." One participant mentioned a Labor-affiliated radio network detective series, "Paul Vlaanderen". Another participant told us that her family had no television for a long time. Now that they do, they watch only the Evangelical network. In one family, the television was always on. Programs referred to as "too risqué" were those of a cabaret and those of the avant garde VPRO network (Fons Jansen and Sjef van Oekel). The anti-religious family listened to and watched the news, documentaries, and leftist programs. They also watched the Catholic network's current affairs program, "Brandpunt", because of the need to know what the enemy is up to.

With regard to newspapers and magazines, the Catholics mentioned *De Volkskrant* [The People's Daily], *Maas—en Roerbode*, *De Gelderlander* regional papers, one unspecified regional paper, and the regional paper of the province of Brabant ("Non-Catholic papers weren't allowed to be delivered in our town"), *Katholieke Illustratie* [Catholic Illustrated, 2 times], *Beatrijs* [a Catholic women's magazine, 2 times], *De Tijd* [a news magazine, 2 times] the Catholic network radio and TV-guide (KRO), *BijEEN* and another mission magazine, "God With Us" published by the priests of Brakkestein, and a blue book with Mary on the cover ("There was a blessing on every subscription"). In addition, there were *De Nederlandse Jager* [a hunting magazine—"Father likes shooting animals"], professional journals for farmers and gardeners, *Margriet* and *Libelle* [nondenominational women's magazines— another participant told us that Mother wanted subscriptions to these magazines but Father wouldn't permit her to have them], and *Engelbewaarder*, *Okki*, and *Taptoe* [Guardian Angel, . . . three Catholic children's magazines].

The women from Protestant milieus mentioned, *Trouw* [a national paper with Protestant sympathies 2 times], *Nederlands Gezinsblad*, [the Netherlands Family Newspaper, which is now *Nederlands Dagblad* the Netherlands Daily Newspaper], *De Spiegel*, [the Mirror, 3 times], a local paper, a regional paper, no paper, the church bulletin (2 times), missionary papers (2 times), *Prinses*, *Margriet* [women's magazines, 2 times], *Panorama* [a popular magazine], *de Lach* [a sexual humor magazine], *Zondagskrant*, [The Sunday Paper], pornographic magazines (in which fathers were shown having sex with their daughters), *Burda* [fashion magazine], knitting magazines, pulp novels, and *Donald Duck* comic books (3 times). One of the participants said that there was no money in her family for magazines.

The woman raised in the anti-religious family mentioned the leftist paper *Vrij Nederland* [Free Netherlands], *De Volkskrant* and *NRC* [two daily newspapers], pornographic magazines for Papa, *Libelle* [a woman's magazine] and *Donald Duck*.

The milieus of the nineteen women we interviewed were quite varied. Some families were closed; others were described as hospitable and welcoming. Some families were dogmatic, others free-thinking. In many of the families, sexuality was surrounded by taboos and not discussed; in others, this subject was an obsession for the offender or the father, and sometimes both. The interviews have left us with the impression that these families are substantially similar to other average families in the Netherlands.

We suspect that sexual abuse of girls fails to occur in all families because the fathers, brothers, and others do not feel the need to abuse their position of power in the family. We see the power of the father and the male members of the (extended) family as the most important factor contributing to the sexual abuse of girls. This power is allocated to men and is divinely legitimated as a result of the patriarchal interpretation of Christianity in Christian churches.

Sexual abuse   Ten of the women interviewed were abused by their fathers; two became pregnant by them. One of these has two children by her father; the other had an abortion. One woman suspects that her father is also the father of her oldest child. Her ex-husband wanted her to continue to let her father abuse her even while she was married. When her husband began to abuse her three year-old daughter, she took the child and left, at the same time ending her own repeated rape by her father.

More often than not, these survivors were not the only ones abused by their fathers. One father abused five of his seven daughters, one father all three of his daughters (two of them were made pregnant by him), four fathers abused at least two daughters. One incest survivor suspects that her father is now abusing her younger sister. The abuse of two participants in the study began at four years of age and continued until they were fifteen. The abuse of five participants began between six and eight years of age, of two others at eleven and twelve years of age. The abuse continued until age sixteen (5 times), twenty (2 times) and thirty-six (1 time).

Two incest survivors who were abused by their fathers were also abused by a brother. One brother abused all of his sisters. One participant was abused by three brothers. This started when she was four years old and continued until she was sixteen. Of the other incest survivors abused by their brothers, the abuse started at seven, eleven and twelve (3 times) years of age. The abuse stopped at ages fourteen, fifteen, sixteen and seventeen. One brother started abusing the participant again when she was twenty-six and continued the abuse for a year and a half. Another woman was approached by her brother when she was thirty-six, at which time she was able to say "no." The offending brothers were between two and fifteen years older than the incest survivors. They all had the upper hand in their relationships with these women, their younger sisters. The words of the incest survivors carried less weight than those of their brothers ("Go ahead and scream; they won't believe you, anyway.")

Grandfather used to abuse his daughter and one of his granddaughters, and also tried to abuse another granddaughter.

Various participants discovered that their mothers had been sexually abused in childhood, one by her father and another by a brother who was a priest. Mother had been afraid to talk about it at the time because she knew she would be blamed.

Interaction with Clergy and Counselors As the study progressed, we were given opportunities to provide information about the study and the related counseling methods; the groups we spoke with included ministers, priests, caring professionals in the medical and social welfare sectors, and law enforcement and judicial authorities. As a result of their questions and responses, we had many opportunities to test our theories and arguments. This stimulated us to formulate these theories and arguments with increasing clarity and to supplement them with new insights. Our dialogue with them was influential in the selection of the various subjects covered in this book.

We were often asked what we considered our main aim: the study of incest survivors, or counseling and guidance for them. We believe that any study of this issue can only be conducted when the participants are already being counseled or when counseling can be arranged for them. Many incest survivors are suicidal. Many have been in therapy for years or in psychiatric institutions, but have not been able to talk about their incest experience or about the negative impact of their religious upbringing on their lives. When they finally do so in order to participate in a study such as this, sometimes after the passage of twenty years or more, one cannot just let them go at the end of the study. That is why we hope that in publishing this book, we shall have have made a start in providing pastoral guidance. By pastoral guidance, we mean offering these women the space they need to identify and come to terms with the religious traumas they have undergone in relation to their incest experience. In addition, we believe it is crucial that priests and ministers as well as caring professionals in the medical and social welfare fields receive training in this area, so that they are able to pick up on the signals of girls and women who were and are sexually abused. They can then refer the survivors for counseling to women who are specially trained in this field. Caring services and support need to be available to such counselors on a permanent basis.

As we talked with various groups while the study was being conducted, many professionals became interested in its final results and in the way we were counseling incest survivors. They urged us to publish both the final results of the study and descriptions of the methods we used in counseling.

The questions and criticisms provided by the women we interviewed and these professionals who have taken an interest in our work have significantly contributed to the quality and content of this study.

Part One:
THE EXPERIENCE
OF INCEST

1
Interviews with Ten Women

Of the nineteen interviews we conducted ten have been edited for publication in this book. In our view these interviews are representative of the various incest experiences undergone by the women with whom we have spoken. We regret that we are unable to publish the other nine interviews in their entirety due to lack of space: those with Karen, Judith, Christine, Barbara, Lisa, Cathy, Theresa, Charlotte, and Tina. Nevertheless, we have taken several quotes from these interviews, which concisely illustrate specific themes.

Three reasons guided our decision to publish these interviews. First, many Christian women and girls will recognize their own experiences in these stories. They will no longer have to feel that they are alone in experiencing Christianity in this way. They will also recognize the long-repressed feelings that have been brought on by these events.

Second, the interviews show that the nature, the circumstances, and the impact of sexual abuse can differ greatly. That is also one of the reasons why it is so difficult for caring professionals to counsel incest victims according to a predetermined plan. The chaos that erupts, within the women themselves, as well as within the families, is the biggest problem that caring professionals face. That is why each case must be studied individually; each age group requires a different approach.

Third, these interviews clearly show that experiencing the religious patriarchal system has had the same impact on all of the women interviewed. In that sense, the ten interviews published here are identical to the nine that have not been included.

Ellen: *I knew that I ought to be stoned even though Jesus stood up for a woman like me. But he also said to her "Go and sin no more."*

Ellen is the middle child in a family of three girls. She was sexually abused by her grandfather. She edited this interview herself in cooperation with the interviewer.

What Is Your Religious Background?   My parents were Dutch Reformed. Father had a cheerful, positive faith in God; in his last letter to us before he died, he wrote, "Please be good to your mother, because you have a father in heaven who's watching you." Mother read to us from the children's Bible and taught us to say our evening prayers. We went to the children's services at the church. After Father died, we lived at Grandpa's for three years; he was a Free Evangelist. Two of his unmarried children were still living with him at the time. As the head of the family, he always led the prayers at the table and read from the Bible, something he'd seen that day on the religious calendar or in a magazine called *Het Zoeklicht* [The Searchlight]. He did a lot of sermonizing on these passages and he always wanted us to listen to sermons on the radio. We tried to get out of it as often as we could. We went to services and catechism classes at the Dutch Reformed church. We also attended Free Evangelist services regularly, where they often sang hymns written by John de Heer (a well-known Protestant hymn writer) and the minister preached from Revelation about the second coming of Christ. Grandpa was part of the Maranatha movement, which believed in eschatological messianism. I thought it was stupid, illogical, and speculative nonsense. The Dutch Reformed church was a lot more interesting. I was very inquisitive as a child, I wanted to know everything, about religion, too. We played the organ and sang.

How Would You Describe the Offender?   Mother later told me that Grandpa had thrown his pregnant wife (her mother) down the stairs once. He had a terrible temper and he couldn't control it. He flattered us when we acted the way women were supposed to; he complimented me because I was so sweet, gentle, modest, and obedient, and because I was a fast learner. But then he criticized me because educated women were nothings, "bluestockings." He sent mixed messages. He always said

whatever he wanted to about women and girls, especially about how they looked, no matter how embarrassing it was. He acted like the patriarch of a big family, you know, like a godfather. A lot of his unmarried children lived in his home and, in the beginning, married ones, too. He was very active in the church. I thought he was a big hypocrite, the way he sat there singing at the top of his lungs. He behaved like a normal member of the community, an entrepreneur, lived in an upper class residential area. He was well liked and had a certain status in his home town and in the church.

How Did Your Father and Mother Relate?   Father had a college education, Mother didn't. He did his work and was interested in community affairs and relations. She took care of the household and the children.

After his death, Mother became very dependent on Grandpa. She was afraid to make any move on her own toward the outside world. Whenever the men spoke, the women had to be quiet. They made her weak, afraid of what Grandpa and the others would say.

How Did the Children Relate to Each Other?   I admired my older sister enormously as a role model. I did everything she told me to. Of course I rebelled sometimes. But she could always get me to do what she wanted by appealing to my sense of honor or my desire to be helpful. I've always had a good relationship with her, especially now that we've talked out some unfinished business. I protected my younger sister, especially against Grandpa. I felt responsible for her.

How Did Parents and Children Relate?   Father liked my older sister better; she was fun to talk to. But he said that I was better at learning, so there was always some rivalry between us. She was prettier, too. Mother always said that she never wanted the two oldest children, especially me. She wanted the youngest one, but she should have been a boy.

What Was the Nature of the Abuse?   I had turned twelve that year. Grandpa was always complaining how much he'd been hurt by love, that he didn't get enough attention, and that he was lonely. I'd been in a Japanese women's camp for four years during the war, so I knew nothing about men, thought they were all

"fathers."[1] I didn't understand his constant whining, and I was tired of listening to it. One day, he asked me to stay with him when everyone else was going out. He started to caress me, sweet-talking me, but it confused me. He always fixed it so that we were alone in the kitchen or he took me with him in the car. I didn't know what to do, how to get out of it without insulting him, and making him mad. It scared me and his old body was filthy. It was too intimate. He kept going further and further, humiliating, until he went too far and crossed the line: This wasn't the way a father acted. I felt like I didn't own my own body anymore. He did it with very gentle persuasion, making me. I was always afraid that I would get pregnant with his child because I didn't know about all that.

Grandpa also tried it with my older sister, but she wouldn't have anything to do with him. That's when his attitude toward her changed. He started criticizing the way she looked, accused her of talking back to him, said she was a sassy little brat. She'd never be able to get a decent husband. There was nothing she could do to stop him. Nobody helped her. I didn't either. I was afraid; I gave in to him. He terrorized us. I made sure he didn't do the same thing to my little sister. We didn't bring any girlfriends to the house anymore because he tried the same thing with them too. I now know that he abused the youngest of his own daughters and that he tried it with other grandchildren, too. When I wouldn't do it anymore, he didn't say anything, didn't criticize me. Maybe he was afraid, but he was very crafty, too. I knew that if I said anything about it, he'd say, "You wanted it too."

How Did Mother Deal with Incest?   I told Mother that Grandpa was bothering me, but she didn't believe me. A while later, I told her again, but she just got really sad. Why did this have to happen to her too, besides everything she'd been through? But then she defended him: That's just the way men are. His wife was gone. I shouldn't let it bother me. She never mentioned it again, so I had to take care of it myself. When I had my own children and

1. Many Dutch citizens living in Indonesia when World War II broke out were interned in segregated camps for the duration of the war. Although the women's camps were not actual death camps, conditions and circumstances were appalling. — Trans.

couldn't stand him touching them or even seeing them anymore, I decided never to visit him again. Mother complained about that. She said I was headstrong. Couldn't I forgive this poor old man? And then she said, "Why won't you go with me? I always have to go alone, and he's still my father." She didn't care about me, about the pain I felt. It makes me so ashamed to talk about it. She kept pestering me about it until recently. He's still alive. Just a few months ago, when I had finally become strong enough not to feel responsible for her any more, her attitude toward me changed. We're getting along better now that I no longer have any expectations of her. Not long ago, she told him that she resented him for what he'd done to me. His reply was: "Oh, well, nobody's perfect; we all slip up a little once in a while." That's all he said. Now that she's realized what happened, she doesn't go to see him anymore either. So the whole family is mad at her now.

What Prevented You from Breaking Your Silence?
Grandpa saw himself as such a poor, pathetic man and it was my job to be loving. That's how it all started. He took me by surprise. He was a smooth talker with women. It happened before I knew what was going on, but it was very hard for me because I had to be sweet and loving. That was my side. I didn't want to get my mother in trouble. He complained to her about our behavior. I felt responsible for her, to some extent, because of Father's last letter. I knew that she needed Grandpa badly in order to get her own house. There was a housing shortage at the time, and he had connections.

It also had something to do with prison. He said something once about prison; that really scared me. At some point, my resistance consisted solely of resisting my feelings. My body wasn't mine anymore.

How did Family and Friends Respond to Your Signals?
Mother later asked me why I had let it go on so long. After it had been going on for a while, my little sister and I asked one of the younger uncles to help us. He said: "It's your own fault; you're young and beautiful and you have breasts." Then he started to wrestle around with us. We panicked and ran away. He also saw me once with Grandpa. I was afraid of running into him after that.

I thought, "He knows; he saw." When I got a boyfriend, I told him right away because I thought he had a right to know. He was so furious that he was ready to do something to Grandpa. I stopped him, though, because I was afraid for Mother. In the end, it would all be on her head. That's the way it goes in families.

How Did Agencies or Institutions Respond to Breaking the Conspiracy of Silence? Once, after I'd been married for a while, I told a minister whom I trusted. He looked a little sceptical and started talking about authoritarian fathers. That was it. He never mentioned it again. The family doctor just nodded and left it at that.

A few years ago, I attended an assertiveness workshop for women. I was supposed to write down what men meant to me in my life. Grandpa ended up on that piece of paper. The other women were pretty cool about it; they were shocked but they didn't deny it, didn't say I was to blame. They blamed it on the patriarchal system. Now I'm in the Association against Child Sexual Abuse within the Family where we ourselves are the best experts; we help each other.

What Impact Has the Abuse Had on You? For years and years, I was so furious that he did that to a child. It was the worst thing that ever happened to me. I was also angry with myself because I'd been so stupid and naive, because I'd allowed it to happen. I felt dirty and bad. It was like this big huge thing inside me. It was suffocating me. I had to get rid of it, I wanted to get rid of it. I thought that everybody could see it. I felt inferior; I was afraid to go to college, and escaped into marriage and family, where I sacrificed myself for everybody's happiness except my own. I thought I was bad because I was so full of hate and couldn't forgive him—not that he asked me to. I thought I was bad because I blamed my mother for things and I didn't go with her to visit her family.

What Connection Do You See with Religion? Sacrificing yourself was always part of religion: being humble, dutiful, loving, and cheerful. You learned to put up with injustice and not to resist. It wasn't until much later that I realized that wasn't necessary. I really thought that the more pain you endure, the

better, but I did stand up to any injustice that was done to my mother or my little sister. I would have gone through hell for them. In sermons, the obedience of women was illustrated by the story of Ruth, who gave her body to secure protection and to bear a son for her former husband. It was her own fault that she lived in poverty because she had left her homeland. David wasn't punished because he was spying on Bathsheba, but because she belonged to someone else. It wasn't about her, but her husband. No one asked about her feelings. I thought that story legitimated what my Grandpa did with me. And that beautiful young girl who was made to crawl into bed with old King David when he was dying? Nobody asked her what she wanted, either.

What Aspects of Religion Did You Experience as Liberating?
I thought Martha and Mary were inspiring. Mary was very inquisitive, too. The story was always explained in a negative sense: Mary was allowed to talk to Jesus, but only if she finished her work first, they always said. I really liked this passage because I had my own secret interpretation of it. Jesus thought that Mary was worth talking to. I thought that was fantastic. I found comfort in Romans: "There is therefore now no condemnation to them which are in Christ Jesus. . . . For I reckon that the sufferings of this present time are not worthy to be compared with the glory which shall be revealed in us" (Rom. 8:1–18). I knew that someday I would be free of all that misery. Into that house full of sorrow, with that complaining mother, one day happiness would come. Now that day has come. Since I've stopped feeling responsible for her, the things I have talked through with her, without being afraid to let her go, she's stopped complaining to me. I only reached this after when I abandoned my faith in God and Jesus, and turned my back on the church.

What Aspects of Religion Did You Experience as Oppressive?
There was something wrong with every single woman in the Bible. The Samaritan woman at the well was a sinner because she went with so many men. Mary Magdalene was a real sinner. She could only receive forgiveness from Jesus. Eve was the seductress. There was always that link between women and sin. The woman who was bleeding touched Jesus. She called attention to her menstruation. The minister preached about that in the

church. I was so embarrassed because menstruation was dirty, something to be ashamed of. In the Bible, it was called unclean. I went through life with my head bowed in shame. I hated those horrible old patriarchs in the Bible who kept adding new young girls to those they already owned and took them to bed. Mary was a virgin; she didn't do anything. Everything that had to do with sexuality was called dirty, except when men did it. Then it was called begetting sons. Women in the Bible were mostly whores, like in Jesus' family tree. They were bad and mean, betrayed their husbands and God: Sarah and Rebecca. The wives of Potiphar, Lot, and Samson were all weak and conniving. There were strong women, like Deborah, but she fought in wars and didn't conform to the norms I'd learned: loving, radiant, caring.

What Male and Female Images Did You Learn from Your Religious Upbringing?

Men? Fathers, those were men. The humbler a woman was, the more she was worth in God's eyes, but men weren't allowed to look down on her. Her caretaking duties were crucial to the family and to the community. Each potato was pared for God. She was self-sacrificing the whole year through. That's why she was praised on Mother's Day. She had to keep silent and cover her head, as if there was something she should be ashamed of. Even within the family, she had to keep quiet about religious matters. She was supposed to leave religious teachings to the men.

What Did You Learn about Sexuality?

Talking about sexuality was unthinkable. Premarital sex was filthy. That was the only sex education I got. You were conceived in sin and born in sin, so it was bad, and doing it only generated more sin. I thought pregnant women were kind of scary, because they'd done it.

What Is Your Image of God?

God the Father could always see us, so we were supposed to be good to Mother. My father was in heaven, too, so I always felt two pairs of eyes on me. I thought that God scorned women, looked down on them because they were always described as belonging to men and subject to them. But all that didn't correspond to the story of Creation in which man and woman were created in God's image and likeness. Then I'd start to think maybe it wasn't all as bad as I thought. I couldn't quite figure it all out.

I was mad at the God-the-Father because he hadn't protected me from Grandpa. He had let me walk right into it. I hadn't deserved that. Something wasn't right. Wasn't He supposed to protect, like a father's supposed to? I had to be really careful because He saw everything. I didn't understand His almightiness, because He didn't intervene and left me to fend for myself for so long. I had the feeling that I'd fallen for the whole thing. If God could see everything and was so almighty, this would never have happened to me. Or was I a bad child who deserved to be punished? That made me even more determined to do my best. I thought God was a very strict person, who didn't understand anything about me. Jesus was kind to children and women, but women were bad and mean-hearted. You were afraid to think about that too much. I knew that I ought to be stoned, even though Jesus stood up for a woman like me. But he also said to her "Go and sin no more." That applied to me because I had had sex out of wedlock. I couldn't believe in the sacrifice of Jesus, because God didn't want human offerings. I thought it was a senseless sacrifice.

What Do You Associate with These Words?

Good: I hated that passage about the good housewife. It was awful, they were always trying to push me into that role. A good wife sees to it that there are no obstacles in the way of her husband's career.

Love thy neighbor: Forgive and obey.

Evil: Sex, dishonesty, intolerance, stealing, those kinds of things.

Guilt: I felt like a sinner, guilty.

Responsibility: People were responsible for their own actions, with respect to each other and to God. Why didn't I scream, wrench myself away? Okay, I was responsible for that myself, but he was a nauseating old geezer. You just don't do that to children. Where was I supposed to go? He would have started in on me with those hateful comments all the time, at the table, the same terrible things he said to my older sister. My mother was responsible too. I understand now that she was boxed in, but at the time it caused me so much pain and sorrow.

Forgiveness: That was the worst. I had to forgive him "seventy times seventy times." It can't be forgiven, even if he were to ask for it—but he never has—even then I couldn't talk about forgiveness. He was a grown man, wasn't he? I was just a child.

Injustice: If Father had still been alive, this never would have happened. A child needs protection, and my Mother didn't give me that.

Where Do You Get Strength?   Praying made me feel strong enough to put an end to the incest. Now I realize that it was my own strength that I brought to the surface through prayer. I haven't prayed for a long time. I get my strength from myself and from other women. They make me strong by sharing their experiences, their understanding. They let me see that they really like me and think that I'm worth their effort. It's a road you make for yourself. You have to fix it up piece by piece: break it down in yourself, clean up the debris, and then rebuild it.

Other Information   Ellen's grandfather had the power to choose the Bible passages he wanted and to interpret them to fit his own plan. That is how he was able to impress on Ellen the belief that all of the women in the Bible were bad and inferior, and at the same time loving, radiant, and beautiful. That idea was validated in the Dutch Reformed as well as in the Free Evangelist church. She felt responsible for others but had never learned to stand up for herself. She internalized her Grandpa's ideas about women. The offender was excused and protected by everyone else in her immediate surroundings. Ellen went to her mother for help, in vain; she then made three attempts to get help from men, all unsuccessful. When she finally got involved in the women's movement, she found understanding for the very first time in her life.

Joan: *My father had very "Christian" ideas about women. Women should be submissive, obedient, servile.*

Joan is now thirty-five years old. She was the eldest daughter in a family of eleven children. Joan's parents wanted her, unlike her older brother, who was unwanted. Mother became pregnant with her brother, which is why she had to marry. Before they married, Mother had been a nurse and Father a monk. He met her when he had became chronically ill. Joan's memories of the first four years are very pleasant. When she turned four things changed. After that she was no longer a child and she was burdened with the duties of motherhood: She was expected to help with the housekeeping and to share the responsibilities for her brothers and sisters. Father worked in the theater. "He worked behind the scenes and never received any applause. That had to be compensated at home." Mother came from a large family. Her father had died when she was fifteen years old. Together with her mother, she took care of the family and the store. As a result, her sense of responsibility for others was highly developed. In her marriage, she led a "slave's existence." Not too long ago, when Joan gave notice that she was leaving the Roman Catholic church, "A huge burden fell from my shoulders." She edited the interview in cooperation with the interviewer.

What Is Your Religious Background?   I come from a very strict Catholic family. My father had been in a monastery. He'd been a monk and he was terribly dogmatic. He met my mother when he was put in the hospital. That's why he left the monastery and ended up getting married. My father had very "Christian" ideas about women. Women should be submissive, obedient, servile.

He went to church with us until I was eight years old. After we started having so many problems he didn't go anymore, but we still had to go. At home, he still read from the Bible. And we had to say the rosary, kneeling on the rough matting on the floor. He sat there like God the Father. He wanted to be worshiped himself. We had to pray to him.

How Would You Describe the Offender?   My father didn't know how to live. He was incapable of taking any responsibility for us. He had terrible fights with his family. He said that they'd always looked down on him and neglected him. That's how he experienced it. His family says that's not true, that it was hatred toward his mother. He turned that into hating all women. He lives like a hermit now. He needed some kind of framework imposed on him from the outside in order to be able to function in

life. After he suddenly stopped going to church he got more violent at home and we had to pray more and more. That went hand in hand . . . I wasn't allowed to scream. He put a stop to that right away. From that moment on, all my feelings have been blocked. The only one who was allowed to show any emotion was my father—and he did that all the time.

How Did Your Father and Mother Relate?   My father had the power, my mother had the strength. He determined what she was supposed to do. Mother ran the entire family; she took all of the responsibility upon herself. But she was afraid to oppose him. When they fought, she always said to my father, "You go to those other women." He went to other women, and my mother knew it. Later on, she said, "At the time, I thought 'Is this what life is like? They say they love you and you lead this invisible, slave's existence.'"

How Did the Children Relate to each Other?   My oldest brother's behavior was so much like my father's. He exercised his power over me at a very young age. He was able to do that because my behavior was much like my mother's.

How Did Parents and Children Relate?   When teachers at school said that I had the ability to go to the high school for business administration, my father said, "You're going to homemaking school. You have to help your mother." It was horrible. I was never allowed to say anything back and, in the end, I wouldn't have been able to, anyway. You become terribly servile because of everything that happens to you. Every single expression of spontaneity from one of the children or my mother was immediately stamped out. We weren't allowed to say how we felt. But whenever he thought something was great, we had to think it was great, too. We always had to respond to whatever he said or did. He was always afraid that he hadn't amounted to anything. He wanted his wife and children to acknowledge him. We had to pray to him. He didn't go to church anymore, but we had to.

What Was the Nature of the Abuse?   When I was about seven years old, my father came to me because he wanted attention; he used me as a shoulder to cry on and told me things about his life. From the time I was seven until I was thirteen, he demanded a lot of attention from me, and I gave it to him. To a certain extent, it was a positive experience, because it gave me the feeling that I was important to him, and I was flattered. At the time, I thought I loved my father. I enjoyed it when he called me by my nickname. And I liked it when he put his arm around me, when he caressed me, . . . but he went way too far. He touched me for his own pleasure, so he could have his fun. He forced me to touch him, to feel him and to satisfy him. One month after my first period, my father took possession of me, raped my body, my emotions, and spirit. At thirteen, he made me his mother and his wife, and I didn't even realize what was happening. Obviously I knew what was happening in fact, what events were taking place, but I didn't know that this was rape. All I knew was that it was horrible. I'd never been told anything about sex, and this is how I first came in contact with it.

As a child, I was obviously unable to oppose my father's power over me, even though I resisted him in different ways. I cried and I screamed, but wasn't allowed to scream. I tried to push him away, which only made him more aggressive and made him use more force. I had to keep quiet and wasn't allowed to talk to anyone. He told me so many times that he'd kill me if I didn't cooperate. Because of all of his threats, his blackmail and violence—he even put a knife to my throat and threatened to kill me—I kept my resistance inside. I was scared to death of my father and the night, lying on my stomach in bed, tensing at every sound, . . . waiting to see whether he'd come or not. Some nights I got some sleep but there were many more sleepless nights full of fear and uncertainty. This humiliating and painful situation lasted for two years and, all that time, I carried my awful secret around with me. I also thought that I was the only one and that this didn't happen to other girls.

How Did Mother Deal with Incest? I'm one hundred percent certain that my mother knew what was happening, even though she's always denied it.

What Prevented You from Breaking Your Silence? As a little girl, I learned to pitch in at home. I always helped with the housekeeping and was responsible for taking care of my brothers and sisters. That's probably the one thing that's most characteristic of my childhood, actually of my life up until now: have to, have to and more have to, whether I want to or not. "What Father wants is the law around here and what I want is . . . ?" Even when I laughed, I did it because it was expected of me. As well as I've cared for everyone else, that's how badly I've taken care of myself.

How Did Family and Friends Respond to Your Signals?
Two of my younger sisters saw everything that happened between him and me. They slept in the same room with me. We never talked to each other about it. Each of us dealt with it in her own way. Not long ago, one of them told me how it had affected her life. It left her with a very bad self-image and guilt feelings. All that time, she was actually jealous of me because Father paid so much attention to me. She thought she was bad because of her jealous feelings toward me while I was being abused by my father.

How Did Agencies or Institutions Respond to Breaking the Conspiracy of Silence?
After thinking it over for a long time and searching around for the right thing to do, I went to talk to a social worker at the Child Welfare Office, who had talked with my parents once. She was shocked by my story, but she said that she not only couldn't do anything for me, but that she was afraid to. She advised me to go to the police. I was astounded and very disappointed. I thought that over for a few months. I just couldn't see my father as a criminal. How could I turn my own father in to the police? The second person I finally went to was the assistant priest of our parish. He was just as shocked as the social worker but he also said that he couldn't do anything for me "because his relationship with my parents was already strained"— can you believe it? He told me—a thirteen year old child—that I should go to the police.

When I was fourteen years old, I made my decision and went to an aunt I was fairly close to. I told her everything. At my request, she called the police and they came and got me at her house. The police took me to juvenile hall in my home town. I was there three days for interrogation and physical examinations. Although the interrogation was awful and really took a lot out of me emotionally, I still felt as if I had been freed from something, even though I was in a six-by-six cell. Not long ago, a counselor in a therapy group said to me: "Can I ask you a question? This might hit you kind of hard, but I think it's important for you." Then he said, "Did you enjoy it?" I blew up at him. He wasn't expecting that at all.

What Impact Has the Abuse Had on You?

When I was ten, something inside me snapped. Before that, thinking about Jesus gave me some kind of security, and I had faith in God. After that, God became untrustworthy and Jesus was like someone out of a fairy tale. That's when everything came crashing in on me. It's becoming increasingly clear to me that incest is the main thing responsible for destroying my faith. I can't stand the Our Father anymore, I just can't say it anymore. When I try to listen to it with no emotions, there are some nice thoughts in it. I used to believe in God the Father and his son Jesus. Because of my father, I threw God away, although I'm very religious. I can still live with Jesus. But God the Father has such almighty power that it's frightening. It was like that at home and at church. That's why my faith in God the Father was totally destroyed. I still have trouble with it. I can't pray to a God, although I'm so religious. Divine power, I experience it, I feel it. But I'm afraid to call it that; I just can't. Now I also know why I got into marriage. I wanted to prove that it was possible to have faith in God and in men. The fact that I married a theologian has everything to do with it. That marriage didn't last very long. My feelings had been blocked for a long time. I couldn't feel anything, only register it. But I couldn't live that way. I saw only one way out: to kill myself. I stole two bottles of aspirin from the medicine cabinet at home and swallowed everything, but it just made me sick. Fortunately, after that I realized that killing myself was ridiculous. My feelings about the past were dead. They had to be in order to go on living. My self-confidence had been ruined. That gradually started coming back, but with it came a lot of emotions. The feelings from that period had been blocked for so long, and I had to live through them. As a child, I completely lost faith in adults. The more self-confidence I got and the more I felt my own strength, the less afraid I was to put my trust in others.

What Connection Do You See with Religion?

My father had very "Christian" ideas about women: Women were supposed to be submissive, obedient, and servile. I used to wonder how incest could happen in such religious families. Now I think that families who practice their religion so strictly live in a closed system, a vacuum. That was sacred. Nothing that happened inside the family was allowed to leak out. My father was religiously dogmatic. A certain image of women was fostered by the church, which enabled men to treat their women that way. Adultery was forbidden when they had sexual needs. The only thing left open to a man was his daughter. In order to protect himself, he forces the daughter to keep quiet. He tells her that she's sweet and good and that she mustn't talk to others about what they do together. Because this was "our secret." That's how fathers get their daughters to keep quiet about incest. With my father, as with so many men, there was a discrepancy between how he believed, what he preached, and what he practiced.

What Aspects of Religion Did You Experience as Liberating?   Jesus stood up when he was twelve years old and left his parents. He stood up in the temple and started to preach. He went his own way, according to his own nature and his own spirit. I really identified very strongly with that. That story had to do with me. It inspired to put an end to the intolerable situation at home. I turned my father in to the police. My real liberation came when I turned my back on the church and had my name removed from the church rolls. A huge burden fell from my shoulders, freeing all of sorts of energy and space so I could think for myself. Until then I always thought through my father and the church. Now I can decide for myself how I want to live my life.

What Aspects of Religion Did You Experience as Oppressing?   My father often said the commandment: Honor thy father and thy mother, and: Thou shalt love thy neighbor as thyself. In the Roman Catholic church, they say that all the time: "Love thy neighbor." That still makes me so furious I could almost explode. I was completely abandoned to his will because I obeyed those commandements. That Catholic morality, they always know what is good for you. Who I am, what I feel, was ruthlessly, systematically crushed out. My father was the only one who knew what was good for me.

What Male and Female Images Did You Learn From Your Religious Upbringing?
Women were supposed to be submissive, obedient, and servile. My father often told the story of the prodigal son. That's how he saw himself. That's how he behaved, too, within the family. We were always supposed to be happy that he was there.

What Did You Learn about Sexuality?
Women have no sexuality. They have to adapt themselves to the sexual needs of the man. Adultery is forbidden when men have more sexual needs than their wives can handle.

What is Your Image of God?
God the Father has such almighty power that it's frightening. My father and God were a lot alike.

What Do You Associate with This Word?

Forgiveness: I used to think that I had to forgive everything that happened to me. It had something to do with hope. The impression they gave you was that, if you'd just forgive, things wouldn't happen to you anymore. But that's all changed now. I'm not so forgiving anymore. Now people have to show that they're sorry for what they do to me before I'll forgive them. I think that, in the end, people can forgive only themselves.

Where Do You Get Your Strength?
Strength is my primal self. It's deep within me. It also has to do with divine strength. The only way I can tap into that is as a pure, innocent child. I identify very deeply, intimately with that image: Children are pure, innocent, unblemished. I respect it and I want to let it come out. For me, that is the essence of humankind's inner being. I recently got involved in the anthroposophic movement. Their ideas correspond very closely to what I believe. I used to feel strength only when I had reached the point that I was just barely still alive. Then I started to fight. My whole being came alive. Now, I start fighting earlier. I realize much earlier what's going on; I can recognize repression as soon as it starts. Then I talk to other people about it. That helps me to deal with it better the next time. There's

still always something in me that causes me to blame myself first instead of thinking that it might be someone else's fault.

___

Other Information   Joan was not only sexually and physically abused. Her spirit and her emotions were also systematically beaten down. Her father took possession, as it were, of her entire identity. Moreover, he determined how and what she was supposed to believe. In the interview, therefore, she always began by telling us what her father thought, felt, and believed. She could tell us how her father used her sense of guilt to force her into silence, but had great difficulty telling us how she felt about it. I asked her, "Can you name any passages from the Bible that made an impression on you, passages you experienced as oppressive or even passages you found inspiring?" Her reaction was, "My father often told the story of the prodigal son. That's how he saw himself." She was finally able to give herself permission to remember a passage she found inspiring. She said, "When you first asked me, I couldn't do that—just a minute ago. All I could tell you was what my father said about religion." Joan wrote down her incest experiences: "He got two years, but I got life—and I wish that I could get off somehow."[2]

At the same time that she gave this interview and partially as a result of it, Joan became aware of the process she needed to go through in order to free herself from what her father had done to her life, in order to go on living with her experience as an independent person. That is when she said, "My feelings have been blocked for a long time. Since then I can only register things. All of my feelings about the past are dead. They had to be in order to go on living. My self-confidence is gradually starting to come back, but along with it come a lot of emotions. The feelings from that period have been blocked for so long, and now I have to live through them."

Ten months later, while working on the transcript of the interview, she says that she has been able to put most of this behind her. This is how she has been able to free herself from the oppression of the Catholic church and her father in her life.

___

2. Association against Child Sexual Abuse within the Family, *De straf op zwijgen is levenslang* [The Sentence for Silence Is Life] (Amsterdam: Feministische Uitgeverij Sara, 1983). 100–108.

Anne: *The worse things are for you here on earth, the better off you are later in heaven.*

Anne is twenty-six years old and had a strict Catholic upbringing. Her family prayed often and the children went to church every day. Various family members were priests and nuns. Anne was an unwanted child, the fifth child in a family of six children. If there had been enough money, the children would have gone to boarding school. Her parents believed that families were better off having sons, then parents ran fewer risks. When she was about six years old, Anne was sexually abused by her brother, who was seven years older than she was. He died a few years ago. Anne was never able to talk to her brother about this experience. When Anne gave this interview, her parents still did not know what had happened. She did have plans to go and talk with them about it. This meeting recently took place. Working together with the interviewer, Anne prepared this account for publication: the interview, the preparations for the meeting with her parents and the chaplain, and the meeting itself.

What Is Your Religious Background?

We prayed before and after meals, and before we went to bed. If we weren't asleep when Father came in to check on us, we had to say our prayers again. We also said the rosary. I didn't understand any of it. Nobody ever explained anything. We had a children's Bible at home, but I hardly ever read it. It was too childish. It was better to pray. I remember being told repeatedly that the Catholic faith was the one true faith. There was a lot of talk about punishment and sin. I was always positive that dead people could see me. Even when I was sixteen years old, I still thought that all those people were watching me. Then I'd always think, "I hope it's dark enough so they won't be able to see me," and, "What will my dead uncles Reverend A and Reverend B think of me now?" I was also taught that I was responsible for everything. One of the examples they used to illustrate this was: If you see a banana peel on the ground and don't pick it up, and somebody slips on it and falls, then it's your fault. I was one of the few children in my class who still went to daily mass. Even in the first grade, I had to go to church every day. The other children didn't have to go to church in the afternoon on Good Friday. So that day I was walking home, enjoying myself. On the way, I started getting nervous; it was too good to be true. Okay, so the nuns had said that I could go home, but I didn't think Mom and Dad were going to be too happy about it. And I was right—everything hit the fan when I got home. I had to do the stations of the cross at home at three o'clock and I was punished. They were yelling at me about sin and capital sin, and they said, "You get down on your knees and pray for forgiveness." I think they were afraid that we were going to break the rules, do something wrong. They really kept tabs on us as far as religion went.

I didn't understand all that Latin in church. The Dutch mass wasn't introduced until much later. I had a little prayerbook and I always held this contest with myself, to see how many times I could read it during mass. I always had to give the illusion that I was listening, because if they noticed that you weren't paying attention, you got in trouble. The children were all separated, boys and girls, according to which grade you were in. One time I was talking to my sisters. They caught me at it and I had to kneel at the communion rail for punishment. Everybody could see me, my parents, too. So when I got home, I got punished a second time. The next day at school, our names were called and we had to come forward again. I thought to myself: "I'm not going up there because I was already punished yesterday". But the nuns knew I was in on it because they'd been in church the day before, too. So, of course, I was singled out. They asked me if I couldn't remember that I'd been talking in church the day before. I was seven years old at the time. I wanted to be a missionary nun. I had the feeling that the only way to get into heaven was to be obedient enough and, above all, not to think of myself anymore. The worse things are for me, the better. Then I will still go to heaven. That's really what they preached, "The worse things are for you here on earth, the better off you are later in heaven."

How Would You Describe the Offender? My oldest
brother was seven years older than I was. Even when he was little he had a very powerful position in the family. How that happened, I don't know. He was the troublemaker in the family, too; he wasn't afraid to scream and hit. When he was older, he developed a chronic illness and everyone was expected to take that into consideration. In the last few years of his life, his illness got worse. He wouldn't take any medicine and wouldn't live by any of the

rules required by his illness. I have the feeling that this was a conscious choice on his part. I was afraid of him at the end, because when he got mad . . . There was some heavy fighting, especially with my father. My brother was very strong physically. But I'd still get in between them and I'd say, "Don't you lay a finger on me." And he didn't. I wouldn't let him touch Father. It scared me to death, the way the two of them fought, the whole house in shambles. One of them would just throw the other one down the stairs. One time, I wanted to call the police to come and get him and lock him up, but they wouldn't let me, because you kept family matters private. You just don't drag strangers into your affairs. He stopped bothering me so much when I moved out of the house.

How Did Your Father and Mother Relate? Father makes the final decision, but Mother thinks it over and does all the preliminary work. Father might think about it, too, but he doesn't say anything until it's time for a yes or a no. Then he decides, but he always acts like it's Mother's decision, "I'll go along with your Mom on this one".

He has absolute power financially. He does whatever he wants and Mother has to hold out her hand for everything. She's given a certain amount of household money and he complains when it's all gone. But he would go out and buy a dog without saying a word to anyone beforehand, and he has magazine subscriptions, too. Mother has never had any magazines, even though she has asked him for them. In the last few years, she's started to speak up, "I have a job and I have money too." But she still can't make money decisions. She isn't poor or anything. I think that she could get the things she wants, but she's going to have to ask for them. She can't go to the bank and withdraw money, so she has to justify the things she wants to him, while he doesn't have to justify himself to anyone.

How Did the Children Relate to Each Other? The oldest ones were the bosses. My oldest sister had some additional power over the other girls. My oldest brother and sister were a team in the family and then came the next twosome: the sisters above me. So I was on my own for a long time. My youngest brother came so far behind me that he wasn't much help until he

was about three years old. That's when he and I became buddies. I was at my best with him because I didn't have to prove myself to him, something I constantly had to do with the others.

How Did Parents and Children Relate?   My oldest brother occupied a very privileged position. The children were the only ones who fought him on anything, particularly me. Whenever that happened, my parents always hushed it up, put a stop to it immediately. "That's just the way he is, now just leave him alone," they always said. Criticizing and undermining his power was seen as an attack on my parents. They were convinced that they were doing the right thing, that he had *his* rights and we had other rights. It was totally biased. I can't remember them being real parents to me. There was no discussion. If I disagreed with something, they didn't listen to me, but just said, "You have to do this or that."

What Was the Nature of the Abuse?   As far as the incest itself is concerned, I only have these pictures in my head that I look at. A picture of me lying in his room. I still can't call it by name. I've talked about it before, during therapy and now again in the association. But I've never called it by name, I only said, "Well, um . . ." I could only remember this feeling lying dormant under the surface, but I've recently learned what that feeling is because more and more pictures are coming back to me. It started when he got his own room. That's when it started for me. He made me look at him when he was naked, touch him, with my mouth, too. He had an attic room with a slanted ceiling. The picture is clear. I'm a spectator, watching through the curtain, even though I know you couldn't see through that curtain. He was lying on top of me and then he tried to get inside me. I didn't know what was supposed to happen. I was six or seven. He was thirteen or fourteen. Something was supposed to go "all right." He would ask, "Is it in, did it go all right?" It wasn't until years later that I knew what he meant, what had happened, and could give it a name. I didn't get any kind of sex education until I was twelve. That was absolutely horrible. I didn't want to hear any of it. I don't know how long it lasted. He didn't hit me or anything, but it hurt. It became more and more clear to me: This is wrong. It had to happen in secret and he was always listening for sounds in the house. He made me

promise to keep my mouth shut. I don't know if I resisted or asked questions. I didn't have any feelings when it happened. I did feel horribly alone and scared. I wanted him to pay attention to me, but he went too far, in other respects, too. He really let me down.

How Did Parents Deal with Incest?   Shortly after this interview, I told my parents what had happened. I used to think that Mother had never noticed anything and I was really apprehensive about telling them. After I told them, her first reaction was, "You know, I suspected it all along. I even asked the other children about it, but no one would give me an answer. I couldn't talk to anyone else about it. In those days, you didn't talk about that sort of thing". She was glad that I'd finally told them. She wondered how it affected Father because he'd never suspected anything. Evidently, she hadn't been able to talk with him about her suspicions either. Mother also said that she'd always considered me a very introverted child, and that if I said yes or no to something, then that was the end of it, because I'd never change my mind. Although my parents were glad that they finally knew what had been bothering me all this time, they also said that they wouldn't have been able to listen to my story or to deal with it emotionally a few years ago.

What Prevented You from Breaking Your Silence?   Mother thought that women shouldn't be assertive toward men. I have a feeling that my brother, who attended boarding school, underwent some kind of sexual humiliation there and that he made me pay for it. This gave him real power over me, even though that now seems pretty strange. It would have been more logical if it had given me power over him, because I had something I could use against him. After he died, I thought for a long time: He can't defend himself anymore because he's dead. If you kept silent for so long, you'll just have to keep silent forever now. That gave me guilt feelings, as if I were guilty. I was there and I didn't say no. I have very clear pictures but when I thought about telling my parents . . . The closer I came to telling them, the more I thought I just imagined it all. Then I started mixing everything up in my mind. I had no proof. The feelings I had when it happened have always been there; I just couldn't bring them to

the surface until the pictures appeared. Sometimes they completely engulfed me and made me confused.

How Did Family and Friends Respond to Your Signals?

During that conversation we had, Father said, "I can
understand why she was afraid to talk about it before, because you
just didn't talk about things like that in those days." That's the way
it was.

How Did Agencies or Institutions Respond to Breaking the Conspiracy of Silence?

It was a long, hard road
with four professional therapists. I kept thinking that it was all me
and that I had to fight these men. Later on, I started thinking: "You
all have power over me, so let's talk about that." The first time I
talked to a woman psychiatrist, she asked me if I hadn't felt
special, chosen. She also asked me if I was against sexual games
between children. I just ran up against this brick wall, this total
lack of understanding, so I just kept my mouth shut. I recently
spoke to a chaplain, who said, "Theologically, it's not a problem. I
don't understand why you feel so guilty about it. There's no need
to feel that way." He also didn't understand why I couldn't be very
businesslike and just tell him what I expected from him, because
I'd already talked to the interviewer once about what had
happened. So I should just be able to talk about it normally with
him now, too.

What Impact Has the Abuse Had on You?

I don't know
how long it lasted. Even when I was able to put a name to it, I
didn't think back on it. I couldn't possibly have fantasized the fear I
felt. Fear has a reason. I didn't start menstruating until I was
fourteen. I often asked my mother, "When am I going to get it?"
She replied, "You always get your period as long as you haven't
been fooling around with boys." I was scared to death because I
thought, "Now I'm going to turn out to be pregnant from what he
did." You had no idea how long sperm survived, or whether you
could get pregnant before you got your period. I also never wanted
to know whether my brother actually succeeded. Sometimes I
think it's important, because I always have this terrible pain in my
lower abdomen whenever I make love with someone. Maybe he

didn't physically destroy anything, but he certainly destroyed something there psychologically. I can only remember things in pictures, and then I'm the spectator. Every time something happens that's life-threatening, I watch myself. For a long time, I thought I could forgive him, but sometimes I think I've invented my own solution for that. I simply have two brothers with the same name. One is bad and the other one good. I only remember the bad one. I did a lot of fun things with him, too, but those memories aren't there anymore.

For a long time, I had the feeling that I didn't have any right to live until I read a book about women's lives.

I'll never be able to have a satisfying sexual experience: It's physically impossible because of the pain; and I can't expose myself emotionally like that, either. I think that I simply won't tolerate men's power over me anymore. Sometimes I think, "Why don't I just love women?"

What Connection Do You See with Religion? I think that the incest would have had less impact on me if I hadn't been brought up in that strict, dogmatic faith, and if I'd had a chance to talk it out. I felt guilty for a long time. I was no longer "immaculate," as they call it, no longer a virgin. I'd ruined it. That guilt feeling played a large part it my life. I also thought that I had no right to say "no." I think that's one of the reasons I've always let people misuse me, because I had the feeling that I had absolutely no rights whatsoever.

Which Aspects of Religion Did You Experience as Liberating? Nothing. I feel this rage rising up inside me that I can't release. A lot of things get covered up because of religion. Faith should be a source of support for me, not something I should have to be afraid of. I think the church could be something good if it practiced what it preached. Now I'm starting to think differently about certain things. I think I'm still carrying around all the problems that went with my childhood religion. The church keeps people down and makes them dependent.

What Male and Female Images Did You Learn from Your Religious Upbringing? I said to my mother once: "Marriage is a question of give and take; you not only have to give

but you also have to take Father the way he is." For a long time, the idea that women have to be obedient to men seemed like the most normal thing in the world. I had the feeling it was supposed to be that way. I just didn't see anything else. There were no women in my surroundings who had a job or led their own lives. And if there was a single woman or a widow, then she was considered pathetic, "That poor woman's all on her own."

What Did You Learn about Sexuality?

Mother thinks everything sexual is dirty, even kisses; she wipes them off. Father hugged me sometimes. For a long time nudity was bad, for myself, too. It took a long time for me to discover my own body. I didn't want anything to do with sex education. Mother tried to tell me how beautiful it was when you loved each other, but I didn't want to hear about it. Sex was just filthy. I thought, "I'm not going to do it with anybody until I'm married, because that's the way it should be." I was afraid to tell Mother the first time I got my period. You weren't supposed to let anybody notice that you had it. It would be a sin to let people know. Sex and sin went hand in hand: It was visible in everything, just beneath the surface. I wasn't allowed to kiss my uncles who were priests, while I had to kiss other people on command, whether I liked them or not. I always tried to kiss my uncles, because then they'd have to explain why it wasn't allowed. There was another message, too: As far as sex was concerned, everything done outside marriage was dirty and bad.

What Is Your Image of God?

I was always really scared of God. I had the feeling that I could do things that were wrong, which I wouldn't find out were wrong until later. They pounded it into you at school that you were responsible for everything. God saw everything and knew everything that was going to happen. What really obsessed me as a child was the idea that God had the whole world in his hands. I'd get upset over that because I couldn't understand it. If that was true, he'd have to have huge, enormous hands; whenever I envisioned that, he was so scary. He knew and saw everything. That really scared me, too. You could never do anything that he wouldn't know about. I could only pray, but everything happened the way he wanted it, anyway. I thought of him as male. Somebody who does the things he does could only be a "he." I once said to Father, "God didn't make the earth, because the earth just happens to be a piece of the sun". Father said, "God made everything, so he made the sun, too.". I think that was one of my few attempts to speak up, but I always had the feeling that I had to prove that it wasn't all the way they said it was. Jesus was different. He loved everyone. I had a beautiful picture of him in my room with children all around him. The stories in the children's Bible were beautiful, too. The stories about Jesus never scared me; it was the church, and the pastors, and the priests that scared me—what they said, and how my parents interpreted it. Everything Jesus did inspired me. I never did understand why he didn't come down off that cross. But there it is again: It was supposed to happen that way. I liked the story about Mary and the Holy Spirit. It seemed completely logical that someone would come to tell you that you were going to be a mother. That's why it could have been beautiful for me, if things had gone wrong, and I would have turned out to be pregnant. Now I don't believe in God anymore. For me, God is having a peaceful feeling inside myself, the good inside other people, and the good in me.

What Do You Associate with These Words?

Good: I think that it won't be good until I'm no longer here.

Evil: That I couldn't forgive.

Responsibility: Enormous guilt feelings.

Forgiveness: Sadness and having no right to be angry.

Love thy neighbor: The message I got was that you have to love your neighbor more than yourself and that you had to give your life for others.

Injustice: That has to do with my brother, with forgiveness. For a long time, I didn't want to justify myself. Now I go after justice, fight on the barricades, if necessary.

Where Do You Get Your Strength?   Sometimes I don't even know myself where I get the courage and the strength to go on with this life. Still, I now feel and know much more clearly what

my life is and what I want to make of it. I have my ideals and I fight for them; I'm not alone in that. It's a good feeling to know that people like me and approve of me.

Anne's Meeting with Her Parents
Long before I decided to tell my parents what had happened, it was on my mind constantly. It bothered me that I'd never spoken up. It took me a long time to get to that point. It took me even longer to get myself ready to talk to them. Whenever something went wrong during these preparations, I'd fall apart completely. That's what really made me realize just how necessary it was for me to tell my parents. Remaining silent was in fact equal to death.

I wanted to find some good support for my parents, and I was thinking of a chaplain whom I knew they really trusted. I didn't have all that much faith in him myself, so the interviewer had a preliminary meeting with him. She received the impression that he was open-minded about the subject and that he wasn't particularly dogmatic. I decided to ask him if he'd help my parents work through what I had to tell them; I also wanted to hear and to see how he'd react to my experience. This chaplain consistently denied my feelings and experiences. This almost made me feel all over again that I was reacting abnormally to what had happened, and to the impact it had on me. He particularly ridiculed my guilt feelings because there was no theological problem in his view, as if, when I was a little child, I could have been able to figure out what was a theological problem and what wasn't. He was more interested in hearing what actually happened between my brother and me than in hearing about the impact it had on me. Often, that impact is no longer proportionate to what actually happened, but it's reinforced over and over again until you're caught up in a vicious circle. He more or less interrogated me and didn't understand how painful that was to me. I no longer had any faith in him as a counselor for my parents. I demanded that he believe what I told him and not twist the facts and not play down what had happened or how it had affected me. I was fighting another fight. I was going to make clear to him how these experiences affect women, and nothing was going to stop me. That's where I had my strength. I mustn't let myself be isolated as an individual, but must show him that my feelings are shared by other women who have survived incest. He couldn't understand why I kept talking about power. It was a bitter experience for me: to feel so tangibly that the position of women in the church has barely changed at all. In a meeting with this chaplain, the interviewer and I showed him how harshly he treated me. He then said that he would have been much more subtle with someone, for example, who had a concentration camp syndrome, because these people had been screamed at, and because they'd experienced humiliation, and had been victims of power abuse. I replied that, as I had experienced it, this was the same thing. My brother didn't scream at me, but he kept his hand over my mouth—for years.

Other Information

The impact of the sexual abuse on Anne became clear during the many conversations we had with her. These can be defined in short-term and long-term impact.

In her childhood, there was fear, confusion, and loneliness. When she began to realize what had happened, there was the fear of being discovered, of being blamed, of getting pregnant, of mortal sin, and of hell; these fears were due to the emphasis in her religious upbringing on the sin of unchastity (the worst sin) and the taboo on talking about these things at home. Finally, she felt that she had no rights because of her guilt feelings about what had happened to her.

On a long-term basis, the impact was: confusion, a split identity, suppression of memory, strong suicidal urge, loneliness, sorrow, little or no trust in other people, little or no self-esteem, and sexual problems.

Because of her brother's death, a lot of unresolved issues surfaced. It became more difficult to talk about her experience with her parents because she wanted to spare them further grief. She started asking questions about forgiveness. She also got the feeling that she kept encountering her brother all the time.

During her preliminary meeting with the chaplain, the interviewer was struck by the open-minded attitude he displayed about this subject and the insight he demonstrated in his way of working and dealing with people. During that first conversation, he did not know which person or family required his counsel. We believe that the subject only became threatening when he discovered who the family was. We think that this created his need to minimize the experience. We realize that this is understandable for someone preparing to counsel parents who are about to hear such a story about their deceased son. However, it meant that

Anne was again unjustly treated. We decided to have two counselors present during Anne's meeting with her parents. The chaplain would look after the parent's interests during this talk, and the interviewer would look after Anne's. It became very clear to us during this talk how difficult it is for male members of the clergy to consider seriously what women say and feel. The father's feelings were met with the utmost understanding and consideration. The mother's feelings, on the other hand, were barely heard or understood. We believe that this situation often arises when women receive pastoral counseling from a male minister or a priest, and that it is essential to recognize the resulting problems. Once this is achieved, women will be able to decide for themselves whether they wish to be counseled by a female or a male member of the clergy.

Margaret: *If the girl had preserved her chastity like she should, the boy wouldn't have gotten out of control.*

Margaret was the next to the youngest in a family of thirteen children, of whom eight survived infancy. Her brother, who was three years older, experimented with her sexually when she was about twelve years old.

What Is Your Religious Background? We had to go to church every day. We went to communion on Sunday, then we had breakfast, and then back to church for high mass. In the afternoon, we went to benediction and catechism, and in the evening back to church again if there was some kind of function. There were prayers before and after meals, and an additional chaplet during the fasts in May and October. It was prayer, dinner, and off to bed. Before we went to sleep, a confession of guilt, in which you were supposed to reflect on what you'd done wrong that day. Everything you did that day was a sin. Then I couldn't get to sleep. I always got scared. Father said: "The worst things happen in bed." I was raised in fear. I was afraid of everything.

Mother would have been a little more lenient, if she'd had the courage. Father was always walking around quoting proverbs. His favorite was, "Honor thy father and thy mother," and: "Work is no disgrace." You just had to be strong and do what you were told. Later on, when you went to heaven, comfort and happiness would be your rewards. You'd eat from gold plates with gold silverware. You weren't supposed to enjoy this life, not enjoy eating, not enjoy sleeping. I was afraid to make one wrong move, because then I wouldn't go to heaven.

The nun, the pastor, and the assistant priest were always right. The deacon was treated like some kind of representative of God. Every year when he showed up to collect money, my parents always gave it to him, no matter how poor we were. That's what they do: First they make people have as many children as possible, and then they come and take money from them. That was seen as a sacrifice for later, in heaven.

At school, we were taught by monks and nuns. There was a picture of hell at school, with people in the fires. Those faces were horrible. They tormented me for years. It was a strict Catholic school. When I was in kindergarten, I picked up my handkerchief off the floor during prayers because it had fallen. I'd learned that I was always supposed to pick up after myself and keep things tidy. The nun punished me because I'd committed a sacrilege; I had thought that handkerchief was more important than God. Once during the war, a classmate gave me a sandwich. I ate it right up because I was starved. I'd committed another sacrilege; I'd eaten it during religion class. That time the whole school ignored me for a week. That was the worst part. Everyone was ordered to ignore me for an entire week. That makes you feel so awful. We weren't allowed to read the Bible or associate with Protestants. I had a Protestant girlfriend who lived across from the school. The nuns told my older sister, who made sure that my parents put a stop to that right away. I wasn't allowed to see her anymore. I was afraid to make one wrong move, because then I wouldn't go to heaven, and things were pretty bad at our house already. Our Catholicism was based on fear, not on our belief in the one true faith.

Our parish priest wouldn't let us do anything. We weren't allowed to celebrate carnival;[3] we weren't allowed to dance. Girls were supposed to stay home in the evenings doing needlework and sewing.

---

3. Carnival is the traditional celebration preceding Lent, well-known for its festivals in Rio de Janeiro and New Orleans (where it is called Mardi Gras), but also celebrated in the Netherlands, particularly in the predominantly Catholic south. – Trans.

How Did Your Father and Mother Relate? The relationship between my mother and father was good, but they didn't express it. They never touched each other when we were around. They never talked about anything; that would cause emotions. You weren't supposed to show that you were sad, or happy. You had to be strong. Father would have liked to talk about things, but he couldn't. Mother didn't want to talk. She'd stand up and turn on the radio.

Mother had a healthy attitude toward life and tried to be as good to herself as she could. Father was a very strict Catholic, because of his upbringing. He always got up very early. He thought that we should get up, too, and he made so much noise at six o'clock in the morning that you finally got up, too. He was really a good man, but he had an awful upbringing.

How Did the Children Relate to Each Other? My older sister took care of the younger children. The nuns had a lot of influence on her. She was in a convent for a while, but she came back pretty fast. She followed all the rules and thought that Catholicism was the one true faith. She always kept an eye on me. The first time I got my period, she could tell that it was starting. We were in a convent at the time because we'd been evacuated. She got me the cloths I needed. I was never supposed to let a boy find out, or to talk about it to other girls.

How Did Parents and Children Relate? Father allowed us to do needlework and sewing on Sunday afternoons if we were finished with everything else, but not if it was the sewing we always did to earn money. I wish Mother were alive today; she should have lived in these times.

What Was the Nature Nature of the Abuse? I think that my brother had heard from his friends what boys do with girls. He asked me if he could try it with me sometime. He didn't mean anything by it. I had the feeling that somehow it wasn't right, but I was afraid to say that I didn't want him to. I was twelve or thirteen when it happened. That was just before or just after the war began. It took a long time before I got my period. I was afraid the whole time the war lasted because I'd heard that a sperm could still be in there. My brother was three years older. The first time he was experimenting. The second time was when my mother died. I was thirty-six years old at the time. His wife was away for a few days. We'd had a wonderful day together, taken a long walk. I'd really enjoyed it. When we came home, he asked me if I would go to bed with him again. I said no. I felt sorry for him. But I was also terribly disappointed that he had asked me to do that because we'd really had a nice day.

How Did Parents Deal with Incest?   We have never discussed anything at all about it.

What Prevented You from Breaking Your Silence?   I understood my brother's needs. I think that he'd heard about it from his friends and was curious. I said no the second time, but I felt sorry for him.

How Did Family and Friends Respond to Your Signals?   You couldn't talk about it. Nobody listened. But it wasn't something you could talk about, either. No, I can't talk about it with my brother, either. We don't talk about that anymore. And he didn't mean anything by it. He was just curious.

How Did Agencies or Institutions Respond to Breaking the Conspiracy of Silence?   I've never talked about my incest experience or about my fears, but just recently, I wrote it all down. (Margaret has been in and out of therapy for years. A few months ago, she wrote down her experiences for the first time in a notebook: about what happened with her brother and about her fear of getting pregnant at the time. Her other fears, such as her fear of death, of the devil, of men, of other people, and of hell, were articulated for the first time during her interview.)

What Impact Has the Abuse Had on You?   For years, I walked around in the constant fear that I'd still have a child. You didn't know anything in those days. I didn't know how long sperm could survive. If you'd sinned against the rules, that was even worse. You can hope for salvation by doing a lot of penance. I denied myself everything. I obeyed the commandments to the letter, and stayed away from everything that was banned.

Whenever someone said, "You're allowed to do this" or "You're not allowed to do that," I did exactly what they said. I still do that a lot, because I've been afraid my whole life—afraid of this, afraid of that, afraid of death, afraid of hell. That's an eternal fire, that will consume everything. It's tormented me for years.

I had the feeling we were doing something wrong. The fear didn't come until later. That's when I thought, we're both going to hell. Then I heard that whenever a boy and girl come together, a baby is born. So whenever my period was one day late, I got scared again. Because I'd heard that that sperm could still be in there. I couldn't tell anyone about it. I've never talked about it. But recently, I wrote it all down. If morality hadn't relaxed the way it has since the sixties, I never would have stopped being afraid. I still have to consciously tell myself: You can sit down now, you can relax now. That takes a long time to change.

What Connection Do You See with Religion? If religious views on sexuality had been different at the time, I don't think it would have been so difficult for me. I was totally convinced that we would end up in hell together, because we'd done something that was absolutely forbidden. All that misery I went through could have been prevented if all those dos and don'ts hadn't been so black and white. You always had to be servile, to serve God. Women were totally ignored. But whenever evil enters the picture, it is always mentioned in the same breath with the word "women."

What Aspects of Religion Did You Experience as Liberating? Nothing about religion was liberating. In my experience, faith was a rope that was being pulled tighter and tighter around me. Religion was being scared to death. It seemed to me that women were always to blame: They were either bad, or diseased, or possessed by the devil. Jesus expelled it and cured those women. I'd like to believe in a God who loves people and wants what's best for them, but the real situation is totally different. Whenever I try to put that into practice, people don't understand. You can't talk to anyone about it, and I have a hard time believing in it myself.

What Aspects of Religion Did You Experience as Oppressive?
That Bible passage about the angels who rejoice for the sinner who repents in the last minutes of his life. That a person like that is welcomed with rejoicing, a person who's lived a life of sinful pleasure. The other ninety-nine who were good their entire lives aren't welcomed with such rejoicing; they're far less important than that one sinner. And the story of Ruth is horrid, that she had to lie at the feet of that man. I thought that was so humiliating for her. Women are always portrayed as evil, like Eve, who incites the man to evil. The woman is always the symbol of evil and of weakness. The snake is a she and a witch is a she. In those days, you weren't allowed to think that, because thinking is a sin too. And it is a mortal sin to think that way. That tormented me every night when I was confessing to God in bed before I went to sleep. Then I always promised God I'd make up for it. If I had a penny, for example, I promised I'd buy something with it and give it to a child who was poor, and I did it too. Then I was able to get some sleep once in a while. I was raised with the word *sin*. Everything was a sin. You know how people say, "That's a sin," and they mean, "That's too bad" or "What a waste"? Whenever they said it at home, they meant it was a real sin. I think the most oppressive thing was that we believed because of fear. We had no choice. Now that I'm not afraid anymore, I don't believe anymore, either. That's no coincidence.

What Male and Female Images Did You Learn from Your Religious Upbringing?
After the war, some of the girls were "going to have a baby from the Americans." Our pastor preached about it in church and everybody at school was talking about it. When one of the girls had to get married, she wasn't allowed in the sanctuary. That was how everyone knew that she had to get married. That's how powerful the pastor was. Girls weren't allowed to even look at a boy, either, because then he wouldn't be able to control himself. It is the woman who gets the ball rolling, they said.

A mother sacrificed everything for her children and for her husband. Being a good wife was one big sacrifice.

What Did You Learn about Sexuality?
Everything was a secret. No one talked about the normal, natural things. Everything

was forbidden. If a girl touched a boy, he wouldn't be able to control himself. For years, I walked around with this fear that I could still get pregnant. You didn't know anything in those days.

You had to be married. Before you got married, you weren't allowed to do anything. Once you got married, the wife had to fulfill her duties. You only got married to have children. That's still true today, when I hear what the Pope says. I don't read that anymore myself. I hear that it's still the same: Whatever you do, don't enjoy it. And if you'd sinned against the rules, that was the worst. The deacon knew how to deal with that. Everything you weren't allowed to do before you got married, you had to do after you got married. When the marriage wasn't going well, it was always the wife's fault, because she was supposed to make sure that the husband got what he was entitled to. At an educational retreat for girls where you were supposed to learn about living a full life, they kept telling you that sex was the girl's responsibility. If the girl had preserved her chastity like she should, the boy wouldn't have gotten out of control. I came home from that retreat more afraid than I was before I went. If views on sexuality had been different at the time, I don't think it would have been so difficult for me. As it was, I was totally convinced that we would end up in hell together, because we'd done something that was absolutely forbidden.

What is Your Image of God?   God was a kind of father who loved all children and wanted the best for them all. I dreamed about that once. We had a picture at school of God on a throne with outspread arms and hands. That's how I saw him in my dream: a man putting his arms around me. But I can no longer accept that God is love. If that were true, then why has my life been like this? When I had that dream, I was having a very difficult time. Fortunately, things aren't as bad anymore as they were then.

God was the powerful one. People existed to serve him, to sacrifice everything for him, to do good, and to be rewarded. He could make or break people. Now, all I can see is the breaking. That's all I want to see. You see it everywhere. I've also explored other religions. Buddha is powerful and Allah is all-powerful. It's the same everywhere. He's always the one who has the power. Why can't people just live with each other in peace? Why does there always have to be one who is more powerful than the people? God is powerful. We must serve God and do his will for his greater honor and glory. The power of God is greater than the power of others. I don't like the word power. I envy the nuns I talked about earlier. They're good to people because they think that is how they serve God. God wants us to be good to people, they think. Why can't they simply be good to people because they want to, for the people themselves?

What Do You Associate with These Words?

Guilt: Penance, being afraid of death, what comes after death.

Responsibility: Weighs heavily on me.

Forgiveness: I never experienced something being forgiven. I'm always reminded of it in one way or another.

Love thy neighbour: I want to do that. But when I see how people treat each other, I think it's a farce. Money is what counts, and prestige, and power.

Love thy neighbor as thyself: I'm learning that now, that I'm allowed to love myself. I was always taught that you were supposed to do anything and everything for the other person, not want anything for yourself.

Injustice: All people who are treated unjustly. Women are still treated unjustly all the time.

Where Do You Get Your Strength?   I don't know where my strength comes from. Our family was very poor. Things got a little better after the war. I was earning good money because I'd learned so much. I had to give most of it to my parents to support the family. Saving was another virtue. Now I have my own house; I've saved for that since I was fifteen. I gradually came to the realization that I can do something by myself, see to it that I get some peace and be myself. When I said that once to a priest, he said, "Our Lord has given you that strength. He'll see to it that everything is taken care of." But I think that I'm going to have to do it myself first. I think that I'll get farther that way than if I wait for our Lord.

Other Information   Margaret was always taught that she should sacrifice everything for another person. She even put this into practice so that her brother could satisfy his curiosity at her expense. She did not want to hurt his feelings. But sex before marriage was a mortal sin; hell was the punishment. The girl was responsible. Girls had to sacrifice everything, including themselves, and then they were to blame. Margaret made excuses for her brother. He was curious. On his second attempt, she still felt sorry for him because she refused him. This is understandable when we realize how heavily her experience was influenced by Catholic morals. In that light, the act and the offender were virtually insignificant. In this family, there was an enormous fear of breaking the rules of the church. Their life on earth was one of bitter poverty, and breaking the rules canceled out the prospect of a better life in the hereafter. So little was told about the offender that it is impossible to draw any conclusions about him here.

Nell: *The Lord Jesus saw everything and he would find a way to punish me.*

Nell is thirty-six years old. She was the oldest of three children, two girls and a boy. She was conceived prior to her parent's marriage and was unwanted. Father sexually abused her for many years. Her husband abused her, physically and sexually, and sexually abused her baby. She is now divorced.

What Is Your Religious Background?   We were strict orthodox Dutch Reformed. Father said short prayers before meals and long prayers after meals, and prayed again before bedtime. During prayers, he named the child who had done something wrong that day. The Lord Jesus saw everything and he would find a way to punish you. It wasn't until a few days later that we received our punishment, because by then Father knew what he had to do. As a child, you were terribly afraid—it made an enormous impression on you that Father heard all this directly from Jesus. Father always said, "The mills of God grind slowly yet they grind exceedingly fine." He also said, "God punishes swiftly". A passage from the Bible was read aloud four times a day. Without warning, you were told to repeat the last sentence. If you didn't know it, you received no food at the next meal, but you had to be present for the Bible reading and prayers. Having fun didn't fit in with our religion. Birthdays weren't celebrated, no presents, and no prayers of thanks. From the time I was very young, I always felt some kind of aversion to evening prayers. I think I was rebelling against it. Wasn't the Bible supposed to be beautiful and good?

I had to go to Sunday school from nine o'clock to ten on Sundays, then to church, and in the afternoon to the children's service. We had catechism every week from a very strict minister who grabbed you and hit your hands with a ruler if you didn't pay attention. I think that I really just let it go in one ear and out the other. I got bad grades for religion at school. I got punished for that. I had to copy a long passage from the Bible, for example.

I never made my avowal. I absolutely refused.

How Would You Describe the Offender?   My father was declared unfit to work and he did a lot around the house. That's why the neighbors thought he was a wimp. Later on, Mother got a job. Father was afraid of arguments. Mother was more aggressive. Later on I noticed that he was acting very peculiarly with a girlfriend of my sister's. Mother noticed it, too, and she told the girl she was no longer welcome at our house. It always came down to the same thing: the girl was the one to blame.

How Did Your Father and Mother Relate?   Father had the final say on religious matters. Outside of that, he did what Mother wanted at home. The only time he put up an argument was when it involved me; then he stuck up for me. Not only didn't they want me, but I was also the cause of their arguments.

How Did the Children Relate to Each Other?   My little sister is still Mother's favorite. She knew more than I did about being pregnant, for example. I was so naive. My brother tried it once with me, too, but I refused. He was willing to take "no" for an answer.

How Did Parents and Children Relate?   Mother didn't want to have anything to do with me. I was an unwanted child. Mother had to get married because she was pregnant with me. You could just feel her thinking, "I don't like you." But then Father

would say, "Even though we didn't want her, she was given to us by God. We're obligated by God to love her; if you won't give her that love, then I will."

When I didn't want to marry my boyfriend because I'd realized that he was cruel, my parents forced me to marry him anyway.

What Was the Nature of the Abuse?   It started with sitting on Father's lap, kissing, and so on. That was nice. But when I had to get undressed for him, when I was seven, I didn't like it any more.

Sometimes he said that mother had to sleep with my sister and that I had to sleep with him, and then he started again. He said this was because I was a terribly nervous child and couldn't lie still at night. Other times, Father would come to get me at Sunday school and say, "Your sister is going to church with your mother and your brother, and you're going home with me." Then I'd say, "No, I don't have to. I want to go to church with them, and I don't want to go home with you." But he said that I couldn't sit still, that he was doing it for my own good, and that he felt sorry for me because then I'd be punished again. I wouldn't be allowed to go to Grandma's after church because I hadn't been able to sit still. It still bothers me that I did say I didn't want to go home with him, and that I always started to cry, but that I still never really refused him. And when he did it to me and I was lying there crying, he'd say that I shouldn't cry: My punishment would come anyway. I wasn't allowed to cry; I was supposed to enjoy it. He did forgive me for crying, because he loved me, he said, and that was as it should be. All fathers did that. Then he'd say, "Go to church with me this afternoon; then you can ask God for forgiveness." Because my crying was what he called "defying your father" and that wasn't allowed. Later, when I started to resist him and really didn't want to anymore, he criticized me for it, and he said that he felt sorry for my husband because he had his needs, too. My husband abused me, physically and sexually. He sexually abused my daughter when she was a baby. When she was about two years old, I took the children and left him. I have no contact now with him or with my father.

How Did Mother Deal with Incest?   Mother always said that she didn't know what was going on, but I find that very hard to believe. It went on for years—until I was thirty-five. When I was restless as a child they'd argue. He'd say, "Let her sleep with me." But she would say, "Her sister sleeps well enough; she's a good little girl." The angels were watching over her, and it was my own fault that I didn't sleep peacefully, because I was a bad girl. When I didn't want to go with Father, she would say, "Do as your father says." She said I was ungrateful and didn't realize how much my father was sacrificing for me.

What Prevented You from Breaking Your Silence?
Talk to Mother about it? No, she didn't like me to begin with. Then I would have nothing left at all. I was scared, too, that no one would believe me. If I didn't accept everything he was doing for me with gratitude, then I would end up in hell, Mother said. I was also to blame for their arguments. They would have been so happy together if I hadn't been born. In the beginning, I loved all the attention Father gave me. The first few times I went to him for a good-night kiss, Mother was shocked and became very angry. Cuddling and tenderness were absolutely taboo with her.

How Did Family and Friends Respond to Your Signals?
My ex-husband said that I should forgive my father. I was bad, he said. I should remember Eve. Men were the ones who were good. The world could have been very beautiful, but a woman ruined the world. He saw women as things, with which he could do whatever he pleased.

How Did Agencies or Institutions Respond to Breaking the Conspiracy of Silence?
I had a nervous breakdown and had to go to a psychiatrist. He only listened to what my ex-husband told him. Those two, my father and my ex-husband, covered up for one another, and the psychiatrist went right along with it.

What Impact Has the Abuse Had on You?
I've always felt powerless, because I knew that things kept happening and I didn't want it. I felt dirty and it made me cry, but that wasn't allowed. He called that "defying your father." My father, my brother, and my ex-husband said, "There's something about you that makes men act like this." So I started to watch the way I acted,

walking with my shoulders hunched, not daring to look at anyone. Mother said that I was ugly. "Don't act so proud and self-assured, because you're nothing," she always said. I deliberately wore clothes that weren't pretty, tried to blend into the background as much as possible. But nothing helped. It went on and on. Then you start feeling guilty again. "What am I doing wrong, that God doesn't make it stop, that it keeps on happening? What is it about me that's so bad?" You don't get an answer.

Mother kept saying that I was bad. Father said that I had asked him to do this to me. Sometimes he said, "I really don't know what I'm still doing with you, because you have absolutely no feeling, you're as cold as ice." Then I thought, "Why do you keep coming back, then?"

I became suspicious. My father-in-law really liked me. He was a good man, but I couldn't accept that because my father had abused me sexually. So I thought my father-in-law had an ulterior motive, too, but he wasn't like that at all.

What Connection Do You See with Religion?   The Our Father says "Thy will be done." That made me feel even more guilty. When I cried for defying my father, I thought, "He's right, of course." When he did what he liked with me, and then I had to sit next to him at the table, he would elbow me conspicuously at the moment that he said "Forgive us our trespasses." As if he wanted to say, "You see? I'm praying specially for you." I always had to ask God's forgiveness for defying my father. Sometimes I asked my father why he kept making me do this. Then he said, "All women are the same as that first woman, Eve. You tempt me. In your heart, this is what you want, just like Eve." I used to pray "God, let it stop." But God didn't intervene, so I thought, either it really was God's will, or I really was as bad as they said, and this was my punishment.

What Aspects of Religion Did You Experience as Liberating?   Once I went with a girlfriend to her children's service. It was such a happy service. I've never forgotten it, that one time, but I was punished for going when I got home.

My grandmother had a children's Bible that she kept hidden from my father. On Sunday afternoon, I was allowed to look at it with her. One picture was of the Lord Jesus with all the little children around him. I can still see every detail.

I didn't want to make my avowal. My parents-in-law were very supportive in this, especially my mother-in-law, who had a much warmer faith than my parents. That also made her a warmer person. She and I were close.

What Aspects of Religion Did You Experience as Oppressive?
Fun things, like birthdays, didn't fit in our faith. That wasn't in the Bible. Being sad wasn't allowed either. When my little girlfriend died I wasn't allowed to cry. In our family, you were supposed to be happy when someone died, because she or he was going to heaven. At her grave we sang "Safe in Jesus' Arms." I was defiant: "You can tell me whatever you want, but I've lost her forever". I was so sad and upset that I went to see my grandmother instead of visiting our neighbors to read aloud to them from the Bible as I did every day after school. They were an elderly couple. They complained to my mother and that same night they committed suicide. My mother said that it was all my fault because I hadn't gone to see them. She kept telling me that over and over and over again; I never heard the end of it.

What Male and Female Images Did You Learn from Your Religious Upbringing?
My father said, "All women are the same as that first woman, Eve." He said that I was bad and that I should think of Eve. Men were the good ones. A woman had ruined the world. He also said that he was better than my mother, because she didn't love me and she should, according to the Bible. He did love me, so he was better. He thought my mother was bad.

There were more bad women in the Bible. Lot's wife was turned into a pillar of salt. We always had to skip over the story of the woman who washed Jesus' feet. As soon as we got to that part, Mother put a stop to it. She didn't want a whore like that to be forgiven. She also didn't think it was right that Jesus forgave that adulterous woman who was going to be stoned. If she'd had her way, that story would have been stricken from the Bible.

What Did You Learn about Sexuality?
We didn't discuss anything about sexuality at home. My mother could hardly bring herself to tell us she was pregnant. She was in tears. My sister said,

"Oh, do you two go to bed together?" She knew more than I did. The first time I menstruated, my mother said: "Oh, is that what's wrong with you?" Her whole face went red and she didn't explain anything. I went to an aunt who did explain things a little. Father said, "From now on, I'll have to use something." And sometimes he said, "I didn't use anything this time, so I hope things turn out all right". After a while he said, "I don't even think you can have any children." He just assumed that I started sleeping with my boyfriend as soon as we met. He said, "Now you have your boyfriend, so it could be his, too."

Nudity was completely taboo. That was something my father was very strict about. The door had to be locked when we took a bath in the washtub. I couldn't understand that. A church elder warned me that I was going to turn out bad when I put my arm around a girlfriend once. When I was eighteen years old, my mother slapped me across the face for hugging a girlfriend.

What Is Your Image of God? God was someone who punished. You had to do everything according to the rules, but we knew from the stories in the Bible that he was also good. That just didn't make sense to me. I was able to keep my faith in a God who punished, but I couldn't believe in a God who was good. I was afraid of dying because I thought, "Then I'll go to hell." Whenever I get really sick, I still get absolutely terrified. All of those old fears close in on me again, "See? I knew it. Now I'm going to go to hell." We had to be really good to get into heaven. But my mother said, "You'll never get into heaven." The angels watched over you at night, but not over me, because I was no good. I could never understand the image of the good shepherd because God wasn't like that in our family. He was always made out to be someone I was terribly afraid of. It didn't make any sense. I used to ask, "God, help me. Make the incest stop." You're brought up that way so you expect that if you pray, it will stop. But God didn't intervene. Then you're disappointed in God and you start to think, "Nothing matters now—I just don't care anymore."

What Do You Associate with These Words?

Forgiveness: When you defied your father, you had to ask forgiveness.

Tenderness: No one was tender; you didn't even get a good-night kiss.

Where Do You Get Your Strength?   Strength? I'm glad I

do have that. I had a breakdown once, but that was because of other things. I stand up for myself. In spite of everything that has happened to me, I have always had the idea that someday things would turn out all right. I was walking around feeling that I should do something about it. Later, I think it was my children who made me strong. These children are mine, I would think.

Does that have anything to do with the church? No, absolutely nothing—not anymore.

Other Information   In Nell's church, women and sexuality

bore the curse of evil, guilt, and punishment. For Mother, sexuality meant only sin. Through her faith, she knew that she was the sinner who tempted men. She deserved to be punished for conceiving a child out of wedlock. She could not see her child Nell as a gift from God, but instead saw in her proof of her own evil. Because Father was considered innocent of all this, he was able to accept the child, but he accepted her as a woman who, unconsciously, tempted him again. As a man, he was able to enjoy sex freely. Did he have no guilt feelings for deceiving his wife and terrorizing his daughter?

Now that Nell has refused to see her father anymore, he says that he is sorry and that he is willing to talk to a social worker.

Nell said that talking to us gave her the release from her father's power. We gave her the room she needed to express her anger toward him, and toward God, and to share it with us. That gave her the strength to refuse to see her father. She said she is now encouraged when others acknowledge and value her capabilities.

She is no longer ashamed of what happened. It is no longer her fault, and the shame is no longer hers.

| Susan: | *I didn't scream because he said, "They won't believe you, anyway."* |

Susan is now thirty-two years old. She is the ninth child in a family of ten children, of which the oldest is also a girl. The tenth child was mentally handicapped, a boy born relatively late in Mother's life. Susan was sexually abused by three older brothers.

What Is Your Religious Background?   My parents are strict orthodox Dutch Reformed. We went to church twice on Sundays. Mother always went. I often babysat my little brother; then I didn't have to go. As a child, I was very religious, but the older children started refusing to go, so I began doing it, too. The girls always had to go to church with my parents with nice dresses on, but my brothers always came in at the last minute with their hair wet from swimming.

Prayers were said three times a day, before and after meals. After the meal, we read from the Bible, a religious diary, and the proverb on the daily calendar. It wasn't something you really felt inside, it was imposed on you from the outside, rules you had to obey. My parents were actually very emotional people, very enthusiastic, but there were a lot of arguments and schisms in our church. They didn't know how to deal with that. I remember only strife in the church. The minister often came to see my mother, but he only came when Father wasn't home. Father didn't want to talk to him. Father wasn't dogmatic enough, and that's why he had no official position in the church. Later, when he moved, he became an elder in the new church.

We were a host family for soldiers and nurses from the church, so we always had a lot of people in the house.

The church dictated our entire social life, school, clubs, and acquaintances. Friends were allowed to come home with us as long as they were from the same church. When I left the church, I received a letter telling me that I was damned. My parents dropped me too.

How Would You Describe the Offenders?   The offenders were three older brothers: the fourth child and the sixth child, who was very aggressive, and another brother who was two years older than I was.

How Did Your Father and Mother Relate?   Father said that the man was the head of the family, but he had rheumatism and was often sick. Whenever Mother had a baby, he always got sick, too. It was as if he did it intentionally. Mother really ran

everything; she's a very strong woman. In our house, the money went to Mother, and Father had his allowance. Our income wasn't large, and it took a lot of hard work. She could never buy a nice dress, so she never joined church clubs. She did have her own friends, from her old job. She went there one day a week. That was her day. Father agreed with that.

How Did the Children Relate to Each Other? The older children educated the younger ones. I was the family scapegoat: "What have you done now?" When my sister left home and I was finally out from under her thumb, I was a completely different child. Still, I know she understood me, because she has accused my parents of emotionally neglecting me. After my little brother was born he was often sick, so Mother had no time for us, the youngest children in the family. She regretted that later on.

How Did Parents and Children Relate? That was very unclear with Father. He had his work and spent a lot of time in the garden. He encouraged me to go to the college prep high school. Mother thought that was ridiculous, certainly for a girl. Mother got her morals from the church. She was a dominating person, but now I think that Father made her that way. She was very no-nonsense. Nobody could stand her. I was the only one who loved her, but from the time I was twelve until I was twenty-two, I positively couldn't stand her either. Before you were twelve, you were raised as a person, but when you turned twelve, your mother had to keep a close eye on you, because then you belonged with the women. From that time on, all I heard was, "No, no, no." I was compelled to do things without any reasonable arguments. A girl had to obey rules. I secretly bought tampons so I could swim when I had my period. Until she found out. She talked to Father about it, although I was never supposed to mention menstruation to men. I felt that she'd betrayed me. Still, Mother was a kind person. No matter what happened, you were still her child. She lets her feelings show more nowadays.

Later on Mother said that she left us to be looked after by the older children too much, but she said she had to because she was so busy.

What Was the Nature of the Abuse?   One brother played sex games with me in the attic when I was four or five years old. He was always touching me, which I absolutely hated. He said that there was nothing wrong with it, but when you could hear Mother coming, it was, "Quick, be quiet." She wasn't allowed to know. I thought, "If there's nothing wrong with it, why's Mother not allowed to know?"

After that came the next brother. I was about eight years old. He had a terrible temper. He played all kinds of games with me and I was really afraid. I was scared to death of him. I ended up isolating myself, had a lot of guilt feelings, and started leading a sort of double life. Emotion and reason completely separated. There's a big hole in my life from the time I was eight until I was thirteen. I had a really nice girlfriend I used to go swimming with, and when he showed up he always had candy with him. She loved candy. Then he took her with him into the woods and made her play all sorts of games with him. He created an atmosphere, with girlfriends and such, that he was the fun brother, the popular guy. It made me sick to see him coming. He raped me in the house. The room where I slept was above the living room where the whole family was sitting, but he said, "Go ahead and scream. They won't believe you, anyway". If I had screamed, they would have come running, but there was something in our family that kept me from doing it—fear and terror.

The third brother was two years older than I was. He and I were best buddies when we were growing up. When he was about thirteen, we were playing that he was a boy and I was a girl. He didn't want to go shopping with me anymore, he said, because everybody made fun of him. I didn't understand that. One of his friends was a real hood. My brother and his friend raped me. They used it to blackmail me, too.

How Did Parents Deal with Incest?   Mother never suspected it. She was very unsuspecting and naive about sex. Last year, when we were talking about the past, my father said, "You wrote that you felt isolated and that terrible things had happened. I think I know what you're talking about." I said, "Oh, really, what?" Then he said, "Never mind." He looked as if he were in pain, but said nothing else. Mother asked, "What are you talking about?" "No, never mind," he said.

What Prevented You from Breaking Your Silence?
Not talking about it had nothing to do with religion that you could put your finger on; it had more to do with the atmosphere, with knowing that my parents would never believe something like that. In our family, no one ever believed me. The way my brother acted (the one who was two years older) was so sickening, so sneaky, so obvious, but I was the black sheep. I know that sounds like self-pity, but that's just the way it was. Now things are changing somewhat; I can feel it. They can't just blame it all on me anymore. I'm the one who decides: You have to take me the way I am or not at all.

As a child, I was crazy about my parents. I wanted our family life to be warm and happy, so I started to behave the way a sweet, affectionate child is supposed to.

Something wasn't right. If it wasn't wrong, why wasn't Mother allowed to know about it?

How Did Family and Friends Respond to Your Signals?
Before I got married, I said to my sister, "I'm an incest survivor," and told her what had happened. She said that she'd always thought so. She told me that she'd been molested once by one of my brothers too. My parents found out about it and kicked him out of the house. She's almost eight years older than I am.

Before my marriage, I told my fiancé about what had happened because I didn't want him to buy "damaged goods" without knowing it. He asked me, "Is that really true?" People can't believe it. He thought I should just forget about it too: It was over and done with. But I was a little suspicious of him as well because his little sister complained once that he always crawled into bed with her on the weekends. She said she didn't like him doing that—she was a big girl. He was very hurt when he heard this because she'd been afraid to tell him herself. He felt rejected. But I think it started the same way for me all those years ago.

How Did Agencies or Institutions Respond to Breaking the Conspiracy of Silence?
I was a member of a feminist group for two years. That's when I became aware of how

I'd always conformed to what others wanted in the past. Now I'm in therapy, using dream analysis; that's where I finally threw that molester out the door. But when it really happened I didn't scream, I didn't do anything.

What Impact Has the Abuse Had on You?   I think that all of my feelings got switched off when I was about eight years old, as if in a dream. I can't get a grip on it. I was at my wit's end, completely desperate. The incest was my fault, I kept thinking. I wanted to kill myself, to be dead. But there is also predestination. God governs all things, that's what they teach. He knows everything and I thought, "Then He also knows that I'm going to die, so I'm not going to do it—I'm not going to give him the satisfaction." But I tried to anyway. You just do that as a child. Through my studies, I became much more aware of my emotions. I met a girl there, and I thought, "God is looking out for me," as my mother always used to say.

I also thought, "God sees everything, but he lets all of this happen. That man doesn't exist, it's just somebody to keep you in line."

In our church, there was a lot of whispering about "pregnancy out of wedlock." Whenever that happened, people said that this man hadn't been paying attention to his daughter. Just imagine if that had happened to me. I was afraid it would. Things got really weird inside my head.

What Connection Do You See with Religion?   It was more the atmosphere at home, the atmosphere of terror. I've thought about this a lot. The oppressive side of religion, the predetermined role for women: It's always their fault. Theology validates that.

What Aspects of Religion Did You Experience as Liberating?   In our church, you had better credentials when you were poor and had a large family than when you were rich and had only two children. That made my father happy. For him, religion was a liberating experience.

It was extremely difficult for Mother to accept the fact that my little brother was mentally handicapped. But in the church, it wasn't seen as a punishment from God. God had his reasons, not only for all of us but for our community, too. This philosophy helped Mother to accept him completely.

What Aspects of Religion Did You Experience as Oppressive?
I remember only strife in our church, being compelled to do things, and total misery. When I left, I received a letter telling me that I was damned. My mother complained to my husband at the time: "I never wanted to tell you this, but I felt sorry for you when you married her." That's just what she said, "Poor man." They got into a big discussion and took whatever he said seriously, because he was still a member of the church, but they completely ignored my arguments. I was bad.

The Bible has revolting stories, like the one about a woman who slept with a man and then put a "nail of the tent" through his head. As a child, I thought: How could anyone sleep with a man, snuggle in bed together, and then do something like that in order to achieve something? I think that's horrible.

What I really found oppressive was that the woman was always to blame. That still bothers me, even now. I still take the blame for things all the time. Oh, you can trace it all the way back to Eve who seduced Adam.

What Male and Female Images Did You Learn from Your Religious Upbringing?
Father thought women were marvelous people, beautiful, God's creation. We had to wear our hair long and be neat. He thought women's liberation was terrible because then women work more for the money than for their own development, and then you get the same situation as in the developing countries. In ten years, the men wouldn't do anything anymore, the women would be doing all the work. He was always very protective of women. I really had a pretty nice father.

We lived by a double standard in our house. If a woman was raped, she was asking for it. Women arouse the desires of men, who can't help themselves. My brothers had to bring the nurses home who'd been at our house and wait until they were safely inside. You had to take care of women.

Mother preferred having eight boys to having two girls, because she thought that girls were very difficult. She thought that raising girls was a lot of trouble, and I was just impossible. Women were loving when they were good mothers and good wives.

Boys are a better breed. Good fathers have sons, and fatherhood means putting sons on this earth. Mother was proud of the fact that she had so many sons.

Eve had tempted Adam. That was the fall of man and, because of it, man had brought all this upon himself. Jesus was brought into this world through a line of whores. Tamar, Bathsheba, and Mary Magdelene were all bad according to the Bible, but God had his reasons. Mary, the mother of Jesus, was a problem because the Catholics worshiped her, so she was unimportant. Women weren't discussed at all, as a matter of fact: No one preached about them, told stories about them, or even talked about them. The sermons were about men, about Jesus, John the Baptist, the people of Israel.

Women weren't allowed to hold positions in the church, either. They had to have something to fall back on, so they had to learn a skill, to be able to be independent if necessary, but they weren't allowed work if they were married. Women were to blame for unemployment because they worked for money. There was that double standard again. That was so frustrating, you got desperate.

What Did You Learn about Sexuality?   My parents lived their life in obedience to God's command: "Go forth and multiply."

My Mother recently asked me what I do about sex when I don't want to get pregnant. She never wanted all those children, she said, but that's the way it was then. At a certain point, she hadn't wanted to have sex anymore, because she kept getting pregnant. She was very naive.

I didn't know anything about orgasms and my husband thought I was a cold fish. We didn't receive any sex education. You just didn't talk about those things, or about your body, or about nudity. In gym class we had gym pants with a special gym skirt over them.

Sexuality was something that happened to women, just like pregnancy. It was disgusting, but also beautiful. I thought, I'll think it's beautiful because my husband thinks it's beautiful. A woman had no sexuality herself. I know I'm really uptight about sexuality. I have this fear of men. I suddenly realized that. My brother looked under my girlfriend's skirt once. When I said something to him about it, he replied, "Then she shouldn't sit like that."

What Is Your Image of God? God punishes justly and harshly but mostly harshly and cruelly. That was our own fault. The little bit you did get, you had to be extremely grateful for. You had to do your best, live according to God's word, but you couldn't earn it, like the Catholics. It was all his mercy.

And then there was predestination. He knows everything beforehand, governs, and makes things happen. When people were really sick, God wanted it that way, but you didn't have to see it as punishment.

Every morning, Mother read from the children's Bible. I always felt good when she read the story of Noah, floating along in a boat on the water. I read the story of Esther myself—fantastic, the way she managed that whole thing. But no one ever preached about that. As for the rest, all I can remember is a feeling of, "Away, get it away from me." I was really, really religious then, and I could imagine what God was and what Jesus was in a hundred thousand different ways. I was really good at that, and I thought it was great.

What Do You Associate with These Words?

Good: Well-behaved, industrious.

Evil: Lying, mischievous, having different views.

Responsibility: The woman is responsible.

Forgiveness: Asking forgiveness in order to escape being punished, nothing positive.

Injustice: The whole system that perpetuates this: "Maybe that girl invented this whole story."

Trust: Giving yourself to someone completely.

Guilt: That's difficult. I was always guilty; I was always the one who had done it—the incest too. That was my fault.

Love thy neighbor: Doing everything for the other person; that's the way it used to be. Now I think: Think of yourself first, the rest will come automatically.

Love: What I feel for my son. I was a constant failure in my parents' eyes, but I know, no one can ever take this away from me.

Where Do You Get Your Strength?   I get strength from women who are warm, just, and honest. I have a lot of good people in my life, women friends. My work is also important to me. There's a will in me to survive. I believe in a good atmosphere. That's all I need for the time being. I have no need of a hereafter.

In the old days, I was denied as a person. That's the way I felt. I had no will of my own. I'm just learning that now. When my own child was born, I started to fight back. I didn't want to lose him. I didn't start to fight back until then.

Other Information   Because of the double standard, the numerous double messages directed at women, and the power of men and boys, there was a terrorizing atmosphere in Susan's home. Moreover, Susan had the bad luck of being the next-to-the-youngest child in a large family that also had frequent guests. Caring for all of these guests was an added burden on the Mother's already considerable work load.

When she answered the questions about the liberating and oppressive aspects of religion, Susan first talked about how her father saw it. Then she talked about how her mother experienced it. Her own feelings and experiences were not explicitly mentioned. They are woven through her entire story. She is in the painful process of trying to achieve self-awareness. This can be clearly seen when she talks about her own child, too. She never put up a fight until he was born. She was still clinging to someone else, not fighting for herself.

It must have been very confusing to her as a child to hear her father say that nothing could happen to girls as long as they were kept inside. Did Father not get entangled in his own theory? He did not intervene when he suspected that incest was going on under his own roof.

During a recent workshop, Susan said that she was getting stronger. Her resistance is increasing. The relationship with her parents is also getting better, becoming clearer.

| Carol: | *Then they point the finger at the church because women have no say there.* |

Carol is thirty years old. She is the eldest in a family of four children, and was followed by a sister and two brothers. She was conceived before her parents married, an unwanted child.

What Is Your Religious Background? Mother was raised in the Dutch Reformed church, but left the church when she got married. Father was anti-religious. He always held Mother's Dutch Reformed upbringing against her. He was a radical liberal and he held Den Uyl's Dutch Reformed background against him too.[4] My father raised me to compartmentalize everything in my life. Everything that didn't fit into one of his categories was either no good or weird. People were pigeonholed according to their political beliefs or their church. He could always find something wrong with you. I was a choir member in high school, but I wasn't allowed to participate in performances given in a church. Father watched the current affairs program produced by the the Catholic-affiliated television network because "one had to know what the enemy was up to." In our family, socialism was practiced like a kind of religion. It gives people extremely high ideals to live up to and people try to do so. Those ideals are unrealistically high, so you're always falling short.

Our family gatherings were like church gatherings in a lot of ways. There was a lot of ritual on my father's side of the family. The entire family got together on Christmas, Easter, and birthdays. Everybody was expected to be there. We always spent the day in exactly the same way; deviation from the standard plan was not permitted. You made your way up from childhood to adulthood. First you ate in the kitchen and then, when you were older, you were allowed to eat with the grown-ups in the dining room. Conversation was always about politics and education, and all the

4. In the 1970s and 1980s, Joop Den Uyl was the Socialist Labor Party Leader in the Netherlands and also served as prime minister. — Trans.

relatives were pretty fanatic. What my parents preached wasn't what they practiced at all; their words and actions were totally at odds. So as a child you had no idea where you stood. Father saw the church as an institution that always caused wars and was against peace. That sounds pretty ridiculous, being brought up in a family as violent as mine. He also believed that churchgoers couldn't be trusted. He could see it in their faces: They were exploiters. According to him, the Vatican was very wealthy. My parents read everything they could get their hands on, but only when it was in keeping with the party line.

How Would You Describe the Offender?   Father didn't come home until I was six years old. Up until that time, he was away studying. He was very lazy and slept a lot of the time. While he was sleeping, you had to tiptoe around the house. He always had to have the biggest piece of meat at the dinner table. He was authoritarian, subject to moods. I idolized him, but it was difficult to fulfill a god's desires and demands. His eyes could make you do things. My relationship with my mother wasn't very good and, as a result, I became closer to my father. I was proud of that, because he was a "Van Dyke". Being a member of this particular family was a big deal to him. It determined Father's whole life, the way socialism did. There was something fascist about it. It had to do with being Aryan, with Wodan and all of that. I had a strong physical resemblance to my father.

Father had girlfriends. Some of them even came to the house. You were supposed to respect one another, but he said once that he respected only one woman, and with her he had a platonic relationship. We lived in an apartment that was much too small. Mother was a basket case for a long time. She later told me that there had been more children between me and my sister and brother but she'd gotten rid of them. She said something about knitting needles. Father had his first girlfriend when Mother was pregnant with my sister. He was also fooling around with the daughter of friends of theirs.

Father had a very bad temper; he'd get physically violent. You didn't dare defy him when he was like that. He had a thing for pornography. Sex was discussed very openly at home, but his porno books and films were stashed away. (Everybody knew where he kept them, anyway.) His drinking got steadily worse, particularly after I increasingly started resisting the incest, when I was about fifteen. He always made a point of displaying his approval or disapproval of a boyfriend of mine or my sister's. We weren't allowed to sleep together in "his" house.

Outside our four walls, he's a completely different person. He's always been very active in the community. Every time he got a new job, his old employers gave him a big send-off. We were the ideal family in the eyes of the outside world. We all contributed to holding up that image.

How Did Your Father and Mother Relate?

At family gatherings, men and women alike discussed everything under the sun, but after dinner the men went for a walk and the women did the dishes. Father looks down on Mother, but he also needs her. He always came back to her. Mother says that she loves him, but I don't think she can see through him. Ever since I was twelve, she's been saying, "We're getting a divorce," but the next day everything was sweetness and light again. On the surface, Father had the power, certainly as far as our upbringing and ethical values went. Mother was in charge of money and how we spent our vacations. She organized that. Mother bought a car, but he decided that she had to get rid of it because it would interfere with the attention she was supposed to be giving the children. She was also a board member of the club she belonged to. She had to give that up. She waited six months and joined another club. She had hysterical tantrums, but even then she didn't get her way. When Father wanted his way, he got into these moods. If he didn't want something to happen, it didn't. When he got that way, he wouldn't talk and then he'd get really mad and physically violent. I hardly ever saw them kiss each other. She tried to, but he always fended her off.

How Did the Children Relate to Each Other?

My brothers were born when I was nine years old. I was given the role of care provider at home. I was a second mother and took care of my little brothers by myself. They still come to see me. I felt unwanted at home, unlike my sister. For a very long time, I felt responsible for her. Whenever she had problems, she'd come to me. I helped her in whatever way I could. She still goes home, as if nothing's happened. I'm the black sheep, because I brought it all out into the open.

How Did Parents and Children Relate? Father was constantly playing one of us children off against another. Mother gave me a little something extra once in a while, but she never stuck up for me. I pity my mother, but I don't want anything to do with her anymore. Every once in a while, she'll call me on the phone and take me by surprise. Then I have nightmares. Mother saw me as a rival, too. She suppressed everything inside me that was uniquely mine. She criticized my looks, told me that I was clumsy, that I wasn't pretty, that I wasn't a good student. I was very outgoing as a child, but everything you said was used against you. For as long as I can remember, I couldn't stand it when she touched me. I always had the feeling that when she touched me she didn't mean it; there was no feeling there. She did have a good relationship with my sister.

I haven't had any contact with my father for five years. I spoke to him just before before the television broadcasts on incest. It wasn't my idea. He said, "I'm telling our friends that you're lying, and I'm telling the family that you seduced me." He hasn't changed a bit. Sometimes I wish he would drop dead in his tracks. I had no choices, no options. I wasn't allowed to do anything. I wasn't allowed to go out. He picked out my clothes. He didn't allow me to smoke, but allowed me to drink. I was a good girl and did all that until I was twenty. When you had to go to the doctor Father always went with you.

What Was the Nature of the Abuse? My first memory of incest was when I was eleven years old. Father says that it started earlier, but I don't remember. It started with him touching me. I didn't want him to and acted like I was turning over in my sleep. We were staying at his parents. There weren't enough beds for everyone and they said, "You two can sleep together, can't you?" Mother was home. For a while after that, nothing happened. Then, he started again when I was about thirteen. That's when he first started screwing me. In the beginning, he kept me quiet by saying, "If you talk about this, you'll end up in jail and so will I." When I was about fifteen, I was able to put up more resistance. I began to realize that I had a certain power over him. Then he went into a nervous breakdown. That was really awful. One time, Mother called the family doctor in the middle of the night. As soon as she got him on the phone, Father suddenly started acting normal again. The next day, he went to the doctor, and so did I. I said, "I can tell you what's wrong with Father." But the doctor didn't want to discuss Father with me. That's when I gave in again, under all that pressure. I felt responsible. I was the one who could make it stop. He molested my girlfriends and he also abused one of my cousins. During those years, he started drinking more heavily.

When I was sixteen, I talked to him about it. At the time, he was in the middle of another breakdown and kept telling me about his girlfriends, over and over again. After my brothers were born he couldn't go to my mother anymore. He said he thought it was really terrible of himself, but he just couldn't stop.

The last period was the worst. I wasn't allowed to do anything at all, to go out, to smoke—I could drink. He picked out my clothes. When I was eighteen, I ended up in a hospital. According to one of the psychiatrists, I had a "hyperesthetic emotional syndrome." I later looked up the description. It fits my experiences exactly. People in concentration camps, who are tortured and woken up at regular intervals during the night, have the same symptoms. The doctor in the hospital was a friend of Father's. I said that I did not want to go home under any circumstances. Nobody asked why. I was put on tranquilizers for a long time, which made me completely apathetic. Those last two years, he tried out entire porno shops on me. I left home when I was twenty. I wasn't allowed to do that when I was seventeen. They said that I'd never be able to make it on my own.

When I was twenty-five, I came home once in a while. Father wanted to start over again, which is when I told him exactly what I thought of him. After I'd been out of the house for a year, I heard that the same thing was happening with my sister.

How Did Mother Deal with Incest? Mother never suspected anything. When Father had his breakdown, she made an enormous effort to cover up what was happening at home. I don't understand that at all. I have a lot of difficulty with her role in all of this. I know it isn't right for me to blame her, but she had economic means. She's involved in everything. She marches in peace protests, demonstrates for all kinds of causes, is always good to other people. She used all different kinds of mental violence in our family. She constantly played us children off against one

another. Father always said to her, "Your father did it with you. You're just like your mother; she was crazy, and you're going to go crazy later too." Grandma spent five years in an institution. The worst times were the weekends when Mother visited her. She didn't understand at the time why I clung to her so and why I was so affectionate, so desperate. She never realized what was happening.

What Prevented You from Breaking Your Silence?
My father saw to it that I kept silent; he isolated me. On top of that, my parents were people who were very highly respected in the community. No one would have believed me. I didn't trust other people enough either. When the people you love the most abuse your trust so badly, it haunts you for the rest of your life. That's the most difficult thing: getting that trust back. I don't really know whether I loved him or not. I was flattered because I resembled him. He was like a god, an idol; I wanted to be in his favor.

How Did Others Respond?
The family doctor didn't want to talk about Father with me. The doctor in the hospital was a friend of his. When I was in the hospital, I said that I did not want to go home under any circumstances. Nobody asked me why not. I was taking a lot of prescribed tranquilizers at the time, which made me totally apathetic. When my sister wanted to buy a present for our parents' twenty-fifth wedding anniversary, I didn't want to go in with her on it, and I ended up having a nervous breakdown. I went to the Dutch Family Planning Association (Rutgers Foundation) so I could talk to somebody. I got fifteen minutes with a doctor, which I had to spend defending myself against his suggestions that I'd had a good time and that I'd enjoyed it. Then he said that I was very good at talking about it. He thought I'd be okay.

My brothers suffered, too, with all that tension in the house. I still have a good relationship with them.

What Impact Has the Abuse Had on You?
After I turned twenty-five, I developed all kinds of problems, not psychologically, but physically. The doctors ran all sorts of tests, but they couldn't really find anything. I later talked to my friends about it, but it was just a vicious circle. They can't really understand what

it's like, anyway. Now I'm in psychoanalysis. That helps, but it costs an enormous effort. Still, I couldn't go on not talking. For years, I was like a pressure cooker. It was all pent up inside, and it had to come out, otherwise I would have been destroyed. I also had this self-destructive streak. A lot of what's inside me is broken. I have to find out what's left inside me, and whether I can do anything with it. I have a feeling that's possible.

What Connection Do You See with Religion? We were dogmatic leftists; everything that wasn't in line with the dogma was wrong. Father's role in our family, sanctioned or not, he saw his wife and children more as property and things than as people with feelings. Socialists and communists have never recognized the oppressed position of women. They're very much male cultures. Even the sexual revolution provided more advantages to men in leftist circles than women. They continued to think: "When a woman says no, she means yes." They never talked about the underlying ideologies. Then they point the finger at the church because women have no say there.

What Aspects of Religion Did You Experience as Liberating? You were raised with the idea that you belonged to a certain group of people who all had good intentions. Belonging to a group with ideals was nice, but when you see what my parents did to me, I wonder, "What was it like for other people in the party?" For me, teachers were role models, people I could identify with. On my report card, it said, "Enjoys helping other children." You were commended for the good things you did. You could be who you were. They saw you for who you really were. Nobody ever did at home.

What Aspects of Religion Did You Experience as Oppressive? You had to suppress your emotions. You couldn't be yourself. You weren't allowed to cry, to show your emotions. You weren't allowed to be enthusiastic, or spontaneous, or happy because you got an "A+." You were supposed to get an "A+." You had to constantly push yourself to the limit and live up to their expectations. They talked about "sharing with each other," while Father always took the biggest piece of meat at the dinner table.

What Male and Female Images Did You Learn from Your Religious Upbringing? Everything was under the pretext that girls were valued just as highly as boys (girls had to learn a profession too), but little brothers were called family heirs, and the women did the housekeeping. Father told pretty stories about love and being faithful, but he never began to live up to them. Mother never once stepped out of line. He had a very high regard for honor, conscience, faithfulness, and honesty.

What Did You Learn about Sexuality? The attitude at home toward sex was very open, but not at school. Father had a penchant for pornography, but that was kept secret. When I was nine years old, Mother told me the facts of life, and she bought a cake to celebrate the first time I menstruated. She was very open about all of her problems with miscarriages. She wasn't allowed to wear white when she got married, because she was pregnant with me at the time. Mother thought sex was beautiful. I'd experienced it with Father by that time and I thought it was filthy. Mother said that she liked it, but I never got the impression that Father gave any consideration to what a woman might want.

What Is Your Image of God? Father said, "God is something people have invented." The church was in cahoots with capitalists; they were in business together. Otherwise, he didn't talk about God.

What Do You Associate with These Words?

Good: Justice, being able to be who you are, not sacrificing everything for someone else, but being allowed to love yourself too.

Evil: Somebody thinking they have the right to decide whether another person will live or die. That's something that's inside people and in the system.

Guilt: If people are really guilty they have to be punished. You can't just gloss over it. People have to hold each other responsible for their actions. That's being responsible, not only for yourself, but holding others responsible.

Responsibility: Discovering your purpose in life and setting goals to achieve it. I still often ask myself why I didn't get out sooner. I should have been able to get out earlier. I have to learn not always to think of others first, because being there for someone else can become the only dignity you have left.

Forgiveness: What my father did can't be forgiven. He affected my whole life and my brothers' lives. Where did he ever get the right and the nerve to do that?

Love thy neighbor: You have to begin with yourself. When I realized that I had problems in my relationships, I could see that it wasn't other people's fault, but that it was because of me. I have to start with myself and learn to love myself. That's a very gradual process.

Injustice: There's a lot of injustice, particularly toward women and children.

Where Do You Get Your Strength?
I'm still here; sometimes I think that's pretty incredible. That's where I get my courage and strength, and from the association. I hope it's possible to change things together with other people. I don't believe in mass political parties, but in people who are close to each other.

Other Information
Carol has filed a complaint with the police regarding her father's sexual abuse of her when she was a minor.

Mary Beth: *As a woman you had to suppress certain talents; they weren't appropriate to your role in life.*

Mary Beth was born the fifth child into a family of four boys. She was clearly a child who was wanted. The first daughter had died three weeks after being born. Two girls and a boy were born after Mary Beth, a total of eight children. She was sexually abused by her oldest brother, who was six years older.

What Is Your Religious Background?
The Roman Catholic faith was very important to my parents. We prayed often: the Angelus before and after meals, the rosary in the evenings, and

evening prayers on our knees, additional prayers in May, the
month of Mary. We had a Bible with Gustave Doré engravings.
The children had to go to church every day. The boys were altar
boys. There were a lot of priests and nuns in Mother's family.
Father was pretty rigid in his faith. You weren't allowed to criticize
the sermon. Father took up the collection in church. Mother knew
the pastor well because of her church clubs. Priests often visited
our house. My parents often invited them, but they sometimes
dropped by unexpectedly. They probably thought, "There's
always plenty to eat and drink at the farm". Mother was always
worried that we wouldn't have a full pew on Sunday morning. We
sat in front, so everybody could see if one of us was missing. A
family like ours didn't sit in the back—that was for the working
class. If we talked in church, Mother gave us one of those "Wait till
I get you home" looks, and then Father gave us the business when
we got home. We went to Catholic schools, but they were co-ed.
One of my brothers was in the seminary for a few years. My
parents were really proud of that.

How Would You Describe the Offender?   My brother
was always trying to be cool; he wore really wild clothes; he was
kind of a hippie. He was always talking about scoring girls, but
that was more talk than action. He had a terrible temper and a big
mouth; he had an answer for everything. Mother had a hard time
with him. Only Father could handle him. He went to boarding
school for a while because he was in trouble at school. He was
difficult to get along with and you knew better than to argue with
him. He looked up to my brother who was in the seminary, but he
was always fighting with my other brothers. He and my sister were
always at each other, too, about the household chores she was
supposed to do. He thought he could order her around. They
usually ended up tearing each other's hair out. He was really
strong and fought mean, punching and kicking. Once he picked
up a chair and smashed it to pieces on her back. He has a good job
these days. He's a model Catholic in terms of church attendance,
which means he can do no wrong as far as my parents are
concerned. At a recent family gathering, he said to me, "You shut
your mouth, because if I ever tell everybody what I know about
you . . ."

How Did Your Father and Mother Relate? At school, we learned that the Father represented the lawmaking system, and the Mother law enforcement. In my experience, that's the way it was. The men talked business, the women discussed homemaking and the children. They sat closest to the kitchen or stayed in there talking. After supper, the men went outside to check out the farm, while the women did the dishes, looked at the house, and examined each others' needlework. The men played cards, too. Father was a closed person, who didn't easily express his emotions. Mother often took the initiative. Things were usually talked out in bed. Mother was more assertive than Father.

How Did the Children Relate to Each Other? It was just taken for granted that the girls served the boys. If one of the boys said, "I'd like some more coffee," and we said, "Well, you know where the coffeepot is," my mother would tell us we were wrong to say that. Making beds, too—I thought that was humiliating, but Mother said; "Oh, come now, that's just part of your job." Father snapped at us. Mother tried to smooth things over, "Now, now, let's not have any arguing. Just go ahead and do it, that's a good girl." When he was a child, my brother always got his way by throwing temper tantrums. Sometimes he got violent. He did it later on by showing off how much he knew. He had an answer for everything. And he kept it up constantly. I was not very good at getting my own way in things that I thought were important. I always took other people into consideration when I wanted something.

How Did Parents and Children Relate? Mother couldn't handle my brother. She often used me for moral support when she had a problem with him. She asked too much of me. We pitched in on the farm when we had to. The boys worked on the farm; the girls worked in the house—and on the farm. The boys never had to do a thing in the house. They couldn't make their own beds or shine their own shoes. We did that. The boys thought that was inferior. Father stayed out of it most of the time, except when it got out of hand. Then he didn't really get mad, he just said: "Cut it out." He'd let me know that he was pleased with me through Mother, or by a pat on the back. I saw Father as a protective figure.

What Was the Nature of the Abuse?

When I was twelve years old, my brother came into my bedroom. He said that he couldn't sleep and that he wanted to talk to me. I felt flattered that he'd chosen me. He took me to his room and into bed with him. He acted like it was an important game, important for me. He started by touching me, and he made me do it to him. Later, he attempted intercourse. I thought it was weird. His smell nauseated me. As time went on, I got more and more frightened. He'd pull me up the stairs when I came home. Mother would be sitting in the other room. I always let him talk me into it, and he kept saying that it was all right. He even tried to convince me that it excited me. I thought that was really sickening. He tried to make me an accomplice to it. He got bolder all the time. He showed me how strong he really was. I couldn't resist him. When I went into the bathroom, he'd be standing behind the door waiting for me.

How Did Parents Deal with Incest?

I told Mother just recently about it. She said that she'd never noticed anything. She'd never noticed that I didn't want to be in a room alone with him. For me, Mother represented all of the morals and values the church imposes on women. Even now that she knows about the sexual abuse I experienced, she still says that I should show understanding and consideration for my brother. She did say that she understood how much I must have been hurt and how terribly alone I must have felt having undergone such horrible experiences, but she still thought that I should go and talk to him. She wanted to set it up for me, but I wanted to decide that for myself. My father supported me in that. He said that he'd never noticed anything either.

What Prevented You from Breaking Your Silence?

I think the image of the ideal woman was crucial to the way I dealt with it: I didn't get mad, but was easy prey. He used me to experiment with. I was obedient, but was also impressed by him and afraid of him. My mother was pleased that I was such a good listener, and that I got along with people so well. Whenever the others fought, my mother said, "You go and calm things down." She increasingly used me as a sounding-board when she was upset about something. I was afraid that Mother would find out about the incest and blame me. Of course, you couldn't talk about sex at all in those days. It was absolutely taboo.

How Did Family and Friends Respond to Your Signals?
My brother grabbed me once in the living room while Father was reading the paper. I started screaming and hoped that he'd realize what was going on, but all he said was, "Quit fooling around". I gave my mother signals, but she did not react.

How Did Agencies or Institutions Respond to Breaking the Conspiracy of Silence?
I don't think I ever confessed it. I probably made it into something else. When I was twenty-eight, I talked about it for the first time, because I had a nervous breakdown. My family doctor asked me to write an account of my life in periods of seven years. I couldn't start on the second period. That's when it hit me. I talked to a girlfriend about it first; a lot of feelings surfaced—shame, pain. The doctor asked me whether I'd talked to my brother about it; he thought I should. My girlfriend didn't react that way; she just listened. I also talked to a social worker about it once. She kept analyzing everything very rationally, like she didn't know how to deal with it. Now I'm in group therapy. I went to the social psychiatry clinic and talked to someone about it. That went really well. I have just read the association's book, *The Sentence for Silence is Life*. I've talked about it in connection with my studies. I've been asked how I feel about telling my story. It is getting easier.

What Impact Has the Abuse Had on You?
What I did with my brother was completely wrong. You're not supposed to do that. I blamed myself. Maybe I'd given him cause. He once said something to that effect, that I should like it. He tried to make me a consenting partner. I thought that was really sickening. He gave me the feeling that I "belonged." That's how he manipulated me. I could have even become a prostitute. I felt very dirty too. I remember students were talking about whores once when I was in junior high school, in the seventh grade. I thought they could tell just by looking at me. Once on my way to school, a car came up

behind me. The man who was driving yelled out the window: "You wanna fuck ?" I said to myself, "You see, he can tell just by looking at you." When I saw how differently my girlfriend reacted, it upset me. I was ashamed that I'd fallen for it, while other people were more confident. I had thought, "That man didn't say that blindly." It's influenced my whole life. I'm ashamed of a lot of things. I feel guilty, even after that, too. I was always afraid that I might say too much, so that people would find out. My body couldn't relax, and I didn't want to look attractive or stylish.

In 1974 I saw the film *The Exorcist*. I was really upset for weeks afterward. I identified so strongly with that girl who was possessed by the devil. People who didn't believe or were bad, like prostitutes, were in the devil's power. Women who prostituted themselves were possessed by the devil in one way or another. I was afraid to talk to anyone about it. My sister didn't understand why that film affected me like that. I had all of these emotions I'd never worked through, feelings of fear and guilt. The incest has done me a lot of damage, particularly in recent years. When you abuse someone like that, you can negate someone's entire identity. It didn't matter to me who I was, what I wanted. It took a long time before I was no longer afraid to be open and straightforward about it. My own identity, my feelings of self-respect, my awareness of my own will were completely undermined. During that time, I always felt like a thing. Since my first conversation about this with my girlfriend and my doctor, I've realized just how deeply this has damaged my life. From that moment on, I've done everything possible to work through these experiences and learn how to go on with my life.

What Connection Do You See with Religion?
Religion was the main determinant as far as sexuality went. Sex was bad and you didn't talk about it. As far as the incest was concerned, the image of the ideal woman was crucial to the way I dealt with it: I didn't get angry; I was easy prey. Afterward, I felt I was a bad person. I thought that if I could be a really good person from now on, God would forgive me.

What Aspects of Religion Did You Experience as Liberating?
Not many aspects were liberating or I wouldn't have sworn off religion. It was more of a problem than a source of

support. Faith was an unbearable burden the way it was explained to me. I thought a lot of things were unjust, particularly regarding women. Leaving the church and traditional religion was my liberation.

At first, I thought Mary was an inspiring figure, religiously speaking. That changed later on. I began to find independent, self-reliant women more inspiring, women who could take care of themselves. I don't remember any examples of that in religion, but I do in films and books. Greta Garbo, Simone de Beauvoir, and Anna Blaman[5] are all intelligent, independent, and have a good deal of psychological insight. That's my ideal.

What Aspects of Religion Did You Experience as Oppressive? Obedience, and that, as a woman, you were always inferior to a man. You had to be subservient all the time, self-sacrificing. At a certain point, I had more than enough of that. I thought it was unfair that you were good if you believed, and bad if you didn't. There are so many other things that determine that, like having respect for others. I found the story about the talents very appealing, but it didn't correspond to what I learned from my religion. As a woman, you had to suppress certain talents; they weren't appropriate to your role in life, In real life you weren't allowed to live up to that beautiful story.

What Male and Female Images Did You Learn from Your Religious Upbringing? The women in the New Testament were very obedient, and yet they were wise women. Mary was the symbol of the good woman who asked for nothing and gave everything. The story that precedes the birth of Jesus, in which Mary goes to visit Elizabeth—I always thought that was about a very young girl seeking support from an older woman. As far as the saints go, I recall the story of Maria Goretti, who was seduced by a young man and wouldn't give in to him. And Bernadette found herself in the field with her younger brothers

5. Greta Garbo (1905/6–1990) is a Swedish-born actress who played in American films. Simone de Beauvoir (1908–86) was a French writer. Anna Blaman (1905–1960) is a Dutch novelist, who is well-known as a lesbian. — Trans.

and sisters and felt responsible for them. I could identify with that.
We used to have lessons from assistant priests. They were nice
young men. Well, men—of course, you didn't see them as men.
We had a very authoritarian pastor. When my girlfriend and I were
accepted at the high school for business administration, he told us
that he thought it was ridiculous. He said, "You're just going to get
married later, anyway". That high school was worthless. He said
that right to my face, and my girlfriend's, too.

What Did You Learn about Sexuality? Sex was never
discussed in grade school or at home. You knew that it was bad; it
was dirty and scary. You didn't even say the word, certainly not
that it was something you could enjoy. Childbearing and
motherhood made it exalted. You had to have as many children as
possible. When I menstruated for the first time, I didn't know
anything. It scared me. Mother said that she was glad, that I was a
woman now and that I had to watch out; for what, she didn't say.
She told me this story, all about having good morals and how a girl
was supposed to behave. My purpose in life was to get married, to
have children, and to raise them with love. Mother couldn't make
the connection between love and sex. For her, love was something
very exalted, and sex had nothing to do with it.

Having an illegitimate child, having to get married—that was a
big scandal. You had to prevent that from happening. The boys got
the same story. They weren't allowed to fool around with girls.
Mother said to me: "You pay attention. Just watch out." Getting
pregnant was your biggest fear. The woman was responsible. She
was supposed to see to it that she didn't have any children before
she was married. Making love and having children were
inseparable. Mother had a book about "falling in love, getting
engaged, getting married." It was written by a priest. Chastity and
purity were part of motherhood. A long time ago a sister of my
mother's had had an illegitimate child. Her brother, who is a
priest, saw to it that an adoptive family was found for the child and
that her mistakes were made invisible. She was thrown out of the
house. I heard this story at home for the first time last year.

Sexuality was a male thing. Men initiated it. They needed it,
and women had to provide it. Sex is all part of the game. You just
have to accept it.

What Is Your Image of God?   God wasn't portrayed as a person, but as a spirit. He had no human characteristics. God saw and knew everything, and if you believed in him, everything would be all right. People who didn't believe in him could never be happy. I believed all that until I was about sixteen; after that, it seemed more and more ridiculous. My faith didn't make me happy. I had a lot of problems with it. It was a struggle between my religious side and my critical side. The critical side won. God the Father was very stern, but he also had a certain justice about him. He resembled Father.

Jesus was different. He was closer. He'd been a human being. His way of life was an example to us all. He was a good person. In the time that I did not want to pray, I still asked for forgiveness before I went to sleep. I asked for forgiveness for the incest, because I thought I was a bad person, and that I had to do a lot of · good to make things right again.

What Do You Associate with These Words?

Good: Love.

Evil: Power that's exercised over you and which you can do nothing about. I get mad about what has been taken from me.

Guilt: More and more, I realize that I am not to blame.

Responsibility: My first responsibility is to myself now.

Forgiveness: Never for my brother. I get really upset whenever somebody suggests that I do that. As long as it's a problem for me, I'll never forgive him; probably for the rest of my life. He'd have to change so much and to admit his guilt. It could happen—I hope so.

Love thy neighbor: Not at my own expense, not anymore. I know now that I have to be able to keep my feeling of self-respect. I let it show too. I used to think it was a virtue to sacrifice myself for others.

Injustice: I've been done a lot of injustice. That realization goes very deep. I am very much aware when someone does me an injustice. I will not put up with it anymore.

Sexuality: It took me a long time before I was able to enjoy it.

Obedience: That gets me really worked up too. I don't want to be obedient in all things. You might be able to say that to a child, but children are people, too, you know; they have their own will and their own needs that have to be taken into consideration.

Love: We all need that; it's something that you really miss out on because of sexual abuse, because you can't ask and you can't give, either.

Trust: It's very difficult to give that. I am easily disappointed in it, but it makes me feel good when other people feel they can trust me.

Where Do You Get Your Strength?

I believe in myself and in my own intuition; now I know inside what's good and bad. I try to see that in others, too, that everybody has something that's good that you should value. Honesty and openness, also being honest with yourself and taking yourself seriously. I think that I've achieved a lot and I've done it on my own strength. I see that all around me: lots of women who have the strength within themselves. I find that very inspiring. It's a sign of strength to be able to live with this sort of experience and to make something of your life, to get your self-respect back.

Other Information

The offender who tyrannized the entire household is still able to silence Mary Beth, and can do no wrong in Mother's eyes, because of his church attendance. He is very difficult in relationships. He exercises power by limiting this behavior to the home front and by helping to hold up the farce of the model Catholic family to the outside world.

The mother is very concerned about the image of the family others receive. The feelings of the children are made secondary to the rules of the Roman Catholic church. The impression given to the outside world is that the rules are being obeyed. Mother sees to it that the morals and values imposed on women by the church are passed on to Mary Beth: The girls are encouraged in a friendly but compelling way to be considerate of their brothers' wishes and to wait on them, while suppressing their own desires and feelings. This is evidenced when she said, "Come on now, that's just part of your job." It is also apparent in Mary Beth's statement, that she represented law enforcement, and Father the lawmaking system. Notice, too, the role of Mother's brother, the priest, in the affair of their sister's unwed motherhood.

Father stayed out of the day-to-day problems of raising the children. He only intervenes when it affects him or when Mother cannot handle things within the limits he has set. He did not protect his daughter against the sexual abuse inflicted on her by his son. "He was pretty rigid in his faith". He owned and managed the farm that had previously been owned and managed by the wife's father.

| Amy: | *Being a person isn't important as long as you're a "true Christian."* |

Amy is the youngest child of a family of two girls and two boys. Although she wasn't "planned," she always felt wanted. She was abused by her oldest brother.

What Is Your Religious Background?   Mother was Dutch Reformed. Father's family was not religious at all, but he became Dutch Reformed when he got married. There was a difference between the way religion was practiced at church and the way we practiced it at home. Things were much looser at home. Faith was not the same for Father as it was for us. He had different ideas, about dying, for instance, "When you've lived a good life, you go on living in the memories of others". In church, it was all hellfire and damnation. The minister always gave these depressing sermons, telling us how bad we were. As a human being, you're nothing. You have to resign yourself. The best you could achieve was subdued happiness, never to be excited or outgoing. We only went to church once on Sunday. You had to sit through the whole service. Afterward, I needed to jump up and down, but I wasn't allowed to because you weren't supposed to play around too much on Sunday. When we were in grade school we had to go to Bible

class after school, but Mother let me start a year late. The church elder wasn't very happy about that. Teachers at the Christian college prep high school I attended were all "true Christians," but they had absolutely no consideration for you as a person.

Religion had something good about it, something I miss now, that feeling of solidarity, of being joined together. We prayed at home before and after meals and read the Bible aloud every day. My parents said a special evening prayer with the little children. Every so often, the minister or one of the church elders visited our house. None of us held an official position in the church, but we always helped with church functions. We were all in the choir, except Mother. She never got around to it, although she would have liked to join too.

We had Roman Catholic neighbors, but we didn't have much to do with the Catholics in our town. My mother used to say, "those stupid papists."

How Would You Describe the Offender?   I liked to listen to popular music on the radio, but my oldest brother always listened to classical. We argued about that all the time. He was a tyrant in his own way. He was a very aggressive kind of guy. The whole family had to make way for him. There was always a lot of screaming and crying. He kept up constant coercion on me. He could make me feel totally pressured by just nodding his head up and down. He'd keep repeating, "Come with me." He'd keep it up until he got what he wanted. After he was married, he was very derogatory about his wife who hadn't gone to a college prep high school. He said that she couldn't carry on a meaningful conversation. He had no respect for my sister, either, but he saw me as more of an equal. He was the apple of my mother's eye, my grandmother's, too. He was a war baby; whatever he says, goes. He could raise hell about anything. He had unbelievable stamina. Whenever he was supposed to do something he made terrible scenes before he finally agreed to do it. By that time it was too late.

How Did Your Father and Mother Relate?   Father was a difficult person, very closed. He sounded more progressive than he really was. In our family, men and women had equal opportunities. Mother was always looking for a compromise. Father decided social things. His attitude was: "I'm right until you

convince me otherwise." Mother just kept at it behind the scenes. Father made the decision about wearing jeans. Mother wanted us to be nicely dressed, and she sewed a lot of our clothes herself. She wanted to talk to the teachers at the college prep high school but did not because Father didn't want her to. Mother did want certain things, but that was very subconscious.

How Did the Children Relate to Each Other?
I don't believe I ever stood up for myself. I didn't have the courage to get mad, because I was afraid that the other person would reject me. Now I know that my life will only have purpose if I have my own identity. Now I want to know what I want.

How Did Parents and Children Relate?
Father thought that I should go to the college prep high school; I was a model child until my junior year, when I had a breakdown. My parents had high expectations of me. They were disappointed and annoyed with me. I was only allowed to be the way Father and Mother wanted me to be.

Don't talk to me about eyes. I am scared to death of eyes. I was destroyed by the eyes of my father and mother. I know that for a fact.

What Was the Nature of the Abuse?
I don't know exactly when it began. It started with fooling around. That happened a lot, in the kitchen, while the others were in the living room. He was so sneaky about it. The worst thing is that I never really said "no" to him and that I couldn't put a stop to it. I think it started when I was about thirteen. Later on I talked to my brother about it and he thought it was around twelve or thirteen, too. It started with just touching. On Saturday, when the rest were gone, I had to go upstairs with him, to bed. I'm just glad it never ended up in intercourse, not really. I managed to prevent that. It lasted until I was about eighteen, and then another year and a half when I was twenty-five, when I'd already left home. He was married by that time. The last few years, the pain has gotten worse and worse. He always said; "You're really worth it, you know; you're so pretty." He never used force; he was always very gentle, a real smooth operator. He used me to gratify his sexual needs. I needed warmth. I lost my own will; I was only allowed to be the way

others wanted me to be. I adapted very quickly to what other people wanted. I was afraid that other people would notice. I am glad I was able to stop it myself. That gave me a certain amount of freedom. When I look back on it, I'm ashamed.

How Did Parents Deal with Incest? I talked to Mother about it. Her response was, "Just don't let his wife find out".

What Prevented You from Breaking Your Silence? I was destroyed by the eyes of my father and mother. Maybe my brother's eyes will start playing a part in it, too. I can't get mad at him. I just feel so powerless. I always think that I have to meet other people's expectations. I needed warmth. I could not get it any other way. He was five or six years older than I was.

Keeping quiet? I couldn't talk about things like that, certainly not about feelings in secret places. My parents would have looked at me so disapprovingly. You can't really be yourself in your religion. If you are, then you're egotistical. When I was finally able to get a little closer to who I really was, I found the strength to resist his power over me. When I developed my own identity and had more self-respect, I was finally able to act against his power. Maybe, I was already in the process of freeing myself from my old religion by that time.

My incest experience is very closely related to my parents' hold over me. The message I got from them was that you aren't allowed to be yourself.

How Did Family and Friends Respond to Your Signals? When you're afraid of being blamed, you don't give any signals. Years later, I talked about it with my sister and my other brother. He'd never had any idea of what was going on. He was really upset when I told him. My sister is very cold, puritanical. The whole thing is hard for her to imagine.

How Did Agencies or Institutions Respond to Breaking the Conspiracy of Silence? At the Netherlands Association for Sexual Reform (NVSH), I found that I would have had an excuse if I had loved my brother. I liked him, but he overwhelmed me. I couldn't handle it. He was five years older than I was. I find that when I make love with women I'm able to maintain my self-respect.

What Impact Has the Abuse Had on You?   I discovered that my "femaleness" was being taken away from me. I feel that I've been made powerless. I lost my own will. I never fully realized what he did to me. I feel so much pain now that I never felt before. I don't even dare to blame him for what happened, let alone be able to talk about forgiveness. I'm afraid to get mad. I'm only allowed to get angry if it's reasonable. So I don't feel anything, which makes me depressed. I feel used. He did things to me that I didn't want; I let him do that to me as if I were not there.

What Connection Do You See with Religion?   In their (the church's) religion, you had to sacrifice your own self completely. You aren't allowed to offer any resistance. So you couldn't stand up for yourself. God created people. People exist to serve God. He determines what your life is like. Trying to find out who you are, that's not allowed. You're not allowed to be the person you are inside. That is because of my upbringing and my religion. That's how it was possible. For a long time I realized that I couldn't get angry whenever a boy molested me. You didn't feel any rebellion, as though you had no right to. I felt used and I no longer want to let people use me.

What Aspects of Religion Did You Experience as Liberating?   When I really became aware of myself, I got depressed. I became suicidal, I was so miserable. I wanted to receive love and to give love. After a year in therapy, I became more self-confident. One day, I went to a cemetery: I parted with death there. Afterward, I walked through the park toward life. I came across some ducks while I was walking. I felt really good and I wrote a prayer for myself, the prayer of an unbeliever. I think that every person has a piece of God inside. That's what life is all about. I can continue walking on the right path because of God who is inside all of us. There are so many good people; that makes life worth living. We have to do it ourselves; God and people come closer together when you experience God this way. It gives you a certain strength; it's not just hellfire and damnation, then. I wrote that prayer down, but now I don't pray anymore. For me, there is nothing liberating about faith. Being gay—for me—that's liberating. It has finally allowed me to discover myself and grow.

What Aspects of Religion Did You Experience as Oppressive?   That always being bad, that hell and damnation. People can do something good only through the grace of God. That grace from that God, who's so threatening. That suffocation, that hypocrisy, that total lack of happiness, not being allowed to be too heathen. Heathens know how to celebrate, to have parties, to laugh. When you're a "true Christian," you walk with a heavy step.

What Male and Female Images Did You Learn from Your Religious Upbringing?   Women in the Bible were either subordinate or nondescript. Mary Magdalene at the foot of the cross, that really made an impression on me. She goes to Jesus. And that prostitute who anoints his feet. The others complained, but Jesus allowed her to do it. Mary Magdalene was important, but Mary wasn't. The mother of Jesus had very little meaning in our church; she was only the woman who bore him. Church people were always quoting Paul about marriage, that passage about the woman having to be obedient to the husband. I didn't think that was fair. Mother always has to be ready and waiting, unnoticeable. She has an eternal love for her children and her husband. There's an old saying, "It is better to dwell in a corner of the housetop, than with a brawling woman in a wide house" (Prov. 21:9). I liked the stories about David and Goliath, and Samson. And that Jesus got angry when the temple was defiled, that was against the hypocrites.

Marriage is a must. You have to get married and have children—especially women. In order to live a decent life, a woman has to be married. Now things have loosened up a little more. A woman is more her own person now.

What Did You Learn about Sexuality?   Sex is dirty. You didn't talk about it. Mother was a very stiff person, who didn't like physical contact. She gave us a little book that told how children came out of Mom's stomach. We knew that the stork didn't bring them. That's what the "stupid Catholics" thought. That's the way our church put it. They sometimes talked about pregnancy in connection with somebody who had a miscarriage, that kind of thing.

Because of our church beliefs, I have the feeling I'm bad and that I've done everything wrong, the feeling that I'm being destroyed. When you have impulsive thoughts, then you're bad. It was always, "You've got to watch out with boys." Always being afraid of getting pregnant. Where did that come from? You weren't supposed to be willing with boys, that was really bad. In religion, it is the spirit that counts and not the flesh. Paying too much attention to your body is narcissistic. That is not allowed. There is something chaste about religion. It's all about spiritual love. Natural, earthly love is profane; it's not for church people. Those are heathen pleasures.

What Is Your Image of God?

Myself, I think, "God is good," but the picture of God you have from church is one of a God who rolls his r's in a big booming voice. A thundering God, the almighty with the pointing finger. God is more threatening than good. I wasn't afraid of him, but you never did it right. You could pray and show remorse, but you never knew whether God had forgiven you. You could be penitent, but you never knew whether it had any effect; it is that double feeling. It was never a generous feeling of "my sins are forgiven." That is the aspect about religion that devastates you: That you let yourself be led by what you considered to be your conscience and you had as much remorse as you could muster, but you were still never sure that everything was okay; you could still be involved in a death struggle. For me, Jesus was a mixture of Christ and a good person who was walking around. That was partly because of conversations I had with my father. He saw Jesus as someone who led a good life.

People were evil by nature. Only through the grace of God could something good come of them, not through their own efforts. People who were good probably did that because they were narcissistic.

What Do You Associate with These Words?

Good: Having pity, clemency. What a bunch of bull. As far as I'm concerned, good has to do with being a good person, trying to be understanding.

Evil: Sinful, screwing somebody.

Guilt: A heavily loaded word, doing things wrong. That word brings a lot of feelings to the surface. The feeling of doing things honestly with good intentions—and still having done it wrong. Being truly guilty is entirely different; that is doing something wrong intentionally.

Responsibility: Knowing what's expected of you and not knowing whether you fulfill it. Never knowing whether you did it right. You always wondered whether it was well-received. Now it is knowing where you yourself stand, what you can be, and what you want to be for someone else.

Forgiveness: Purifying sins. I don't mean that in a cynical way. It has something beautiful too; being able to put things behind you, such as having a girlfriend who accepted me the way I was.

Love thy neighbor: In the church, there is something dogmatic about it that has a bad ring to it. On the other hand, you need people who can do that, who can be open to others, empathize. But first you have to be something yourself; only then can you open yourself to others.

Injustice: Being powerless. You are often made powerless. Often it isn't meant that way. I find it difficult to counteract that. It's inherent to the system. For me, that's the final blow. It grabs me right in my neck. It has something to do with "no right to exist." Now I only want to find people I can be myself with.

Obedience: Being a sweet girl, a nice girl; a straitjacket, a sacrifice.

Love: Receiving and giving warmth, and at the same time, security.

Trust: Something I really need. That you have to be honest to get it. I can always see when people aren't being honest. Maybe they're doing it unconsciously, but people often have subconscious goals. That makes you powerless.

Where Do You Get Your Strength?   I believe in the warmth and friendship people have for each other. There are a lot of good people. You have to watch out that you don't lose yourself. I get a lot of strength from my inner self. I feel dynamic and full of life. I experience strength in just being the way I am. I love classical music. I am a member of the Dutch Society for the Integration of Homosexuality (COC) and I conduct bisexual women's groups at the women's center. I have a good career, a fashionable job that allows me to work closely with people. I love my work and all my activities at the women's center. My friendships with women are really essential to me.

Other Information   Amy's interview is filled with hard characterizations about religion. Her parents exerted a lot of pressure on her to mold her according to their ideal.

Mother's powerlessness comes up again and again, but Amy fails to acknowledge it. For example, "In our family, men and women had equal opportunities," but, "We were all in the choir, except Mother. She never got around to it, although she would have liked to join too. ... Mother was always looking for a compromise. Father decided social things and said, 'I'm right until you convince me otherwise.' Mother just kept at it behind the scenes." Mother did not talk to the teachers because Father did not want her to. Father decided about the children's clothes, but Mother sewed a lot of the girl's clothes herself. There was never a problem about it. "Mother did want certain things, but that was very subconscious."

In addition, Amy made the discovery at the Netherlands Association for Sexual Reform (NVSH) that she would have had an excuse if she had loved her brother, in contrast to her realization that her "femaleness" and strength have been taken from her and that she is in so much pain.

Ingrid: *I know now that I'm not to blame.*
Ingrid is twenty-nine years old. She is the fourth child (and fourth girl) in a family of five girls and three boys. She was "another girl" when she was born. She was sexually abused by her father, by whom she had two children. Father also abused two of her other sisters, by whom he fathered a total of four more children.

What Is Your Religious Background?   Mother and Father
were from two different Dutch Reformed churches. In addition to
his regular job, Father was the sexton at the Netherlands Union of
Protestants (Nederlandse Protestanten Bond) building. There was
a lot of work involved, which Mother largely did. As sexton, Father
only went to worship when he had to help with special services
and at Christmas. Mother seldom went. We didn't do very much at
home in the way of religion. We went to Sunday school until we
were fifteen, then we went to Bible class, and after that you were
on your own. I loved going to Sunday school, and to church with
my grandmother on my father's side, also because it got you out of
that atmosphere at home for a while. When I was sixteen years old,
I bought my own children's Bible. I went to meetings at the
Salvation Army for about six months.

How Would You Describe the Offender?   The threat of
violence was always there. Father once threatened my mother with
a knife. She never did anything right as far as he was concerned.
He said that, as a child, he had always been the black sheep of the
family. He drank. That was generally known outside the family,
but he was such a friendly person that he stole everybody's heart.
That's what's so frightening. The whole family revolved around
him. Nothing was ever his fault. He was always sorry when he'd
sobered up. Then he'd cry and say that he hadn't meant it and he'd
promise that he would shape up. He usually made the decisions,
but difficult decisions had to be made by someone else. Or he'd
play it so that he came out smelling of roses.

How Did Your Father and Mother Relate?   Father had
six women in the house, so he lived like a king. When he came
home, his slippers were brought to him, his beer was cold, his
paper was waiting, supper was served on the dot. Before she got
married, Mother had worked in a store and that's why he always
said she knew nothing about housekeeping. Women belonged in
the kitchen. He looked down on Mother with contempt; the man
wore the pants in the family. He was a tyrant. You never really
noticed her; she was just there. She never said a bad word about
him to us. Even after the divorce, she didn't try to keep us away
from him. She did not want to see him anymore because of

everything he had done to her. I don't think he thought that all
women were really bad, but Mother couldn't do anything right. He
put her out of the house once in the winter, in the middle of the
night. He let her pay for his taxis with her body, but she managed
to refuse in the long run. She went to the police, but they sent her
away. The police knew he drank; they couldn't do anything about
a domestic fight. We had debts all over town because of his
drinking. That's why Mother went to the city on Saturdays to
shop, but he was against that, too. According to him, the debts
were because Mother spent money like water, and she squirreled it
away for herself for later on. She was always the last one to get
new clothes or shoes, but he was always dressed to the nines. He
let her make the decisions; then it wasn't his fault when things
turned out wrong. Mother? I don't know what she wanted. You
didn't see any signs of resistance, but then she filed for a divorce
after twenty-five years. She never let him into the house after that.

How Did the Children Relate to Each Other? My
brothers were waited on hand and foot by us women. We cleaned
the house with Mother and took turns doing the dishes. Even
when I was in high school, I always had to do the shopping, set
and clear the table, and do the dishes. After Father moved out of
the house, my brothers had to help clear the table. They
complained about that for ages. I get along really well with them
now, but there used to be a lot of fighting. I have a good
relationship with my youngest sister these days. I was exactly in
the middle. I was either one of the older children or one of the
younger ones, depending on the situation, but I always had to
"know better". Mother had no time for us, so we raised each other.

How Did Parents and children Relate? Mother worked
her fingers to the bone for the church—because he was sexton, in
name, anyway. But she did all the cleaning, lit fires in the stoves
early on Sunday mornings, kept up the library. That's why we had
to help her clean the house on Friday afternoons. She cooked. She
never had time for us, so everyone begged for her attention. When
you were sick, you were allowed to lie downstairs. Then she
tucked you in and gave you juice in bed. That felt good. She liked
to sit with me in the afternoon while I did my homework. She
always went to school nights with us. She put some lipstick in her

purse to make herself up a little. When she got on the bus with me, I thought she looked beautiful. The money that was supposed to support the children went largely to pay Father's debts. We walked around in broken shoes and other people's hand-me-downs, but he always had nice clothes to wear. He said that we were careless with our clothes. When he went down to the bar on Friday nights, we all ran to get him a fresh shirt. Then we shaved him, combed his hair, nothing was too good for him, as long as he got all the attention. I did what I was told. "No" was *no*. If I put up a fuss because I thought I was right, stamped my feet and cried, then they said I was hysterical. And then it was, "Okay, upstairs", with a smack on the behind. That's how they dealt with it. They say I was even worse when I was little.

What Was the Nature of the Abuse?   It started when I was eight years old. He didn't have to use force or violence, the threat was always there. Father slept upstairs in the double bed, alone or with one of us sisters, and Mother slept downstairs. I was a good listener, he said, and he kept talking and talking at me. He had so many problems. During the week, things went all right, but on Friday, the fear started to mount: He's going out to the bar tonight, he'll come home drunk. What is he going to do to us this weekend? He put a lot of pressure on my oldest sister and on my youngest, but they were always able to refuse him. When the youngest one was next in line, he had already left the house, so it was easier for her. But we all took a mental beating because of it, the boys, too. They had to watch while he did it, or he wanted us to do it with them. I always refused to do that; I think the others did, too. He abused me and my second oldest sister the most. He didn't do it as often to the others. We did it to protect the others a bit. You never talked about it but you thought, "Oh, God, if they have to go through this too". You could call it sacrificing yourself. We didn't say it in so many words, but we were saying, "I'll go up to the attic tonight, then he won't be able to find me". or, "Please don't let it be my turn tonight."

When I was almost eleven years old, he took my virginity. I was still in grade school. He always took the initiative. He'd start this begging, pleading story that could last half an hour or even forty-five minutes; he'd be in bed in the other room, pleading with you to come to him. Then you thought, it just goes on and on.

Finally, you couldn't take it anymore, so in the end you went; you gave in. Mother really gave it to him when he went on like that. You were more afraid of his whining than of the act itself, more afraid of the power he had over you. I never want to see him again. I'm afraid that the power will come back.

I got pregnant when I was thirteen. That's real fear and you don't talk about it. I tried to hide it as long as possible, but at certain point, you can't anymore. Then you tell your father and he says: "Oh, what am I going to do now?" Not what was *I* going to do now. I stayed at home pregnant for eight months and he took me out walking in the evenings, because that is good for pregnant women. They have to get their exercise. And all the time, he's talking at me. Finally, a social worker came and Father spoke to her. He said she didn't have to ask Mother because Mother wouldn't come anyway. Mother didn't go, either; she was tired of fighting it. The night before I had to go to the home for unwed mothers, I cried all night. When you're used to something, whether it's terrible or good, you miss it. I had never been away from home before, and I didn't want to go. That was the only world I knew. I had to go and have the baby. It was really horrible. I lied at the home and told them I had been out in the field with three boys.

The second pregnancy happened when I was fifteen. My sister and I wanted to go to the police, but he tried to convince us not to. He realized that something had to give. I think that he felt guilty, too; it had all gotten out of hand for him. He talked to a social worker, but he only admitted to being responsible for my second pregnancy. He voluntarily admitted himself to a clinic so he could dry out, and he was there for two years. After a year, he was allowed out on the weekends. I wrote a letter to him every week and I went to see him because I felt guilty: he was in there because of me. So he still had a lot of power over me, still influenced me. I only felt free of that power after he threatened me again, came to see me, and raped me all over again. This time he used physical force. Then he got a three month suspended sentence, with two years probation, and a thousand dollar fine. For the first time, he had a police record.

I put up both children for adoption. You have to. They keep talking you into it until you agree. The only information I gave them was their first name.

How Did Mother Deal with Incest?   Mother really gave it to Father when he whined like that. I understand why she couldn't do anything, because I'd seen him beat her up. I never talked to her about that.

What Prevented You from Breaking Your Silence?   The fear in the house: "If you ever dare to say one word . . ." Father said that all fathers did that with their daughters. He also said that Mother was abused by her father, which I don't believe. He said his father was supposed to have done it with his daughters, which might be, because that Grandpa always wanted to wash us when we were in the washtub. I never wanted him to. I didn't trust him. I never saw Father as a real father, because he made up other fathers for all of us, except for my oldest sister. That was his way of saying that Mother had been unfaithful, that we weren't his own children, so it wasn't incest. I really had a problem with that, because we all had his eyes. The father he made up for me had the same eyes and the same chin, so I didn't know what to think. He created a lot of confusion. He also wanted you to like it; then you'd come back and he wouldn't have to feel guilty. Your body responded, but you felt that it was wrong, because Mother wasn't allowed to know and you weren't allowed to talk about it. You just had to obey him, no "ifs", and no "buts". But, of course, his story was that I was asking for it. He said that I was responsible. Mother was responsible, because she wouldn't do it, he wasn't getting enough from her, he said.

People at school and people around you knew it, and nobody asked about it. There was no sense in telling anybody about it. You were afraid too: If you told, they would think you were bad. It was because of that whining that you gave in. Did you want to? Nobody understands.

How Did Family and Friends Respond to Your Signals?   The neighbors had some suspicions about Father, but he denied everything. Our minister liked Father, too. He was good to his family, wasn't he? They saw him out walking with us, buying an ice cream cone, working in the garden. We'd all help. And Mother hardly ever came out of the house; she had no contact with other people. Father did drink, but well, with a wife like that . . . When Mother wouldn't let him in the house anymore he gave one of the neighbors a big sob story, so the neighbor came over the next day to put in a good word for him.

How Did Agencies or Institutions Respond to Breaking the Conspiracy of Silence?   After I had the first baby, not one teacher at school said anything to me, although they all knew. One teacher gave me the lead in a play. He spoiled me a little bit that year. With the second pregnancy, I ended up in a home in another town. The director took me to school the first day and explained that I'd been raped. The sewing teacher told the girls. When I came to school the next day, the students all acted friendly and very relaxed. I couldn't go to school the last few weeks before the baby was born, but not one teacher gave me an extra lession to make up, except for the history teacher. So when I came back, I had to work like crazy for finals.

I went to a psychologist, who was good and very friendly, but she didn't understand why I had let him in that time when he was drunk again, standing in front of my house, whining and raising hell, and raped me again. She didn't understand the power of his whining.

What Impact Has the Abuse Had on You?   I had to do well in high school because I was so bad in everything else, and guilty. I always had something to compensate, something that had to be really good. I still have that: I'm a perfectionist at everything I do. Being good at sports because you work at it so hard. And that's all you have, nothing else, because you're bad and guilty. Father had a good time. For a child, it's absolutely terrible. It's no fun. My sister knew how to play it out when she wanted something. She got further than I did in separating her mind and body.

For a long time, I thought, "I've forgiven him, it's just that I can't forget it." Maybe that's because you'd always learned that you must forgive people. I liked thinking that for myself, too, because I thought, then I can learn to live with it. But it's not that way at all, because I've felt really furious about it lately; it's bothering me more and more. Even when I was in the home, they said, "You should get mad. You're so calm about it, so understanding about everything."

Maybe I didn't feel guilty until I got pregnant. That's when it became so visible. My fat little stomach, that I tried to hold in with rubber girdles, not wearing belts. A loose shirt in gym class. They still asked you questions, "Have you got a hernia?" And when you had to get up in front of the class . . . ! I think I was living so many lives at the time that I could forget it now and then. I loved learning. I had friends there, but I never took any of them home. I fantasized these marvelous stories about home, that it was so great at home, because I was afraid they would notice something.

I don't want other people to "eat me up," to want too much from me. I'm afraid of being powerless, hypersensitive to power being exercised over me. I don't want to be hassled by men who think they have the right to do that to me. Because you're alone in that and people can't understand it, you start to have doubts about yourself: "Do I really think only of myself? Do I whine about it all the time? Why can't I be like her and put it out of my mind? Why can the others get along with him—and I can't?" My youngest sister is the only one like me. The others think I'm egotistical. I think only of myself, they say. They would rather not talk about it anymore, or about the rest. They have suppressed everything. I don't want him to know that I'm still trying to work through it, either, that I'm still having trouble with it. For him, that would be a sign of victory, a sign that I have not been able to get rid of it. I don't want to give him the satisfaction.

In the shower, after playing sports, I always thought, "They can see it from the scars on my stomach." Every time there was a new girl, I would think, "Oh, she's going to see it and what am I going to say?" Now I think, "Okay, say she asks me something. I'll get confused again, but I'll say that I'm an unwed mother because I was raped. Then I'll come out on the other side of it a stronger person." The last time I was in my support group at the association, a woman asked me: "Do you have children?" I said no again, but the next time I'm going to set the record straight. I'm going to tell them. That's my way of making progress.

I am also more self-confident toward my parents-in-law since I have been in the support group. Now, I think, "They can just take me the way I am." My father-in-law used to say to my husband, "Couldn't you get anything better?"

What Connection Do You See with Religion? I see no connection with religion.

What Aspects of Religion Did You Experience as Liberating? I had six years of Sunday school, Bible classes, and going to church with Grandma. She was a good woman, knew nothing about it. It was wonderfully quiet there, peaceful, and God was good. I was crazy about singing. They talked about evil, too, but as long as you didn't dwell on it, it didn't affect you. There was a certain bond with each other, so many people with good intentions. At the Salvation Army meetings, you could clap your hands and sing. To me, it felt like being at a party.

Which Aspects of Religion Did You Experience as Oppressive? After her divorce, Mother had no money for three months. Father was the sexton in name, but she was the one who worked herself to death all those years, did everything. The church gave her nothing. My sisters were working by then, and they helped her out until she got her welfare money.

At the Salvation Army, I found out that an unwed mother was not allowed to have her baby baptized because the baby was supposedly a sinner. I never went back there after that.

No, no more church and no more Salvation Army, not as far as I'm concerned.

What Male and Female Images Did You Learn from Your Religious Upbringing? Ruth was a good, strong woman. Eve was really bad, but Adam was no saint, either; he let himself get talked into it pretty fast. I don't recall that many women: the prostitute, and the woman who was stoned because she had committed fornication.

What Did You Learn about Sexuality? Sex was good, as long as it produced children and it was only allowed within a marriage; so it was not allowed before marriage. At least, that's what you learned in church. It was not discussed at school or at home. Mother was always dressed, we were too, but Father sometimes walked around naked. He thought that was great, a kind of show, I think. Then he just disappeared again. There was no tenderness or cuddling, although he did fool around with us.

What Is Your Image of God?   The Lord is my shepherd. God is good, he's your friend, and you can go to him when you're in trouble. I don't believe that God just takes everything filthy that people do and makes it right. If God wants to, he can step in, but if we make a mess of things in this world all on our own, why should he be the one who has to take care of it? In any case, I think there is something that guards over us. Jesus is very good. God is good, and Evil is the Devil. This is what you were taught: Bad people are the heathens and the unbelievers, people who didn't live according to the rules, people who were divorced, or single, or gay.

What Do You Associate with These Words?

Good: Harmonious, real.

Evil: Injustice.

Guilt: People who have committed a crime, but are acquitted because they had a difficult childhood, or because they are mentally unsound. I think they are guilty.

Responsibility: As adults, you're responsible for what you do with your children.

Forgiveness: That's a loaded word, learning to have more understanding for each other.

Obedience: A bad feeling; it's important as long as you are not misused.

Love: I love people. I want to see the good in them.

Trust: I have to be very sure of someone if I'm going to trust that person.

Where Do You Get Your Strength? I get my strength from my faith. I asked forgiveness for the incest, and I received it. I saw the light. I didn't do anything wrong in God's eyes; I don't have to have any guilt feelings about that. You draw strength from yourself when other people validate you. You're good at your work—can write good pieces for the sports magazine, for example. When people compliment you on that, you're happy with yourself.

Other Information Along with all the terrorization and destruction, Ingrid had some favorable circumstances: a loving mother, who stands up for herself in the end; several good months in the home for unwed mothers; sessions with the psychologist. Ingrid also has a husband who understands her.

Everyone in Ingrid's surroundings, family, teachers, neighbors, the minister, police, and social workers believe the powerful family member with his smooth story. Even the psychologist underestimates his power. The accommodation syndrome has begun with the mother: not showing her defiance in order to survive. This model was a determinant in the daughters' development. They learned to show understanding, forgive, and forget: In short, they took the path that society and the church call the path of harmony, on which the powerful person can exceed all limits unimpeded. Ingrid thinks that she, too, has chosen this path of understanding and forgiveness in order to survive, but she has not been able completely to bury her own will, her rightful anger, and her pain. She was sometimes overcome by depression. Since she started talking to us, individually and in our support groups, she has been able to give way to her feelings. We made room for her tears and her rage. Now she is becoming more self-aware, as she herself describes in the interview. In our last conversation, she said, "I'm not as afraid of confrontations with people who can hurt me. I feel stronger toward myself".

2
Child Sexual Abuse and Power within the Family

The title Child Sexual Abuse and Power within the Family refers to any inappropriate intentions or actions toward children by older or more powerful family members. The crucial element is the offender's unilateral position of power, which limits the child's freedom and her options. An important motive for the offender is actualizing his (sexual) desires. The offender does not always have to be older. A girl can be harassed by a brother who is the same age or even younger, but who is more powerful than she is.

In literature on the subject, a random age discrepancy is generally used as one of the standard criteria. Dutch law does not use this criterion, but refers to violence or threat of violence and force "to commit or allow lewd acts" (*Penal Code*, section 246). Although use of the term "lewd" censures the indecency of the act more than the resulting damage to the child, this section of the *Penal Code* does acknowledge that the power discrepancy is more significant than the age discrepancy. In the Netherlands, if the offender is a minor himself, he goes to juvenile court where, depending on the offense, the judge has a talk with him or decides to take further measures. Sexual abuse may progress along a sliding scale of seductive behavior, beginning with intrusive cuddling or with sexual innuendos that can be threatening to the child because she does not understand exactly what is intended. In reality, no or nearly no age limits exist for incest victims. The abuse can go on for years because the woman's will is suppressed by the ongoing incest or because she cannot release herself from her rapist's power due to her situation. Sometimes, the child initially represses the emotional damage she has undergone, and only when she reaches adulthood does she become aware of the trauma resulting from what has been done to her.

We avoid the term *victim* as much as possible because it evokes associations with "pathetic," "sick," and "treatment." This can lead to stigmatization. People who have been damaged by incest often benefit more from official recognition of their trauma than from patronizing treatment by the "healthy" members of our society. If the problem had been recognized in time and if the signals of the child as well as of the offender had been recognized, fewer women would have been victims; fewer would have entered the negative spiral of self-destruction in which alcohol, drugs, and prostitution frequently play a prominent role.

Defining xual Abuse According to popular belief, and unfortunately very often in the fields of medicine, criminal justice, and social work, a distinction is drawn between two forms of sexual assault; molestation as the less serious form, and rape as the serious form. Rape cannot be constituted unless coitus has taken place. In this masculine usage, the body of the man is the key element. His penis must be shown to have penetrated the vagina. Ejaculation has generally also taken place. In this definition the woman is reduced to a uterus, because the concern is that coitus and ejaculation can lead to pregnancy. Men, of whom women are traditionally possessions, do not want a suppositious child. When sexual abuse meets this definition of rape, men consider it a serious offense. Most people are no longer aware of this line of reasoning. They have remembered that sexual contact is not labeled such unless coitus and sperm are involved. That is the proof, according to a supporting argument.

When we approach this from the viewpoint of the woman's sexuality, however, the rape occurs at the moment that her erogenous zones, in the most serious case those around her vagina, are in any way violated against her will. This definition is based on the woman's feelings, because it is she who is raped and, consequently, she who knows what rape is. It is sad to hear a girl say: "All he did was molest me," although she has been forced to undergo or perform every sexual act and verbal rape possible with the exception of coitus. Her vagina may have been penetrated by his finger or by objects. The result is that many survivors have been internally deformed for the rest of their lives. The consequences of this oppression are sinister: Women have internalized the masculine approach to sexuality and sexual abuse. Women do not take their bodies or feelings seriously and thus unwittingly contribute to the perpetuation of their own exploitation. In this study, therefore, we do not draw a distinction between molestation and rape. We speak of sexual abuse, which covers all forms of rape as women experience it.

Available statistics on incestuous child sexual abuse are based on representative samples of the population. In the United States, these percentages vary from 4 percent to 16 percent of the girls and about 1.5 percent of the boys. In the Netherlands, the statistics are between 5 percent and 15 percent of the girls and about 1 percent of the boys.[1] An American study indicates a 200 percent rise of sexual violence against children since 1976.[2] In light of the stream of cases currently being reported, we expect the actual percentage to be closer to the high estimate than the low. In the city of The Hague, reports to the police in the first eight months of 1984 numbered four to five per month.[3] Of course, many cases are not reported to the police; this does not include cases reported to doctors, the youth advisory center, the children's hotline, and other social and child protection services. A representative sample taken by P. Vennix[4] in which 257 men and 272 women participated, showed that in 95.3 percent of the cases, the offender is a man and in 4.7 percent of the cases a woman. In most cases, these are normal, authoritative men who function well in the

---

1. N. Draijer, "Seksuele Kontakten tussen Kinderen en volwassenen of ouderen" [Sexual Contacts between Children and Adults or Elders], in *Seksueel geweld en heteroseksualiteit: Ontwikkelingen in onderzoek sinds 1968* [Sexual Violence and Heterosexuality: Research Developments since 1968], (The Hague: Ministry for Social Affairs and Employment) p. 32. See also chap. 1, n.1.

---

2. R. S. Kempe and H. Kempe, "Child Abuse and Neglect," *The International Journal*, no. 2 Harvard University Press, Cambridge MA (1984)

---

3. Verbal confirmation by E. Anneveldt, head of The Hague vice squad, September 1984.

---

4. Draijer, "Seksuele Kontakten," p. 30.

community, and who know exactly what they are doing.[5] The behavior of the incest offenders in our study cannot be labeled abnormal within the patriarchal structure, either, because men are not limited in how or to what degree they may experience their sexuality. They are expected to be the initiators and they are permitted to harass women sexually anywhere and everywhere by making remarks and touching them, while similar behavior is not tolerated from women. A prostitute is bad; her clients are looked on charitably. Sexual abuse of children is the ultimate consequence of the gender power relations in our society that we call normal. The child does not construe this behavior as normal, but society teaches her to do so by ignoring or minimizing both her signals for help, and the offender's power abuse signals. The dominant group in our society has created the conditions to abuse children and has not permitted these children to express their feelings about what has happened to them. Sickness or psychological disturbance cannot be an explanation in itself; if it were, the numbers gap between male and female offenders would not be so overwhelming. Something else has to be wrong.[6] A more plausible explanation is that gender power relations between men and women are disturbed, meaning that our girls are born into a society that deforms men into dictators and women into their slaves who, in order to survive, contribute to perpetuating the system.

mily Power Dynamics Human relationships are built on a series of encounters. The encounters with one person are more frequent and take place on a lower or higher level than with another person. During each encounter, there is the matter of who takes the initiative, who determines the length of the encounter, and its progress. The more equal the relationship, the more this input is equally proportioned over both partners. For the purposes of this study, this dimension in the relationship is termed

---

5. H. Acker and M. Rawie, *Seksueel Geweld tegen vrouwen en meisjes* [Sexual Violence against Women and Girls] (The Hague: Ministry for Social Affairs and Employment, 1982), p. 93.

---

6. The idea that the sexual desires of women are less activity-oriented has been rendered obsolete by the modern sexual revolution. Moreover, that prejudice existed largely in Western, Christian culture. The Islamic religion, for example, credits women with an active sexuality.

"power," and we use the sociological definition of this term as "one person's (or a group's) ability to impose his own will or influence, even when faced by resistance from the other person or group". Power can be categorized in two ways:

— *Direct power*. A public accounting can be demanded when direct power is involved and, when one does not have enough, one can lodge complaints through official authorities.

— *Indirect power* is power derived from others, also called "power behind the scenes." A public accounting cannot be demanded when indirect power is involved, or may only be done with great difficulty, and the same is true of complaints to public authorities. When that does happen, one is accused of washing one's dirty linen in public.

In general, housewives have a certain amount of indirect power, but no direct power. They are not trained to articulate their opinions. When they have too little power, they have nowhere to lodge a complaint. However, when a housewife fails to fulfill her role according to traditional standards, her mistakes come to light by way of social control, society's back door. Society can lodge a complaint against the wife in this indirect way, but she cannot lodge a complaint against society, or can do so only with great difficulty. A wife who makes a mess of the housekeeping and neglects her husband and children, soon has a reputation as a bad wife. What men do and do not do at home is well concealed in deference to their professional careers, and because of their solidarity with the dominant group.

Power resources are necessary to power. The most important resources are money, status, knowledge and experience, language, physical and psychological power, and allocated power or authority. The family also has a structure that can be described in terms of power. While the man has more muscle mass, the woman has the power to bring forth life. Nevertheless, her physical power is limited by the patriarchal ideology of motherhood, that it is her purpose to produce children, preferably male heirs. Whoever has the direct power also possesses most of the power resources. He can also shift the responsibility for his acts on to the less powerful person. The less direct one's power is, the fewer power resources one has.

The interview questions concerning power dynamics within the family were divided into the three categories discussed below.

_____

The Father–Mother Relationship   In all of the interviews, Father has the direct power. He makes the important decisions, is the family spokesperson, and determines how the family practices its religion. He has the most power resources: money, status, knowledge, experience, physical power, and the power allocated to him by society, his authority: "Father really knew how to get to her by using his superior knowledge. He had two degrees, so he knew a lot" (Charlotte). Father also shows Mother his contempt: "Whenever we had visitors and the conversation started to get interesting, he sent Mother for coffee" (Christine). Father determines sexuality: "He complained that Mother wouldn't try the different positions illustrated in the Netherlands Association for Sexual Reform (NVSH) magazines" (Christine). "Later on, Mother admitted that she, too, had suffered under patriarchal religion, which took only the husband's sexual desires seriously" (Susan). Mother remains responsible for his sexuality: "I thought, 'Mother claims she's sick, so what else is he supposed to do?'" (Judith). When Mother also has money, knowledge, and experience, she is prevented from deriving power from these resources through her own internalized gender role, her double burden, her many pregnancies, or Father's physical strength. In all of the interviews, the mother is psychologically or physically abused by the father. Four of the women speak of physical violence against the mother. Moreover, Mother is aware that society will not allow her first-class status, so she accepts her second-class position willingly or unwillingly along with the indirect power allocated to women: "When I was a child, she considered it a great honor to take a back seat to her husband so he'd be able to shine in the spotlights" (Christine). Social control works to her disadvantage because she cannot go to anyone with her problems: "Mother said that I was never to tell anyone about the whole thing and I could see that she was ashamed" (Tina).

Father lets Mother run the day-to-day business and manage affairs that he considers boring or insignificant. When necessary, he puts pressure on her by playing the underdog or by ignoring her. All of these fathers allow themselves to be waited on by the mother. Mother holds the purse-strings when income is tight; he holds them when there is more room financially. Mother accommodates him, but also tries to use psychological power resources and to get what she wants in a roundabout way. In eight of the interviews, Mother takes the role of provider upon herself in addition to doing the housekeeping. She runs the business or farm, sometimes with her son; does the work involved with father's position as sexton; handles his social responsibilities and helps others when that is required by his position; provides his pupils with temporary lodgings; works in a store; is a seamstress or a cleaning lady.

The Children's Relationships   Power hierarchy followed seniority and gender: The oldest children have power over the younger ones, the boys over the girls. The oldest daughter does have authority and direct power to a certain extent, but she is undermined in this position by her dependence on and her servitude toward men, which are demanded of her as a woman: "My brother hit my oldest sister on the back with a chair and smashed it to pieces because he didn't want her bossing him around" (Mary Beth). The girls have less freedom, less allowance, and are responsible for others as well as for the housekeeping: "Saturdays after Brownies, I still had to wash the windows and roast the meat for Sunday supper" (Judith). They also work in the family business or in the vegetable garden. Moreover, all of the girls take care of the boys and the men: "The boys didn't have to do any housework but they always had plenty to say if they thought we weren't doing a good job" (Barbara). Outside the house, girls are dependent on their brothers' protection (Susan, Theresa). Rivalry among the girls is stimulated by the men (Ellen, Charlotte, Tina) and by the mother (Nell, Carol). In doing so, they pay particular attention to the girls' bodies and to the virtues which are considered to be womanly. Because she's a woman and because of her position in the family, the woman interviewed feels unwanted, responsible for others, very alone, inferior, that she is not taken seriously. She has to meet the parents' expectations, to keep everything pleasant in the house. She is unwanted because she was conceived before the marriage, was "another girl," the youngest, or the umpteenth child in the family. The women in the interviews protect their other sisters from incest, or believe that their submission prevents it from happening to the others.

The brothers are powerful family members by virtue of their gender. Their power resources are: status (male heir and protector of the weaker sex), money, knowledge, experience, physical, and psychological power. They have direct power, more so than the girls, because they know that the parents will listen to them and take their wishes seriously: "The boys came into church at the last minute with wet hair from swimming, but we could never get away with anything like that" (Susan).

The Parent–Children Relationship According to the women we interviewed, their fathers' behavior corresponded to traditional gender role patterns. All of them name their fathers as the authority in the family. He is absent and doles out postponed punishment. This threat also allows him to rule the house during his absence. It also gives him the law-making power in the family. Otherwise he tyrannizes the entire family: "You had to do what Dad said; he wasn't used to having to say something twice" (Judith). He punishes in the name of God or threatens with divine sanctions: "I was afraid of making a wrong move because of Father because then I'd lose out on heaven" (Margaret). As to the children's upbringing, Father concerns himself mainly with religious matters. However, he also intervenes when he feels like it, for example, when it concerns Daddy's little girl or his son. He also intervenes in order to stimulate the rivalry among the daughters or between mother and daughter. As a ruler, the women did not feel safe with Father or validated by him. Father thinks boys are more important. He says so: "Good men father sons," or he shows it in his attitude. Girls don't need to study because they are going to get married anyway. Otherwise they have to learn a skill or trade to be able to fall back on, but that doesn't exempt them from household chores, as it does for the boys. Mary Beth says that she sees her father as a protective figure, but when she sends signals about her brother, he doesn't take them seriously. When the woman interviewed is Daddy's little girl, she also serves as his sex dolly. The minute she shows any resistance, his loving treatment evaporates.

Mother has adapted herself to her traditional gender role. She, too, suffers from the accommodation syndrome. When the road to open resistance is cut off, the only method left is that of the powerless: making compromises; being pathetic, weak, dependent or a household drudge; escaping the family through charity work or shopping. Mother shuts off her emotions, partially or completely. She joins forces with the children: "She was one of us" (Ingrid), or she and her daughters form an alliance of tolerance toward Grandpa and Father's religious and sexist indoctrination, as described by Lisa who was raped by her uncle over a number of years. Lisa's mother is a positive exception: "The little bit of self-esteem that I do have, I have from her. She thought the world of me, and she protected me against Father". The other mothers have internalized their oppressors and don't protect their daughters against the men in the family. They teach their daughters that women are in the world to serve men. Or, in the event of conflict, they invariably say to the girls: "You be the one to give in; you should be above all that". But the girls do defend their mothers when necessary. In their interviews, Amy and Tina aptly describe the powerlessness of their mothers in the face of their dominant fathers, but they are unaware that their mothers' attitudes towards them are directly related to this powerless position. Mother is always making compromises—the conflict-avoidance strategy—of which the child is the victim. Rivalry among the children is actively stimulated by both Nell and Carol's mothers. In Nell's situation, this could be explained by their strict, orthodox religion in which conception out of wedlock is a grievous sin. Mother transfers her resulting guilt feelings onto the child. But things are not much different in Carol's leftist milieu: Mother is not allowed to marry in white. *Her* clothing, not the bridegroom's clothing, had to reflect the blame. This mother has so many traumatic experiences in her childhood and marriage, that she is an insurmountable problem for Carol. Barbara's mother physically abuses her children and exploits Barbara. (No information is available on this mother's childhood.) This family lives in an environment of terror.

Father is the authority figure, outside as well as within the family. The mother is said to be bossy or dominant at home. These terms correspond with the sort of power she had, namely, power derived from Father to deal with or take care of things that do not interest him or things that do not provide him with any status.

Power that leads to Abuse In these interviews, the youngest age group at which abuse begins is four to seven years. This is sometimes following a period involving increasingly intimate cuddling from infant and toddler age leading up to the actual abuse itself. Physical as well as psychological violence are used.

In ten cases cousins, girlfriends, other sisters—sometimes all of these—are abused. An attempt to abuse Susan's oldest sister is blocked because she starts calling for help. Ellen talks about mental incest in connection with her older sister who, because she resists her Grandfather, is verbally attacked in front of everyone about her appearance and her unladylike behavior. Charlotte, who was repeatedly raped by her uncle over a number of years, says that Father committed mental incest with her: He read pornography and books in which fathers do it with their daughters. Mother was always terrified for Charlotte's sake. Two women say that they succeeded in protecting one of their younger sisters. In other cases, the offender abuses the sisters in the same room (Christine and Theresa) or turns the abuse into group sex or "multiple incest" (Cathy and Amy). Susan is abused by three brothers in succession and Lisa by her Father and brother.

The frequency and length of time of the sexual contacts differ, varying from every night to once in a while, over a period of about two years or of ten to fifteen years. This uncertainty as to when it will resume traumatizes the child, similar to the concentration camp syndrome. Nell's father forces her to submit again after her marriage. He also gives her money, which she needs to pay her husband's drinking debts. Her husband is a sadomasochist who abuses her baby daughter, at which point Nell escapes to a shelter for battered women (*Blijf van mijn lijf*) and stops seeing her father. Four women are harassed or raped again by the same offender after moving out of the house. Nine women talk about their fear of pregnancy during the period when they were abused as children. One of them, Karen, had to undergo an abortion. Between twelve and sixteen years of age, Ingrid had two children by her father. Two of her sisters also became pregnant. Lisa and Cathy also mention pregnant sisters. Two women say of coitus interruptus: "The worst part was the sperm on my stomach." Father keeps his own calendar, so he knows when it is safe.

Four women say that Father was an alcoholic, or that he drank a lot, or drank more than moderately. Carol's father started drinking more after she started refusing to allow him to have sex with her when she was fifteen. How much he drank before that is unclear. Barbara's mother drinks sometimes. Karen's and Carol's fathers give their daughters alcohol.

Overstepping the Girl's Boundaries   Blurring boundaries and overstepping boundaries are closely related and exhibit the following patterns: The offender slowly builds up a relationship of trust with the child; he comes to watch while she undresses; he creates a cozy environment of "just you and me" until he expands his fondling to include her erogenous zones, or forces her to undress. Barbara was placed in an orphanage after her birth, because her parents were temporarily unable to care for her. When she was seven years old, they began visiting her again. Her parents sat at a table with staff from the orphanage. Father took Barbara on his lap and put his hands in her panties under the edge of the table. After a year of Sunday visits, she was returned to her parents' home, where her father forced coitus on her.

The offender creates situations so he can be alone with the child: walks, bicycle and car rides, an evening at the disco. He visits her in her room at night to tuck her in or goes to her room first when he comes home from the nightshift. After the fondling phase comes the attempt at coitus; prior to the coitus, a finger or object is frequently used over a period of time to prepare her for penile penetration. This results in infections or injuries, as Karen described.

The offender manipulates the child's self-worth by implying that he takes her seriously. Anne, Susan, and Mary Beth are allowed to play with the big boys, the older brother. Ten women say that the offender misled her by appealing to her strengths: She was such a good listener, was considerate and sweet to others, gave him so much understanding while he felt so lonely and unhappy. "He just kept talking and talking at me . . .," Ingrid says.

The offender gives the child sex education and introduces her to how that feels. In his experiments, he doesn't consider whether the girl wants to go that far at that particular moment or whether he is the one she wants to do it with. He determines the onset, the intensity, and, in three cases, the final phase. In seven cases, he pretends it is good for her and that all fathers, uncles, or brothers do that with their daughters, sisters and nieces.

Father, and in general the older offender, is sometimes genuine in wanting to provide the child with physical pleasure, as nine women indicate: "Then he knew I'd be back" (Ingrid). This also reduces his own guilt feelings and makes her an accomplice. She knows that he can blackmail her with it, so she soon tries not to respond and, in the end, not to feel anything at all anymore.

The Girl's Suppression of Feelings Sexual abuse is an extreme exercise in suppressing feelings, physical as well as emotional. In four cases, the subtle beginning ends up in hardhanded measures when the girl displays reluctance, or the offender starts demanding more: "During the last phase, he tried out whole porn shops on me" (Carol). Ingrid describes an extreme form of mental violence: "I was more afraid of his whining than I was of the act itself." All of the interviews describe how, with or without the aid of Bible passages, the women are played off against each other by the offender or by other men in the family and their direct surroundings. The stories are filled with threats of violence: "There was always an atmosphere of terror," Ingrid says. The girls all suffer verbal rape.

Brother is sometimes more awkward and rougher than Father, especially when he is not much older than the girl.[7] He can cause her a good deal of pain. Brother experiments with her. He involves others in it, or demands access to her girlfriend, too. By doing this, he creates a very humiliating situation for the child. Brother brings candy, money, doll clothes, and promises many things he never delivers. (Susan's brother threatens to tell their parents something about the girl if she does not cooperate.) The stricter the parents, the easier it is to put this kind of pressure on the child. The cases of seven women involve hardhanded rape by the father or uncle, complete with physical and mental abuse. Father actually puts a knife to her throat when she will not give him what he wants, or verbally threatens to kill her. The girls try to keep their rapists

---

7. This view is confirmed by David Finkelhor, *Sexually Victimized Children* (New York: Free Press, 1979) who "suspects that more force and physical violence are used when the age discrepancy is smaller, as this decreases natural authority" (cited in Draijer, "Seksuele Kontakten," p. 45).

away from them in every way possible. Screaming, yelling, or crying make little impression or are labeled "rebelling against Father," for which forgiveness from God is required (Nell). Sometimes, her resistance only makes him more aggressive, so he hits her a few more times.

Mother Blamed as the Cause   Father shifts the responsibility from himself and to Mother. He complains that Mother does not give him enough attention, love, and care, will not or cannot make love (sometimes because of sickness or pregnancy), or will not do it the way he wants her to do it, a new way. Mother is never good enough: Either she does not have a higher education, or she is not a good housewife. Karen says: "I had to be nice to him because Mother was away so much". Not only does Father complain about Mother, he deceives her too, sometimes in the presence of the child (Nell), or makes up lies about Mother (Ingrid).

Trying to End Incest   Fifteen of the girls did put an end to the incest themselves. For three girls, it stopped when their brothers found girlfriends. Anne does not remember how long it lasted or when it stopped. In the beginning, the children organize various attempts to escape, which fail, such as running away (Barbara and Carol), or asking for a lock on the door (Judith and Christine). They send signals asking for help. In some cases, they are able to put an end to the abuse when they are fifteen to twenty. They find themselves a boyfriend, or they become so tortured by self-recrimination, moral dilemmas, and fear of pregnancy that they themselves find the strength to resist successfully. By this time, they are older and stronger; they have acquired more knowledge about and insight into their own situation through conversations with friends, or from books, radio, and television. Sometimes, talking with a girlfriend or family member gives that last encouraging push. Carol said, "When I was about fifteen or sixteen I was better equipped to resist him. I started to realize that I had a certain power over him." In six cases charges were brought against the offender, or the survivor threatened to bring charges, which resulted in the offender voluntarily committing himself to a clinic.

Pressure to Continue Incest   As indicated above, the offenders did not always accept the ending of the incest with equanimity. They sometimes exerted enormous pressure on their victims: Father had a psychological breakdown, suddenly started drinking too much, or forbade her to move out of the house into a little apartment (Carol). He made terrible scenes, alternating between begging and rage (Barbara). Father does "a 180 degree turnaround" and suddenly starts treating her like yesterday's garbage (Judith). In Christine's house, things get more tense. Karen is no longer allowed to go out, her allowance is stopped, and Father brings her to school in his car and picks her up afterwards. She is not allowed to finish her education. Judith is finally kicked out of the house, literally. Karen and Christine leave home of their own accord after a time. Ingrid ends up in a home for unwed mothers, and Joan in a children's home.

After her marriage, Nell's father forces her into incest again. He also gives her money, which she needs to pay her husband's drinking debts. Ingrid, too, is raped again while living on her own. Margaret's brother tries again, but she says no. The strength with which these children resist this dominance is remarkable. They use whatever power resources they have or those they are gradually securing: knowledge, insight, language, outside support.

The men and boys in these interviews have not learned to set limits on their own sexuality or to respect another person's limits. Men overstep these girl's boundaries and entangle them in their own sexual chaos.

Women Afraid of Rage   We observed that these women frequently displayed more aggression toward their mothers during these interviews than toward their offenders. It was difficult to get them to talk about the offenders. It cost them a great deal of energy. They said their throat squeezed shut, they felt they were suffocating, felt hot or cold, were falling apart, or even that they were disintegrating into nothingness. In talking with other girls and women, I [I. Jonker] have observed that they, too, often avoided talking about the offender. They talk around him when they tell their story or they talk about him in a monotone. Within the limited scope of this study, it was not possible to set a process into motion through which the women dared to let go of their anger so that we could learn more about the offender. Such a process costs a great deal of time. The women say that they are afraid of their own rage toward him: They are afraid of its destructive power and of letting go of it. During training courses for caring services professionals, I have also found that professionals have a tendency to excuse the offenders too easily and to hold mothers responsible for the harm men do to their children. Consequently we closely examined the feelings these women had for their mothers.

Three Types of Offenders
In literature on this subject, the offenders are divided into three categories: promiscuous men who cannot pass up any woman; men with pedophilic tendencies; and men suffering the consequences of emotional neglect in their childhood, who have not worked through their own experience of abandonment.[8] It may be possible to fit the offending fathers described in these interviews into these categories. However, this still leaves us with several questions.

Perhaps with the exception of Lisa's brother, the offending brothers in these stories have, at the time of the sexual abuse, not noticeably suffered from emotional neglect, nor have they been abandoned by their mothers. Their mothers give them the status appropriate to a male heir, care for them, and allow their sisters to wait on them. Grandmother and Mother are proud of them. They do not suffer from the consequences of being born into a large family any more than their sisters. All the brothers (except Anne's who died young) later marry and have their own families. Do they fit into the offender categories?[9] It seems more likely they are experimenting around and, in doing so, unscrupulously overstepping their sisters' boundaries. In-depth research on brothers as rapists is urgently needed.

8. Samuel K. Weinberg, *Incest Behavior* (New York: Prentice-Hall, 1955).

9. See, for example, Association against Child Sexual Abuse within the Family, *De straf op zwijgen is levenslang* [The Sentence for Silence Is Life] (Amsterdam: Feministische Uitgeverij Sara 1983).

Promiscuous women and women with pedophilic tendencies exist also.[10] Moreover, we may logically assume that approximately as many women have suffered from emotional neglect in their childhood as men. In light of the very small percentage of women who commit incest (4.7 percent), we conclude that the explanations do not sufficiently explain the incestuous behavior of men, certainly not when our data on brothers is taken into account. In our view, the explanation must be re-examined and supplemented with data on the gender power dynamics between men and women and its connection with their psychosocial development, on the differing norms learned by men and women in their childhoods.[11]

10. D. Van Den Bosch, *Daar sta je dan . . . alleen* [You Are Left Standing There . . . Alone] (Eindhoven, 1984).

11. Sarah Nelson, who generally writes about father–daughter incest, also ridicules these rationalizations for men's guilt: "Not one of these theories links his behavior to the total system of social norms and values regarding sexuality and the family in which he lives." *Incest, feiten en mythen* [Incest, Facts and Myths] (Deventer: Van Loghum Slaterus, 1984), p. 67.

3
The Aftermath of Incest Trauma

The Girls' Response Some of the girls put up immediate resistance. Others left home or had a psychological breakdown, but couldn't find a safe place and either returned "voluntarily" or were sent back home. When the girl continues to resist, mental or physical sanctions follow. In the end, she gives in and can only continue to resist internally, which results in the adaptation or accommodation syndrome. She will continue to interpret many situations in her life that she perceives as threatening within the framework of this syndrome until she becomes conscious of it and manages to conquer it. Some girls do not send any signals, however faint, until weeks, months, or even years have gone by.

The most important aspects in the development of the accommodation syndrome are: first, the girl's fear of the offender's authority and of being terrorized by him; second, her lack of knowledge; and third, her defenselessness because she has learned to suppress her will and her emotions. This suppression has a profound effect. Resistance turns inward; it goes underground, but it continues.

The Silence of Fear The survivor had nowhere to go. Even if she did have a place, she would have to explain why she was running away from home. People would be unlikely to believe her, or she would have to go through life without a family, cast out as the black sheep. "You know what you have, but you don't know what is going to happen to you out there," Ingrid says. A threatening prospect. The higher the family's standard of living, the more difficult it can be to walk away. The survivor tries to stay in the family as long as possible. "I was crazy about my parents. I wanted our family life to be warm and happy, so I started acting the part of a sweet, affectionate child" (Susan). The resulting tension saps much of her energy. She shuts herself in her room, tries not to be alone with her father, takes long walks or bike rides alone, and is always on the lookout. The evenings that Mother goes out are the worst; so are the sleepless nights full of fear and worry. She asks for a lock on her door, but Father has an extra key or he manages to pry the flimsy latch open. She wraps herself up in her blankets like a package or sleeps on her stomach. She lives in two worlds: home, and school (where it is pleasant and safe). Or she displays behavioral problems in class, which are attributed to puberty.

Until a few years ago, intrafamilial sexual abuse was nonexistent as far as society was concerned. The signals went unnoticed or were not taken seriously. The magnitude and the gravity of the problem were not recognized. Sexual abuse by a brother or brothers has been a sensitive issue in the Netherlands for judicial authorities and caring services professionals. In their view, the age discrepancy outweighs the gender power discrepancy. They examine the boy's intentions: He was only curious, was playing a game, didn't mean any harm. She is not allowed to take offense because his intentions were good. Even now, the case judgment is based on the motive and the goal of the more powerful one—the boy. The girl has already experienced the effect of power in other areas and knows that it is futile to argue. She has internalized this masculine prejudice: "He didn't have bad intentions; he was just curious" (Margaret). She makes her own pain subordinate to excusing the offender.

The survivor's will is systematically suppressed, curtailed. Boys had more freedom, were made to do less housework, or none at all, and received more allowance. The girls had to wait on the boys. Boys were allowed to study. Cathy often browsed in her brothers' books so she could pick up some extra information. The girls wanted to be boys "because you'd be allowed to do more". The parents, and grandparents say: "Good men father sons"; "It's better to have sons—less trouble for the parents"; "A girl makes you happy; a boy makes you proud". When Charlotte was sixteen: "You'd better hurry up, or you'll end up an old maid". This gender power imbalance between boys and girls and men and women is evident in all nineteen interviews.

Some of them felt they were not taken seriously due to their position in the family. The girl's capacity to express herself verbally is also diminished by this feeling of inferiority. The sexual abuse reinforces the feeling of inferiority; with others, sexual abuse causes its development. Judith, for example, says that she had a wonderful childhood prior to the incest.

Resistance is countered with the following negative sanctions: she is not allowed to finish her education; she gets less than the other children; she is intimidated; her freedom is drastically curtailed; she is ignored; she is threatened with murder, or brutally beaten, or thrown down the stairs. If she talks, she, or he, or both will end up in prison. He threatens her by saying that Mother will not be able to handle it or will blame her. Moreover, she is guilty, too, because he says that she seduced him, or that she is an accomplice at the very least; otherwise, why did she not walk away? Yet, if she resists or leaves, he will carry out his threats. She is boxed in.

Physical or mental violence is always present or threatened. Even when she is his little favorite, she is afraid of his temper tantrums, of his power over her. It happens in a threatening environment: in the attic or when Mother is gone. Although Mother seemingly managed the household ("Mother ran the show"), Father is the authority, and his will decides. He terrorizes the family with his temper tantrums, the frequency of which ranges from once in a while to constantly. When necessary, he alternates this behavior with whining and being pathetic, going into depression or drinking more heavily. That is just as threatening, since he is the breadwinner and the family cannot afford to let him fall apart. These women also say that Mother tends to make allowances for her sons, to overlook more with them than she does with her daughters.

The girl does not see Mother as an ally. As a good parent, Mother must force her child into the traditional gender role. "Mother would rather have had eight boys than two girls, because she thought that girls were very difficult. Before you were twelve, you were brought up as a person. After that your mother had to keep a close eye on you, and then you were forbidden to do anything. All I heard was: no, no, no, being compelled to do things without reasonable arguments. All these rules, you had to obey because you were a girl," says Susan. Margaret tells us: "you had to stay in at night, because you were a girl, doing useful work like sewing and knitting. You weren't allowed to look at a boy, either, because then he wouldn't be able to control himself." Mother makes her take care of the boys and wait on them. "Making their beds, I thought that was kind of humiliating, Mom would say: 'Come on, that's part of your job'" (Mary Beth). Father is able to stay in the background as the "good" or quasi-protective figure, which makes his role unclear, according to twelve of the women. Every so often, he is unmasked. In five cases, he refuses his daughter a good education. Father says: "Boys are a better breed" (Susan). He forbids his daughter to have male friends or, in complete contradiction, forces her to marry against her will. He doesn't protect her against the violence committed by the sons (six cases). In her interview, Mary Beth says: "He'd let me know he was pleased with me through Mother, or by giving me a pat on the back. . . . He didn't get mad easily, he just said, 'Cut it out'. I saw Father as a protective figure. . . . Once, my brother grabbed me in the living room. . . I started screaming and hoped that [Father] would realize what was going on, but he was reading the paper and all he said, was: 'quit fooling around.'" The daughter cannot expect an alliance with the woman who curtails her daughter and teaches her to serve men—and who herself is submissive and subservient to men. Ellen and Tina asked their mothers directly for help. Ellen had been in a women's camp during the war and knew little about men. Due to the absence of a patriarchal structure during those years, she was a naive child and mistakenly saw her mother as an ally. Tina's mother does intervene, but forbids her daughter ever to mention it again and never brings it up herself, either. In six cases, the offender simply forbids the girl to talk to anyone about it: "If you even dare tell your mother . . . !" In the other cases, the offender does not need words to let her know she had better keep quiet. It had to be done in secret; he was always listening for sounds in the house.

Father makes it impossible for the child to see Mother as an ally by denigrating the mother: He portrays her as a foolishly extravagant woman who keeps him on a tight rein, who is dumb and insignificant. She does not give Father enough love, he complains. According to him, she is either a hard woman or an insignificant, pathetic, and weak creature. The girl has internalized this message: Mother spent all the money, wasn't interested in anything intellectual, or the radio, or nature, like Father. The daughter already knows that Mother is hard and dominant. When Mother is weak and insignificant, the daughter cannot expect any help from her against the powerful male stronghold. All of the women interviewed saw that their mothers were weak-willed where their fathers and other men were concerned. Some of the women think their mothers are strong outside the family or they see that their mothers are playing the weak role: "Mother was really the strongest one, but she took on the role of the weakest", Christine says. Mother isn't weak; she is made weak. She evokes the same aversion in her daughters that an overseer evokes in his fellow slaves.

Expectations work in favor of the person in power. The daughter has learned to feel responsible for others. She has developed a deep feeling of obligation toward her mother and father, the other members of the family, and—when the offender has his own family—toward his wife and children. If she were to talk, the immediate as well as the extended family would suffer; his name would be tarnished; the family income would be endangered. All of the women interviewed were deeply convinced of their obligation to maintain family appearances. That was instilled in them at home. "Keep quiet, don't wash your dirty linen in public. That gives the offender security! Handle it within the family. You see a lot of that in Dutch Reformed families," Charlotte says. Most conspicuous was that all of the women say the same thing about their own church or social class. Mother has an active part in it, because the outside world holds her responsible for keeping harmony within the family. The higher Father's position, the more difficult it is for the daughter to talk. Moreover, she fears that the police will be involved. In that case, it is better for her to be self-sacrificing, to be the more humble one. The resolve to become a martyr, to make this sacrifice, is strengthened by religion. For the woman who continues to be raped, being able to give herself this aura can be her only means of survival.

In part, she makes this sacrifice in order to preserve harmony in the family, or to spare Mother who has enough trouble, as seven of the women say. Because Mother does not make love the way Father wants, the child gives him what he wants. She sacrifices herself for Mother, or for her little sister: "You thought, 'Oh, if she has to go through this, too . . .'; you could call it sacrificing yourself" (Ingrid). She is sympathetic toward the offender's desires. She has learned that he needs this. She has learned not to stand up for herself, not to resist, to be self-effacing (eleven interviews). It is often suggested that incest happens to girls who feel responsible. These women show us that a child who is confronted with incest at a very young age *is made* into someone who feels responsible for the offender, her mother, and the other family members. Later on, she becomes aware of this: "I was systematically taught to be responsible."

Her self-reproach also keeps her silent. She fears her own feelings. She despises herself: She had to allow this, although she did not want it to happen and sometimes suffered severe physical pain. Or she may have enjoyed it against her will: "My body let me down." She is ashamed that she let it go that far, feels like an accomplice, and feels guilty. She is afraid of being reproached, because she already reproaches herself. She is proud and does not want to admit that this has confused her. She suppresses her feelings because she does not want to be her mother's rival. Incest raises so many problems in her relationship with her mother that she is no longer able to manage them and decides to remain silent. Each of the women we interviewed has experienced this self-reproach in one form or another.

She thinks that she is the only one struggling with this problem. Her other sisters do not complain about it. She thinks this does not happen to other girls. This means that other people will think it weird. It would be better if she did not talk about it. Besides, you just do not talk about such a blatant attack on your person that takes place via the erogenous zones. The longer she keeps silent, the more guilty she feels, but: "Whether you talk or whether you don't talk—you're still guilty" (Anne).

The church provides her with the last problem: "If you had sinned against the rules, that was the worst. You hope you can be saved if you do a lot of penance" (Margaret). Barbara never talked about it in confession, because this was something really bad, the worst. Cathy did confess it: "I was in a moral dilemma because if I didn't go to communion, the others were going to ask, 'Why aren't you going?' I was committing a mortal sin three, four times a week and I had to confess, always in different churches because I was ashamed to admit it to the assistant priest. Once, I hadn't gone to confession and I went to communion anyway, but I couldn't sleep for weeks afterward" (Cathy).

The Lack of Awareness

The child is warned against strange men, but not against men in the circle of family and friends. So she does not know the proper code in which to speak of what has happened. It has no name. She knows little or nothing about sexuality and certainly nothing about her own sexuality. She only knows that pregnancy and sex are things that "happen to" girls. For boys, sexuality is much clearer. They are more familiar with their own genitals, the purpose, and the feelings that go along with them. In eighteen families, emotions, tenderness, sexuality, and physicality were discussed with detachment, hardly talked about, or not talked about at all, "certainly not about feelings in secret places. My parents would have been very disapproving" (Amy). Charlotte's mother did sometimes tell Charlotte and her sister how they were born and how happy she was with them. Only in Carol's anti-religious milieu was there a very open attitude toward sexuality. Mother thought sex was beautiful, while her daughter experienced it with Father as something filthy; she also received the impression that he had no consideration for women's feelings.

The offender says that this is normal. "It's part of life. It's good for her" (five interviews). "He acted like it was an important game, important for me" (Mary Beth). Father spins a web of lies around her: His wife has always deceived him, so his children have other natural fathers and therefore this is not incest. Or he says that Mother also experienced incest as a child and so he may abuse his daughter too. He also knows that she is ignorant of the law and that he can threaten her with it.

What did she learn? A woman must conform to expectations, be subservient, stay in the background, be quiet, sweet, and caring, and above all care for and serve the men. She must also meet the emotional desires of the man. She never learned to stand up for herself. She knows that men cannot do without sex. They have to spill their seed, but it must not go to waste. It is obvious that he cannot go to his wife, so . . . The girl learns that men have a need for tenderness and does not realize that they are looking for sexual contact. She believes that he has chosen her especially, which makes her feel important and flattered, until she realizes that she is simply being abused.

The myth that she wants to be conquered works to her disadvantage. When she said "no," she means "yes." Experience teaches her that resisting doesn't help. According to the myth, that just means "yes," which is why she is better off accommodating him and letting him do what he wants. But she is also aware of the myth that a girl who has been raped is the one to blame: She should not have been there, should have run away, should have resisted. In this way, the child learns to separate reason from feeling: She is stricken dumb.

The myth of motherhood also encourages silence. Mothers are supposed to understand everything about their child, without a word having passed between them. Mothers have to solve their children's problems. The child thinks that Mother understands this problem, too, and will solve it without the child having to talk about it. In reality, Mother sometimes does know or suspect that her child is being abused, but much of the time she has no idea. The offender makes sure of that. When Mother comes in, he acts as though nothing is going on. "The next day, he acted so normal, as if nothing had happened. A man with two faces," Charlotte says. Mother does not know the code, either. She believes in the stereotype of the child molester. Why should she distrust the men in the family? That would be unfair to them. Everyone knows that incest only happens in antisocial families. That is the very last thing she expects in her own family. Moreover, she has learned to accept the sexist behavior of men in her immediate surroundings with "a sense of humor." Should Mother have to act like a police officer in her own family? Could men not take part of this social control upon themselves and start watching each other's signals?

The Intertwining Religious Trauma   Lack of awareness is reinforced by myth and ideology. These women indicate that they have not only undergone an incest trauma, but a religious trauma as well. Such a trauma can also develop in a family with a different sort of dogmatic ideology, as Carol described in her interview: "In our family, socialism was practiced like a sort of religion. It gave people unrealistically high ideals to live up to, . . . so you always fell short." The effects of one trauma are not necessarily piled on top of the effects of the other. In our view, it is more an intertwining whole. The survivors described this trauma. Religion reinforced the fear, the moral dilemma, and the lack of power to resist. The most important message a woman hears in church is: *obedience*. Eve was disobedient and that's why sin came into the world. A daughter sees this obedience in Mother, with whom she identifies herself. She must honor her father and mother. Amy says that she was destroyed by Father's and Mother's eyes. Nell learned that she had to ask God to forgive her for resisting Father. A woman must keep silent. That was quite normal in the church. A girl has to stay in the background, is not allowed to be an altar "boy." She must love her neighbor and be self-sacrificing. Girls are not allowed to be aggressive. Boys are commended for their assertiveness. For the same behavior, girls are called catty or bossy. Mother teaches her to be nice, then she will turn out all right: She must always smooth things over, otherwise Father would get mad. Forgiveness is the single most important aspect, so a girl has no right to be angry. She fears going to hell: you must do endless penance, because sex outside of marriage is a mortal sin. She learned from the Bible that she is the property of men, someone "in relation to others." This aspect plays a role in all of these women's lives, with the exception of Carol. In her socialist milieu, the equality of men and women was paid a lot of lip service, but was practiced just as infrequently as elsewhere: "What my parents preached wasn't what they practiced at all; their words and actions were totally at odds. So as a child, you had no idea where you stood."

Twelve women thought that this was evidently God's will, because almighty God would otherwise have intervened. God wants this to be your punishment, because he knows and sees all: "He had the whole world in his hands" (Anne). What happened is unavoidable, simply because she is a woman, and that arouses sexual desires in men. It happens unconsciously.

There is very little discussion of sexuality in the family; the Bible is full of it, but in a masculine form in which the existence of female sexuality is denied. Still, women are responsible for the sexuality of men. Men supposedly have irresistible desires, and when they have been aroused, they can no longer control themelves. Women have to be careful not to put men in such a situation. Anti-religious ideology is also familiar with this masculine approach. Carol's father says, "I'm telling our friends that you're lying. And I'm telling the family that you seduced me." The offender knows that the family will believe that story. A man is permitted to overstep a woman's boundaries; a woman is forbidden to overstep a man's.

Religion forces women to forgive their rapists, although those rapists have not asked for forgiveness. They were commanded to love their enemies. Moreover, Christian churches stress the love of one's fellow human being so heavily that the words "as thyself" following "love thy neighbor" have very little meaning for these women. When Karen as an adult, talks to a minister about this, he reproaches her for never having understood Jesus' words correctly. An official representative of the church has a strong tendency to defend the church and, in doing so, blames the woman for not having listened well enough when she was a child, or for not having been able to understand adequately what was taught.

God the Father wants only the best for her. He is Almighty and merciful. When something happens to her and she wants it to stop, she must pray hard. "God saw and knew all. As long as you believed in him, everything would be all right," Mary Beth thought. Perhaps he is punishing her because she's bad. She is uncertain about this. God sometimes asks people to suffer and to make sacrifices. This, too, is part of His plan: She is being tested or she needs to be chastened. In doing this, God demonstrates just how much He loves her. To a certain degree, Cathy saw her suffering as her cross to bear. God sees everything, including the bad things that the offender does to her. When she allows it to happen, she is also responsible for and guilty of the acts her rapist commits. Theresa also feels this way, and later thinks that she could have escaped sooner if she had used more strength. She wonders whether thinking this way is a form of self-torture. Out of all of these possible responses to her questions, the child never gets a definite answer, so she has to keep all of these options open simultaneously, with one possibility weighing more heavily one moment and another the next.

The survivor experiences this inconsistency as God's arbitrary treatment of people. Her spirit rebels in vain. She refuses to accept this kind of treatment. She believes that she has the right to know where she stands, to be treated as conscientiously as she herself is required to treat others. Her will is strong and she keeps fighting. In the end, she is so battered from this inward struggle that others regard her behavior as strange, judge her unstable. In answer to our final question, Barbara says: "Strength? Courage? I think it was more *rage*. I have no faith anymore. I don't even think about it these days. The church has no meaning for me now."

It is particularly difficult for a girl not to weaken her will to resist. The role models she was exposed to are all women whose main task was to preserve their chastity. A girl who is sexually abused has clearly failed in fulfilling this obligation. Catholic women have three principal role models in this area: Mary was the prime example of virginity and obedience; Maria Goretti, the martyr of chastity, allowed herself to be murdered rather than lose her virtue; and Saint Lidwina patiently bore her suffering. The girl fails to live up to the examples of Mary and Maria Goretti due to her incest experience, and the example of Lidwina only encourages her to accept her fate. Working out this dilemma is impossible. An adult could not succeed, and certainly not a child who has no one to talk to about it. Cathy says that her experience made her believe that she could never achieve certain goals because she could not accomplish what these saintly women had accomplished. As a child she was already a failure in this sense. Mary and the command to obedience caused the most confusion. She must obey Father who is deceiving Mother? She must obey Mother who orders her to give in to her brother in arguments, while she really needs practice in resisting him? She must obey God and his complicated command of chastity, pregnancy, and bearing a son who has a higher place than his mother? The girl experiences what the priest calls a mystery as being misled. "Grandma kept silent. 'She knew, but stayed silent; she kept all of these words in her heart.' That was in her death announcement. My uncle (the offender) wrote it. Evidently, it was considered a virtue. Women kept quiet" (Charlotte). She had to keep the misleading words in her heart. That means that the resistance turns inward and the rage destroys herself. What these children picked up in church, catechism, and Bible classes about God, parenthood, sexuality, and love did not correspond with the deception they experienced in their own lives. Because they were not allowed to speak about their own feelings, they had to search for their own explanations.

Survivors tried to rationalize their emotions in various ways:

— regarding the offender, "I must have given him some cause, so I'm to blame," or, "I'm not allowed to say 'no,' so I'm powerless";
— regarding God, "God allows this to go on, in spite of all my prayers. So this is evidently right and, in doing it, I am serving God's purpose, which is known only to him—they say that God works in mysterious ways"; "I need to be punished. I must be very bad"; "I have to do penance for the evil done by the offender or by other women. I am sacrificing myself"; "I must be chastened. I am a martyr and deserve sainthood."

Her sound spirit, which sees through the misleading nature of these rationalizations, continues to resist them. In the long run, this inward struggle saps both her physical and mental strength.

The more frequently God's word is preached by the offender, the greater was the survivor's tendency to identify God with the offender.

Her Own Strength Due to the dynamics of the powers around her, the girl has gotten a feeling of being rejected, of being let down, and being betrayed. She can only break down the suspicions built up in her mind after a long struggle with herself and others. An endless amount of patience and effort is required on both sides. She does not want to be taken by the hand any longer, to be treated like a child or a victim. The reaction of outsiders is often: "Oh, the poor girl." This is painful to her. She is not a poor girl; she is not pathetic, she does not need pity, and she does not want to be treated that way. Sixteen women said that they find their strength within themselves. Such women can hardly be called pathetic. They display a normal reaction to a sick system that is perpetuated by the taboo on talking about power relations.

Response of Others to Her The reactions of immediate family members and friends differ very little from those of caring services professionals. These reactions, as described in our interviews, varied from a new rape to solidarity. Between these two extremes, we found disbelief and denial, minimization, blame, not recognizing the seriousness of the problem, no verbal response, and clumsy attempts to help (which were sometimes offensive).

The New Raping

One child confided in an uncle who responded with a wrestling match. Another girl later received guidance from a pastor. When she told him about her incest experience, he began fondling her. When questioned, the pastor said that he did it because he wanted her to experience that sex can also be enjoyable. This woman's will was thus restricted anew; was he determined what was good for her. Such responses only increased the confusion of these women; their feelings of inferiority and dependence became stronger, and their distrust grew.

Disbelief, Denying and Rejecting

Mother evades all discussion. When the girl does try to tell her, Mother does not believe her at first. The survivor's husband asks: "Is that really true?" The assistant priest says that she is fantasizing, the family doctor will not talk to her about her father, and the doctor at the hospital is a friend of Father's. The psychiatrist does not believe her. When asked by the police, Mother denies ever noticing anything wrong, although she once witnessed it.

Minimizing

The girl goes to Mother once again, who says that she should not take it so seriously; men have these needs and that is life. Mother said something to an aunt once about Father's behavior. If Mother knows, she plays an active part in the cover-up. The survivor's husband says: "That's all in the past." A girlfriend says: "You enjoyed it." The Netherlands Association for Sexual Reform (NVSH) tells her that if she loved him, that could be an excuse. The minister or priest doesn't see any problem theologically and does not understand why she feels so guilty about it. The child protection agency talks about projection. The social worker analyzes with cool rationality. The psychiatrist hardly responds at all. The minister thinks that "There are men who are 'touchers.'" The sexologist who is supposed to treat Father calls what happened "erotic games" as long as coitus didn't occur.

Blaming Brother accuses her: "The way you act, you're just asking for it; you bring it on yourself." Uncle says it is her own fault because she is young and has breasts. Mother is ashamed and forbids her to speak of it again. Years later, Mother blames her: "I don't understand why you tolerated it for so long." Mother blames her daughter for the entire mess and beats her. A husband accuses her of being punished for something, because this sort of thing does not happen to other women. A therapist asks "a hard question for your own good: 'Did you enjoy it?'" A psychologist doesn't understand why the girl let him in the house in the first place. Other people, friends, caring services professionals, do not respond at all: Silence can mean anything, and these women interpret it as rejection because they are accustomed to that.

Ignoring Suspicions The offender forbids the girl to speak to anyone and uses all sorts of threats; consequently, any signals the child may send are usually weak. She says things like: "He keeps bothering me"; "I want a lock on my door"; "I don't want to go"; "I want to be in bed with Mother instead of Father." Sexual violence is so unspeakable, and male authority in the family is so dominant, that the taboo works two ways: the victim works just as hard to cover it up as the rest. Anne says that she did send signals to Mother, who did not respond, but she also says she was afraid that Mother would find out, and blame her. In therapy, social work, and the criminal justice system, the girl herself refers to incest only in vague terms or keeps it a secret.

Due to the imperviousness of the family, those who are confronted with sexual violence keep quiet, repress what is happening. This happens to the girls themselves, but it also happens to caring service professionals. In addition, the family doctor is the doctor of the man of the house, the breadwinner. Father determines who the family doctor is, sometimes on the basis of financial considerations. The same applies to those providing religious guidance.

It is inconceivable that the nuns in the convent where Barbara had lived for seven years before being reclaimed by her parents did not intervene when she tried to get back into the orphanage. With iron-willed perseverance, she kept coming back to the only safe place she knew year after year, daily during some periods. No one asked her, "Where did you get those black and blue marks? Why are you late for school? What are you feeling?" In the interview she said, "I heard about God, that he was almighty and saw everything. I started thinking, Where is God now? I think that's why I later left the Catholic faith, because they're just cold words, words without meaning. I cried rivers when I tried to walk back to the orphanage with the nuns after school, but it didn't make an impression on them. How can you just give someone away like that?"

Some mothers later insist that they honestly did not suspect anything. In retrospect, they are able to connect sounds and signals. For the daughter, it is inconceivable that Mother did not pick up on what was happening. She feels rejected by Mother. Nevertheless, the expectations of Mother generated by the myth of motherhood are too high. Mother cannot meet them and the child is misled by them. Mother is supposed to have a special antenna for everything concerning her children, to see to her husband's emotional needs, to run a (large) family, in addition to dealing with all of her own resulting physical and mental tensions. During the birth of her ninth child, Judith's mother began hemorrhaging and Judith had to help her: "Mother was so ashamed and had more of a problem with me helping her than I did. She even had to go to the hospital."

In the interviews, Mother's position is described thus: Mother has money doled out to her or she manages the money, sometimes after Father's hobby or drinking money has been deducted, until times get better. Father keeps the money in his bank account and Mother has to keep asking for it. She has to be a good cook and keep the place neat. She is responsible for good relations with members of both sides of the family, organizes parties. In addition, she sometimes has to run a farm or business, clean the church if her husband is sexton, and carry out other duties when her husband has a prominent position in the community. Because the incest problem overshadows everything else in the child's life, she thinks that it must be so for everyone, and that it must be visible, evident. But even if no one else notices that something is wrong, Mother certainly should. Lisa often thought, "She sees that I feel awful, doesn't she? She sees that I cry?"

Mother does suspect something, but she cannot or dares not confront it (two cases). Even if she wants to do something, there are various factors that stand in her way. In the first place, she knows that she is responsible for fulfilling her husband's sexual desires. If she were to say something about Father's incestuous behavior, she would be blamed for not giving Father what he needs, or she would blame herself, because she has internalized this sense of obligation for Father's sexuality. Everyone else in society will also agree, so the community will be quick to accuse her as well. That is why it is so difficult for Mother to call in outside help. Through our work in the women's movement, we meet many women who tell us that they hear this accusation at most agencies and services where they go with marital problems. Charlotte's mother is worried that her husband will use his daughter to actualize the fantasies in his erotic books and magazines. She keeps a careful eye on her daughter, but stays with her husband despite countless humiliations. She remembers her Grandpa's commandments on the duties and virtues of the woman. Later on, the daughter calls Father's attitude toward her: "mental incest"—you just feel it, by the way he looks at you. The interviews indicate other factors that stand in Mother's way: She herself was frequently threatened with a knife, beaten, and raped (in three cases) or forced into prostitution by Father; she is an incest survivor herself (three cases), she has gone to the police or to a social worker but not been taken seriously. All of the mothers had learned at home to keep silent. Some had internalized their oppressors, and made the traditional choice within the patriarchal system: for the offender. Mother knows her husband's power resources: He can take away her "Mrs" status; she will suffer most in the event of a divorce because she will have lost her "job" whereas he will not. At that age, with no experience, and having to care for the children alone, she will not be able to earn very much on the side. Every human being wants to survive. Not everyone is a rebel. Even the church is not a sympathetic employer: It refuses to pay the sexton's wife one cent after she throws her husband out. This woman cleaned the church for twenty-five years, lit the stoves every Sunday morning, and took care of everything that needed to be done.

Finally, nine mothers also exploited these daughters in one way or another: The daughter had to listen to their problems, keep the peace in the family, or do the housework. This exploitation may be a form of power abuse, but it may also be caused by powerlessness against the patriarchal system.

In addition to the myth of motherhood, there is the myth of fatherhood: the protective father. In these interviews, there is little evidence to support this myth of protection. Theresa's mother lets her daughter know that she is aware of the problem. She doesn't blame her, but makes a rather clumsy attempt to help her, and says that her daughter must call out to her if necessary, or, if she would prefer, call her father. Father is evidently also aware that his own daughter is being raped by his stepson but stays out of it. The girl calls no one. Tina's mother forbids her son to bother the child anymore, "because otherwise he'll ruin her." Tina later says that she was afraid to talk to her father about it. She could not do that anyway, because she had to adhere to the norms, and keep up the appearance of the model family. She would be blamed, just as she would be if Father were the offender. Tina understands, and later says that she no longer bears a grudge against her mother. Susan's father either knew or suspected, as he later admits. He adds: "Forget it." Mary Beth's father lets his daughter scream. She calls him a "protective figure," although she is also afraid of being blamed by her mother. This fear is understandable because she has experienced the firm hand with which her mother teaches the norms of the patriarchal culture; one of these norms is that the woman is responsible for sexual encounters between women and men. Women who got pregnant before marriage were seen as the guilty party. Ellen, too, believes in the myth of fatherhood: after four years in a women's camp in Indonesia, she sees men as "all fathers," but she doesn't think Grandfather's behavior is very fatherly. He is not the just, benevolent, protective figure. She does not know the code for his actual behavior and therefore says: "I had the feeling that I'd fallen for the whole thing". Many more women have had that feeling.

Believing, but Failing to Act   People who failed to act feel badly for the victim but do not ask or say anything further, and never pursue the subject. This also gives the woman the feeling that she has been rejected. This was the mother's reaction in three cases. Others described this response from a sister and a brother. Theresa told male friends and one girlfriend but no one followed up on it. The same also applies to a minister, a doctor, a priest, a therapist, and social workers from the child protection agency. The assistant priest says that he can do nothing for her "because his relationship with my parents was already strained" (Joan). He does refer her to the police station. But you don't just turn your father in to the police! The priest does not go with her. The church does not like getting its hands dirty.

Believing, but Acting in an Offensive Manner

Helping victims of sexual violence is extremely sensitive. If the person who has been approached proceeds too quickly or in a clumsy fashion, she or he could block a solution for years. Carol, who had a psychological breakdown, went to the Dutch Family Planning Association (Rutgers Foundation) where she attempted to explain to a doctor that she had not enjoyed it, as he suggested. He said that she was very good at telling her story, and thought she would be all right. Karen's aunt guessed at the truth and asked her if she was all right. Karen's trust was evidently not strong enough, because she did not answer. Mary Beth's mother heard the story years later, showed a great deal of sympathy (as it turned out, she was not all that bad), but wanted the girl to talk it out with her brother: "She wanted to set it up for me, but I wanted to decide for myself, and my father supported me in that." One woman had six counseling sessions at the Dutch Family Planning Association, wrote down her life story, and then froze. She is now in therapy elsewhere, but wonders: "Am I in the right place?" Another woman says that her therapy treatment was threatening. Ten years pass before she summons enough courage to go into therapy again. One woman tells us that she has had four professionals from various caring services and says: "I kept thinking that it was me."

Believing and Supporting

These women have found many people who show their solidarity. Sometimes family members are good listeners; A boyfriend or husband takes her seriously. These people create a bond of trust, but do not make new demands. They do not put words in her mouth and allow her to determine her own speed in working through the experiences, to take her own steps. They do share her anger and hurt. They see that the woman is actively working toward her own healing, and they are willing to listen to her story as often as necessary. By asking open questions, they give the woman the opportunity to order the chaos in her mind. Seventeen women receive this kind of support from girlfriends, consciousness-raising training, feminist support services, support groups, or in the association.

Some of them find a husband who shows genuine solidarity. The woman usually tells him about it up front, because she does not want him "to buy damaged goods" and believes he has a right to know with whom he is getting involved. She also looks to him for protection and support. Many men truly give this and want to listen. However, this protection sometimes goes too far. In his honest outrage, he starts organizing everything for her, running her life, determining what is good for her. A new relationship of dependency is created and the woman is once again silenced. Many men find it difficult to acknowledge sexual violence as the ultimate consequence of the patriarchal system. They try to turn it back into a personal problem. They are bothered by a collective guilt feeling, are afraid that their wives will become "radical feminists" or—in their view even worse!—lesbians. Once again, limits are imposed on the woman's choices.

The Remaining Family Tension Incest is a breeding ground for mutual distrust and blackmail in the family circle. When sexual violence occurs outside the family, the loyalties that cause the enormous tensions and pain resulting from incest are absent. Under favorable circumstances, the woman who has been raped can sometimes work through her experience to a large extent with the help of good counseling or therapy, but the offender counts on her silence. Father says that it must remain a secret, otherwise the family will fall apart; the child doesn't want to be blamed for that. As soon as Father begins to have doubts about her silence, he starts manipulating. As a powerful person, he can still use "divide and conquer" methods, but the atmosphere is ruined. Because women are responsible for harmony in the family, they will sacrifice themselves and each other to keep the peace . . . Until all hell breaks loose.

In the end, when everyone in the family more or less knows or suspects what has happened, the closest bonds may be torn apart by divided loyalty conflicts: bonds between father and mother, mother and daughter, the sisters, sister and brother. Then there is the family-in-law, which has its own interests. Choices are sometimes made for purely material reasons: the inheritance, for example. Some family members try to maintain a "good" relationship with both parties, which leads to complicated situations at family gatherings and celebrations. The end result is that the woman who has been raped begins to feel more and more alone. She cannot count on her family's solidarity, because solidarity means: "Your struggle is my struggle." Even when Mother knows the nature of the sexual abuse the daughter has undergone, she still says that the daughter must show her brother her willingness and understanding. The offender rarely wants to realize what he has done so that he can truly ask forgiveness; if he does so, the woman is then able to consider whether she is willing to grant him that forgiveness.

The other children and the mother also deserve attention. Sexual abuse is the most extreme form of a range of abuse including exclusion of the powerless and women, sexist language, offensive jokes, pornography at women's expense, and authoritarian behavior culminating in macho behavior. The other children are also exposed to these tensions in the family. The most powerful are constantly trying to overstep the personal boundaries of the others. When the son is not an offender, he finds himself in a conflict of loyalties toward Father and the abused sister. He is sometimes so conditioned that he chooses his father's side. The advantage is that Father's power continues to reflect on him. In the worst case, he will verbally abuse his sister for being a "whore." This attitude toward what has happened has an adverse effect on his later relationships with women. In the reverse situation, Father sometimes tacitly sides with his son(s) when he (they) commit sexual violence.

Little research has been conducted on the behavior and signals of offenders. In order to prevent sexual violence, it would be wise to make a survey of their signals as well, instead of concentrating solely on the reactions of their victims. How does a man treat the girls and women in his immediate surroundings? Who are the potential offenders in our society? When it comes to a crime as frequent and serious as sexual violence, we must ignore the hindrances of social control, and start keeping an eye on the offenders.

We have attempted to classify the reactions of the girl herself, of her surroundings and of caring services professionals, in a spectrum progressing from being accomplices up to solidarity. The child can be turned into an accomplice, and she needs strength in order to start taking her feelings seriously again. We have examined the mother's role and have tried to do her justice without minimizing the pain her daughter has experienced because she felt unprotected by her mother. Many incest survivors display more aggression toward Mother than toward the offender for whom they either have an excuse, or from whom they no longer expect anything. As long as you hate someone, you still have expectations from him or her. As a participant in the patriarchal culture, the girl also holds the woman responsible for much of the evil that befalls her. Mother is the primary role model for her psychosocial development. If she has a negative mother-image, she will also develop a negative self-image. Her own guilt feelings and Mother's guilt will reinforce each other.

Finally, we have seen that fathers do not fit the psychological, secular, and Christian fatherhood myth. This is self-evident when they themselves are offenders, but fathers who are non-offenders protect their daughters just as poorly against intra-family sexual violence as mothers.

The Impact of Incest The trauma of incest is caused by the combination of violence and failed resistance. Even babies resist violations of their person, and show their displeasure when they are neglected or treated roughly. Children's resistance originates from a pure, unbroken will, which is much stronger, and stays stronger, than previously thought. The strength of our will is evidenced by the stories of concentration camp survivors. We can compare the resulting wounds with someone caught in barbed wire: The more one resists, the more damage one sustains. On the outside, it sometimes seems as if one has stopped resisting, but one's resistance usually continues on the inside. This inner struggle against injustice manifests itself in the visible damage or occasionally abnormal behavior discussed below. The symptoms these women relate are an indication of the ongoing resistance of a still unbroken will rather than of a person who has been forever broken and tamed. Only through the abuse of drugs and other addictive substances is the will temporarily, and in the end permanently, incapacitated.

In analyzing the impact of incest, we were conscious of the stigmatizing effect a summary of impact issues can have. Everyone wants to be treated with consideration, but an incest survivor is quickly branded as someone whose trauma has made her distrustful. She can be safely insulted, because her angry reaction is understood in terms of her trauma, rather than being directly related to the insult she has just received. A failed sexual relationship can also be attributed to her incest experience, so that the partner escapes all blame. When a person has been so labeled, no one takes her resistance seriously. She is considered pathetic; people do not talk with her, but about her.

Incest survivors have experienced gross injustice and will therefore be extremely sensitive to every form of injustice, abuse, and exploitation. This is not, however, a qualitative difference in their emotional lives; it is more a difference of degree in relation to how "other people" feel. These women do not wish to be labeled as special patients, but only want their experience and their feelings to be taken seriously. Even now in the Netherlands, doctors, caring professions, and police often try to keep a sexually abused girl in the family too long. The child feels inferior and therefore runs a high risk of getting involved with a boy on the social fringes, one who is also more likely to help her escape. If she does not get to a child-protective service or agency, she may end up in a squat with adolescents who are addicted in varying degrees to drugs and alcohol. These children can end up in heroin prostitution. Increasing numbers of these young women contact the association. Under more favorable circumstances, most of them end up in better situations, but they are badly damaged. It is crucial to provide an overview of the impact of incest so that the caring professions can acquire more insight into the mechanisms that develop and the traumas that accompany them. We hope that the children being abused today will receive more adequate help and counseling as a result.

We do not make a distinction in the seriousness of the trauma. This difference is partly dependent upon factors, such as inherited strength of mind, intelligence, place in the family, role of the mother or other family members, adequate help at a later age, or a more tolerant religious upbringing. A comprehensive analysis of these factors does not fall within the scope of this study. We have also not distinguished whether the sexual abuse was effected by use of physical violence. A girl who has not been physically forced may have experienced such a degree of mental coercion that she is badly damaged psychologically. Moreover, she can accuse herself of being an accomplice to the abuse. To make such a distinction, we should also have to classify the nature of the threat or of the actual violence. A single-incident rape within the family leads to agonizing uncertainty: When will he do it again?

We talked with women who contacted us of their own accord and who were able to articulate their experiences, although this sometimes cost them a great deal of effort. Many others are unable to do this. They have disappeared silently and lead an invisible existence, sometimes in the closed wards of psychiatric institutions where their stories are given little attention. The women we interviewed there told us that their experiences have affected them in these ways, insecurity, loss of identity, fear, and pregnancy, split identity, prostituting effect, negative self-image and victim role, and loss of faith.

Loss of Identity   Each woman says that she has lost her identity, and her personality, and her femaleness. She lost the freedom to determine what happens to her own body. She no longer belonged to herself. That happened during a period when she was scarcely conscious of an identity. Karen says: "It meant that I was his slave, and wasn't allowed to have a will of my own." This resulted in her inability to develop into an adult during adolescence. She remained a child, without a future, a young bird with a broken wing who could not achieve flight. On the other hand, she was never able to be a carefree child, because, as a child, she had had to perform the duties men desire from an adult woman. A balanced growth from child to adult was either interrupted or made impossible. That's why she is often naive and sometimes gives the impression of being chaotic. The worst part is not that her father has fallen from his pedestal and that she has become his lover, but that she has lost the right to control her own erogenous zones. According to all of these women, this is the most serious consequence. They base this on their own will, person, and body.

She has learned to feel responsible for others and tends to sacrifice herself for them. She does this partially to compensate for the evil she thinks is in herself, for her failures, her shame. This may result in a tendency to be a perfectionist. As a result of her servility and her fear of making mistakes, she will be repeatedly abused in her life. This confirms her in her role as a victim and in her inferiority feelings. She ends up in a negative spiral of victimizing behavior. Depressions and suicidal tendencies cause her to develop new guilt feelings about her own weakness. This may have resulted in a poor ability to concentrate in school and college; it is often combined with inappropriate and acting-out behavior or the opposite: silence and withdrawal.

Her deepest feelings have been betrayed: her affection for her parents or brothers, her sexual feelings, and her religious needs. Her whole being has been negated. As we have seen, the age discrepancy is less significant in brother–sister incest than the gender power discrepancy. Susan is more badly abused by the brothers who are slightly older, than she is by the oldest brother.

Sexual abuse by an uncle, grandfather, or stepfather can be just as traumatic as father–daughter incest. The degree of blood kinship is less significant than the power relationship and the living situation of the offender and his victim in the (extended) family. The cousin suffered from sexual abuse by an uncle and from the mental incest practiced by Father. In Grandfather's house, where Ellen lived with her mother and sister, there was a great deal of physical violence in addition to sexual abuse and intolerant, sexist religious practices. Seeing grown people fight is threatening for a child.

The woman engages in a lifelong search for her identity, one aspect of which is testing everyone: Is this true love? Are you really taking me seriously? When are you going to overstep my boundaries? Interpersonal relationships are very important to her, focused on the other person but looking for herself. With every disappointment, she feels that she has been stripped of her own personality all over again. The longer this continues, the deeper the trauma becomes entrenched. She seldom has the courage to begin an intimate relationship with anyone because she fears coming to the point when she will have to tell her story. Will the other person still accept her? That fear, and her fear of a new violation of her personal boundaries, often ensure that she keeps a substantial margin of safety between herself and others.

People with no identity have no language, either. She was not allowed to talk about the worst thing that ever happened to her, about the subject of her thoughts day and night. She suffocated in it. She knows, too, that she is worthless. What is there left for her to say? Nobody believes her anyway, right? She is stricken dumb and can only hope that someone will see that she is in suffering. The secrecy isolates her completely: "The worst part was that you were so totally alone."

Insecurity, Fear and Pregnancy   While the incest continued, she lived in uncertainty: when will it happen again? Will I have the courage to say "no"? She is afraid of being watched. He undressed her with his eyes, or watched her through the keyhole. Open doors may cause her to panic; she is afraid of being seen, turns off the lights everywhere; she fears footsteps on the stairs. She associates sex with fear, terror and suppression. She is absolutely terrified of getting pregnant. The offender does not realize that these fears are suffocating her. She is often very poorly educated about sex: She did not know how long sperm survived after ejaculation; she had thought that she could get pregnant before menstruation because sperm survives for some time. In her fear, Anne sought something to cling to and found it in the story of Mary who had also become pregnant out of wedlock; to her, that was beautiful and good. Perhaps it could be like that for her too. But for a girl made pregnant during puberty, things do not go as well as they did for Mary. The girl has to attend school in this situation and goes through a hell of scandal, shame, and disgrace. She invents lies so she does not have to admit who the father is. Caring professionals try to talk her into putting the child up for adoption. But it makes no difference in which family her child grows up; someday that child will want to know who its real father is. Should she tell it the truth? What effect will it have on the child? She is ashamed and waits far too long before going to a doctor or clinic. By that time, it is sometimes too late for an abortion, or the required procedure involves complications.

Split Identity   A split identity is one of the potential effects of oppression. For example, the discriminated black always sees himself through his own eyes as well as through those of his oppressor.[1] Women suffer from this problem due to their low social status,[2] but rape exacerbates the situation. When rape is committed within the family, the woman's emotions and reason are ripped apart. Each of these women says that she became a person with a split identity. This process more or less follows the pattern described below.

The eyes of her oppressor are those of her rapist, but they are also the eyes of her parent (or parent-figure), or of a trusted and authoritative member of the family. Although Father does not interfere with her upbringing very often, the child still knows that his social status, his career, and usually his philosophy of life are the factors that determined her upbringing. The perfect family image projected to the outside world must be maintained. As his future successors, the brothers share in Father's position, and his norms are learned by the girl. Thus, her rapist completely determines how she is supposed to think, feel, and behave. He knows what is good for her, however humiliating and painful. She knows very well that there is something wrong with this, but she does not know the code in which to express herself. She is not permitted to develop the power resource "verbal language usage." She has difficulty talking to people and sometimes thinks: "Oh, they can see what I mean by the look on my face" (Cathy). She knows only *his* codes and they can be summed up as: The more she acts like his slave, the better. Because the position of female slave is unbearable, she starts deluding herself that it is not so bad: She makes excuses for him and punishes herself, alternating between her rebellious feelings and her behavior as an accomplice. An ambivalent love-hate relationship develops, a relationship of dependency with her rapist. She learns from him that women are despicable creatures, deceitful, and cunning. She lets herself be beaten down and, with every blow, she reads the deep contempt in his eyes. When she has an authoritarian father who exhibits

---

1. See, for example, W. E. Dubois, *The Souls of Black Folk* (New York: Washington Square Press, 1970) and Ralph Ellison, *Invisible Man* (Westminster, Md.: Modern Library, 1963).

2. Paulo Freire, *Pedagogy of the Oppressed* (New York: Seabury Press, 1970; Harmondsworth: Penguin Education, 1972), p. 34.

macho behavior, she can internalize Father's norm: tough, independent, and contemptuous of the weak.

During the interview, she tells us what he demands of her: Don't behave like a victim; be tough. She still wants to meet his expectations of her; she has internalized her oppressor. You're beaten but aren't allowed to cry, or he thinks you're weak and insignificant, and then he ignores you. This is how the oppressed are silenced, and how the powerful can do whatever they want. The girl isn't permitted to cry, yet she is not allowed to be strong and to exercise her own will, because Father hates strong, independent women. He despises Mother who behaves in a womanly and dependent manner, but he feels threatened when a woman does not look up to him. The daughter becomes entangled in the chaos of this patriarchal system of norms in which pain and sorrow are identified with insignificance, being invisible, and death. In the most extreme case, she refuses to see those who are helpless, hates the weak or abuses her children. Still, she feels guilty about her attitude, because it is not in keeping with her conscience or with the Christian norm of mercy. As long as she refuses to recognize the weak, she refuses to recognize herself, because is she not one of them? She has indeed lost herself. One of the effects of the interview is that the woman becomes aware of these contradictions. In the follow-up sessions, many women say that they will be fit again only when they have managed to rid themselves of their rapists' norms. A long road of consciousness-raising lies before them: they will have to go through the pain and come out on the other side in order to free themselves.

With brother–sister incest, too, a girl feels guilty of betraying Mother and herself although she knows that she could not successfully resist. The feeling of guilt toward her mother becomes unbearable and she therefore tries to shift the blame on to Mother who was not always kind to her, did not always understand her, and did not protect her. She is living in two worlds, the world of deception and the world of truth, or the world at home and the world at school. Many of these girls like going to school: It is an orderly place, and they are taken seriously there, are considered persons. When a survivor's girlfriends talk about sex and boyfriends, she feels left out, does not know how to react. This isolation blocks her normal growth into a young woman. Inside, she has turned to stone, but on the outside she goes through life laughing. She may talk in a flat, sometimes loud, piercing voice and she laughs a lot, even when she is telling us the most terrible thing that has happened in her life.

Because she has to meet the expectations of others, she can be misled by her strengths: "You're such a good listener, you're so sweet." She thinks she is unique but finds out that she has been used, feels manipulated and is ashamed that she *let* herself be fooled like that. Because she is constantly confronted with the offender in the house or at family gatherings, she is afraid of accusations if she suddenly starts acting differently. Thus, she remains an accomplice, which only contributes to her self-recrimination.

She could threaten to tell others; however, she does not exercise this power because he has more effective power resources: money, status as a trusted adult male, verbal violence, knowledge, experience, and physical strength. She toys with the possibility in her thoughts, but her feeling of responsibility for the other family members, and shame for her own coerced part in the situation, prevent her from taking the risk. She accuses herself of being a coward and lives a double life: two entities continually chasing one another in a vicious circle.

When the offender gets his way by managing to get her to pity him, she feels even more responsible for him. When she realizes that she is just being used, her house of cards collapses. In order to survive, she continues to excuse him. She must suppress her rage because she is not allowed to display it. This survival mechanism may be the response to any variety of oppression. By pitying him, the oppressed girl attempts to make the powerful offender smaller. Although he is powerful, he can be pathetic and weak in reality; he then has this weakness in common with her, making her more equal to him. A king's subjects enjoy hearing that he, too, has the flu or is unrequited in love. In this way, they can bring him down to their level. The powerful offender usually tolerates this pity gladly, because it disguises his real power. A woman also primarily pities a man because he, too, suffers so cruelly under his own system. According to his own norms, a man isn't allowed to express his emotions and his love, but may only translate them into sex. How sad that he has to work so hard to be a successful breadwinner in this dog-eat-dog society. A woman is much better off, because she is allowed to really love. She will have to do it for him, play the role of surrogate, loving sufferer in order to redeem the man, his family, and his society. Thus, the circle is complete: from suppressed anger through pity to self-sacrifice and martyrdom.

The survivor gradually begins to doubt all her feelings: are they real? Is it right for her to give in to an orgasm that he has aroused against her will? Is it right to feel pain for deceiving Mother? Is it right to feel anger at him and at herself, at her surroundings for not responding to her signals, at God for allowing this to happen? Because the events are so utterly wrong, her anger is so intense that she fears its destructive force. She suppresses her emotions, physical as well as mental, because she feels rejected by everyone. She suppresses her memories. An incest survivor sometimes has gaping black holes in her memories. The repressed fears manifest themselves in physical pain, nightmares, or attempts to hurt or destroy herself or someone dear to her. She cannot give love, and does not want to receive it. Every once in a while, Karen escaped outside herself. She was temporarily able to free herself of her burden by leaving her body. There are also echoes of this extreme form of splitting oneself in Anne's story: She says that her memories consist only of images in which she is watching herself through a curtain.

When she does not break completely with her family, she is confronted with the person who raped her for the rest of her life. This situation still allows him to exercise power over her, until she decides not to expect anything from him anymore. After a confrontation with Father during which he admitted that his actions were wrong, Christine says that she is letting him go for her own good. The more she works through it, the less important it becomes; she is then able to let him go.

A woman who has not yet reached this point may still be in his power, although she may never see him again. This manifests itself in that she refuses to use his surname, she does not want to resemble him, fears meeting him, or fears talking about him because her throat tightens with anxiety.

Prostituting Effect   She distrusts her body because she has learned that it seduced men, or because it has let her down against her will. She has learned to see herself as a whore and fears that outsiders also consider her a slut. When a man harasses her on the street by making some remark, she thinks: "They can tell just by looking at me." She dresses plainly and modestly. She engages in sex outside of marriage and is paid for it in material favors or attention, or in return for harmony in the family. It keeps him quiet, stops him from bothering the others, from whining, or it makes him drink less. All of these women say that they felt like whores. Whenever a Bible story or a sermon involved a whore, they saw themselves in that role. To paralyzed and blind people whom he has cured, Jesus says: "Sin no more." An incest survivor cannot imagine that these people have any sins. She can, however, identify with the adulterous woman whom Jesus rescued from stoning and to whom he also says that she must not sin again. The survivor did sin again, and should therefore be stoned. It does not occur to her that there can be no adultery without a male partner. Of course, the Bible does not mention him either. The entire problem rests on the woman's shoulders.

The prostituting effect is reinforced by her negative female image. She has learned to despise herself, and to despise and detest the man. She looks down on him when he acts pathetic to get his way, but often continues to be subservient and to look up to him. She knows no other language in her relationships with men. Approximately 65 percent to 75 percent of the female prostitutes and very young heroin prostitutes in the Netherlands are incest survivors.[3] Girls who have experienced incest and are placed outside the home frequently behave so provocatively that many caring services professionals respond: "No wonder she was sexually abused; she was asking for it." They do not understand that the girl's behavior is the product of her home environment. She has learned that men expect her to act this way and that she will be rewarded for it. The reverse result is a total aversion to and fear of men. When a man approaches her, she gets confused, becomes insecure and evasive, and distrusts herself and him; this is due to the norm she has learned that says she should be subservient toward men. An incest survivor's behaviour may fall anywhere between these two extremes. This prostituting effect is detrimental to her psycho-social self-image.

---

3. B. Neeskens and A. Klein Herenbrink, "Wat heet incest?" [What is Incest] (Master's thesis, University of Nijmegen, 1984), p. 99.

The effect is manifested in a less extreme variation when a girl latches on to the first boyfriend who comes along for protection. She gets into a new dependency relationship and knows that she is giving him her body in return for safety and money: the Ruth syndrome. "The story about Ruth, that she had to lie at the feet of that man. I thought that was so humiliating," Margaret says. From the outset, this new relationship is based on her subservience: she feels sorry for him because he has chosen a defiled woman. Other girls who have been raped are incapable of beginning or sustaining any type of relationship at all where sex is involved. They don't want just to pretend.

Negative Self-Image and Victim Role   The survivor has learned to think and talk about Mother in the negative wording of her father or rapist. She also blames Mother for not protecting her. She transfers her own repressed feelings of guilt toward her. Because Mother is the most important woman in her young life and is also her first gender role model, this negative female image exacerbates her own negative self-image.

In her naiveté, she often thought that the oppressor was abusing only her. Sometimes, she did not realize that the younger sisters would get their turn the moment she left home. She did not warn them. This violence is unspeakable. The shock she feels when she hears, sometimes years later, that others were abused simultaneously or after her, destroys her remaining self-esteem. She thought that she had protected the others. Her only consolation had been this belief, which she had nurtured deep inside in order to survive.

Loss of Faith   The child who has faith turns first to God, her savior in need, or to Jesus, always praying, reading the Bible, doing penance, making sacrifices, confessing. In every way imaginable, these children try to live a good life for God and for those in their immediate surroundings, in the hope that the Lord will show them a way out of this chaos. Karen found great comfort in the lyrics: "Teach me to follow without question; Father, what you do is good. Teach me to bear only the present, with calm and peaceful courage. . . . Do not allow me to decide my fate; Were I permitted, I would not dare. O, how I would fail if you left the choice to me."[4] This hymn supports the accommodation syndrome. The author did not write these words in order to make a sexually abused child accept her fate more wholeheartedly or to eliminate her own will, but a child is not aware of the author's intentions. She thinks that the hymn applies to her because she is in such a hopeless situation that she cannot discuss it. God does not punish the offender; there is no miracle that makes the incest stop; nobody helps her. She usually has to solve this problem all on her own.

The older she grows, the more insight she acquires into religion's inconsistencies and its oppressive mechanisms. The church is for sinners and criminals, not for little girls doing their very best. "The angels rejoice for that one sinner who repents in the last minutes of his life . . . [more, than for] the ninety-nine who were good their entire lives. So there'll be more rejoicing for him up in heaven than for me when I get there?" (Margaret). The offender knows that too. After first trying to deny everything, he says: "I have sinned, but that doesn't matter because my redeemer will grant me forgiveness" (Ellen). When she runs away from home or breaks the taboo on speaking out, the offender is consoled. The minister visits him. The prison chaplain teaches him to pray. The sexologist and the psychiatrist nod sympathetically and believe his pathetic story: He is sorry, he will never do it again; his feelings of love just got out of hand, or his daughter seduced him; he had problems at work, or with alcohol abuse.

The survivor sits alone in her room. No one bothers about her. She is inconsequential to the church until she comes to ask for forgiveness. If she contacts a priest or minister or a therapist, she is given a story, full of accusations, about forgiving trespasses. Why cannot she forgive her offender for what happened? She must go and talk with him, to be the first to make amends, lovingly. Not the other way around? Should not the offender not go to her? Should she grant forgiveness before he even asks for it, or while he still tries to deny his actions and her pain? If the priest or minister cannot think of anything else to say, he says that in God's plan, all

---

4. By J. Van Der Waals, in *Dutch Reformed Hymnal*, No. 300.

things work together for the best. To suffer is noble. Can she not see this bad experience as life-enrichening? No, unfortunately, she cannot.[5]

She turns her back on religion and the church and makes her own religion. Priests and ministers can react very nonchalantly: "If she's not happy with us, she's better off leaving." But to whom does the church belong, then? Is it not *her* church, too? Faith is not a jacket to be slipped off. Leaving the church is accompanied by struggle, disappointment, and pain. The criminals remain members, while the survivors—who have also been wounded in their souls—flee the church and miss the community of faithful spirits. They may find a good alternative in the women's movement or the gay movement, but why does the church community not acknowledge them, and take their problems seriously? The church follows a strategy of conflict avoidance; it seeks to reconcile the faithful and evades conflict. Thus, the conflict remains with the less powerful person, the one who has been hurt. Although she continues to resist alone, she cuts herself further on the barbed wire, until someone is willing to face the conflict with her, so that she can find room for her anger.

Double Messages The dominant group in society uses contradictory commands or messages with a double content. Thus, the oppressed person is always wrong and the powerful person is always right. The interviews and follow-up sessions show that these messages increase these women's confusion and insecurity. The following list has been compiled from the nineteen interviews.

1. All women are bad because of Eve. But you are bad, because this doesn't happen to other women.

2. You must obey your elders, but sexual abuse is your own fault: you should have said "No."

3. Women are very special, beautiful creatures; you must particularly honor your mother. Nevertheless, the woman's body

---

5. These women's negative image of professionals has been confirmed in the many counseling sessions that I have conducted in the last three years with approximately sixty women and girls and in consultation with a number of therapists. In these cases, the professionals reinforced the offender in his pathetic behaviour and minimized the survivor's story. Fortunately, many other professionals in the field have not acted in this fashion, and the mention of this negative image is in no way meant as a slur on their professionalism.

is a temptation to men and it is unclean. Therefore, women are forbidden to serve at the altar.

4. You must resist sex outside of marriage, but you may not resist incest because you must always be protected. Moreover, you are not allowed to stand up for yourself because then you are a castrating bitch.

5. The eyes of the punishing God always see you. He will punish you. On the other hand, you must forgive your offender seventy times seventy times.

6. Father and brother are authoritative, but they are also pathetic; they get too little love, so you have to help them.

7. You have learned always to think of others first. But with sexual advances, you have to think of your own interests first. And what's in your interests? If you refuse, you're not a good girl. A woman must be good, always radiant, the sunshine in everyone's life.

8. Offenders have the tendency to minimize what happened: "You're making a big deal out of it; it's not that serious." But you have learned that sex outside of marriage is bad, that a woman who commits adultery should be stoned, and that she must keep her body pure, like Mary. Therefore, you have sinned.

9. You are not allowed to lie, but you are not allowed to tell this to Mother—ever.

10. You learn from the Bible: "Honor thy father and thy mother," and from Father: "Honor thy father and deceive thy mother."

11. You learn to love your neighbor and to be your mother's rival.

12. You are not allowed to talk to strange men, but if you show any resistance toward family members and friends, you have no sense of humor.

13. You learn that you are not allowed to overstep the personal boundaries of others, and you experience that men are allowed to overstep yours.

14. You must do your best in school and learn a profession so that you can stand on your own in case you are "left over" or become a widow, but your purpose in life is running the household and motherhood. Which career are you supposed to choose?

15. A prostitute is bad, but the offender rewards you with all sorts of extras, such as attention and gifts.

16. A prostitute is bad, but Mother allows herself to be paid too.

17. I must be a big girl, do not carry on. Do not cry when you are hit. But I must also be sweet, insignificant, weak, and womanly. Look up to men, let them protect you.

18. You are not supposed to be eager with boys, but you also have to see to it that you are not "left over."

Incest Trauma and Religious Trauma The traumatic impact of incest is related to the negative consequences of an oppressive religious ideology. We will define both traumas and indicate the correlation between the two.

An *incest trauma* means that the development of the will and the personality are deformed, so that all later life experiences are interpreted on the basis of the incest experience. Positive experiences cannot be freely accepted, and negative experiences are viewed as consequences of the sexual abuse. The course of every human contact is influenced by this abuse.

A *religious trauma* is the interpretation of all relational experiences on the basis of fear of and anger toward a God by whom one feels rejected, deceived, and punished; one also feels this anger toward a church community by which one feels cast out, threatened, and deceived. One may experience the community as an obstacle on the road to God.

In the interviews, we found a correlation between, or an intertwining of, incest traumas and religious traumas: All sexual, relational, religious and theological texts, symbols, and actions are interpreted on the basis of both traumatic experiences. This means that a woman with these traumas is particularly receptive to everything in religion related to evil women, seductresses, punishment, blame, guilt, and penance; to patriarchal sexuality in which the man is the central figure as the procreator of (preferably) male descendents, with his seed (which is precious and must not be wasted); and to the servitude his male potency demanded of her. She sees these themes in relation to herself, and her way of experiencing them is so all-embracing that she has no sense of other religious and theological ideas and experiences. The negative feelings generated by both traumas were unspeakable until a short time ago. The road to God and to people is blocked.

She will curse God because he deceived her as a child, but that curse makes her feel more guilty toward God. She becomes increasingly more afraid. In the end, she is afraid to accuse her rapist because she is expected to forgive him according to God's commandments; however, she cannot be content with the thought that he will go to heaven without admitting his guilt to her. When she is unable to see him as a "neighbor" or fellow human being who deserves forgiveness, she feels even more guilty. She knows that she is innocent, but still thinks she will be punished. When she can no longer live with these inconsistencies, she will either turn her back on God and her service to him, or no longer see any purpose in life and want to end it. This tendency to suicide already existed due to her incest experience and is exacerbated by the intertwining of the two traumas.

Too often, the church still preaches a theology of forgiveness that confirms the evil and guilt her offender has talked her into feeling. A liberation theology gives her room for her anger and teaches her that she is not a bad woman, but a "child of the kingdom."

4
Lessons from Working with Survivors

Because incest was unspeakable until recently, there are at present no accurate research-based statistics. The establishment of the Association against Child Sexual Abuse within the Family in 1981 made research on this subject possible for the first time. Large-scale research is presently under way, but comparisons with the past remain impossible.[1]

New and Old Myths   Incest seems to be more prevalent now, because the conspiracy of silence has been broken. Incest may also actually be increasing on the whole due to various factors that were formerly scarce or nonexistent. The most significant of these modern factors are examined below, along with a number of new and old myths that are still widely believed. When I (I. Jonker) refer to survivors or victims, I am referring not only to the women we interviewed in this study, but also to the women I've spoken with (approximately sixty in number) as ombudswoman for the association in the province of South Holland.

Changing sexual morality.   Sex used to be taboo. Now, everyone is more or less expected to like sex, regardless of with whom, when, and how. The person with the most power resources is in control. The number of abused young toddlers and babies reported by third parties is growing. Children under ten years of age are subjected to

---

1. See N. Draijer, 1988, Introduction, n. 1.

excessive and humiliating cuddling sessions, wrestling matches, or to actual "sex education." They become overstimulated and sometimes express their resistance by developing anorexia nervosa at a young age. Father, stepfather, brother, or the boy next door subjects these children to every kind of sexual act imaginable, or engages them in pornographic games. Fathers force their children to look at pornographic pictures or to watch pornographic films and videos. Child pornography is becoming increasingly violent. Now that incest has become an "acceptable" topic for discussion, it has also become a hot commercial item. Pornographic books, magazines, and videos are available in which the daughter plays the familiar role based on existing myths, and the father plays the poor, pathetic hero.

The myth of the pedophile. I'm often confronted with questions about pedophilia. The inquirer usually believes that pedophiles love children and are good to them. In a world where children have no place, pedophiles stand out for their supposed altruism toward children. A myth has emerged, comparable to those of motherhood and fatherhood.

In my view, every child has its own sexuality which she or he experiences: with herself or himself; in careful embraces with others; or in the open approach with peers inside a framework that is as equal as possible for everyone concerned. I have learned from conversations with young boys who have reported their abuse to the association via the children's hotline that pedophiles use power in the form of money, presents, trips, more knowledge, experience, a better vocabulary, and superior status. They give children attention and love with the premeditated goal of achieving their own sexual satisfaction, just as the offenders who were described in our interviews. Young men also tell me that they experienced sexual contacts during their childhood as damaging because they felt degraded to the status of an object.[2] Adults forget that the violation of a person's boundaries is not experienced by the powerful person the same way as the weaker person: An elephant does not feel the mouse he stands on; the mouse does.

---

2. See J. Frenken's observation in *Strafbare seksualiteit* [Criminal Sexuality], ed. J. Doomen (Deventer, 1984), p. 139.

Sexual relationships between elders and children within the extended family are always subject to the power dynamics and manipulations that have been examined in the preceding chapters.

Divorce.   Part of the tragedy of our world is that every liberating force has its own limitations. Being able to get a divorce is a positive development, yet divorce can contribute to incest. Two significant elements can be singled out: visitation rights and stepfathers.

Many children complain that Father bothers them during their weekend visits. Fathers accuse their ex-wives of inventing these stories in order to turn the children against them or to deprive them of their visitation rights or custody. Law enforcement, judicial, and psychiatric professionals are inclined to disbelieve the mother, especially with regard to very young children. Nevertheless, young children should initially be taken seriously; the truth can be subsequently discovered by using good, responsible methods of investigative interviewing. If this fails, or if the children are too young, the only remaining course is to educate the father. Visitation rights could be made contingent upon his reading a required book on the subject and discussing this book with a social worker.

The second problem is that of the stepfather, Mother's new partner. Cases show that when Mother acquires a new boyfriend or remarries, this new partner often abuses her daughter. The child is afraid to speak up because of her sense of responsibility toward her mother. Mother has had so much trouble in the last few years and now she is finally happy. Besides, Mother might think that the child is inventing this story because she cannot accept her new father. The girl thinks it is better to keep quiet. The accommodation syndrome begins. Child protection and social services agencies must be alert to situations like these occurring with minor girls. Adequate information and education for divorced mothers and their new partners is necessary. The child should also be present at such sessions. Relationships benefit when people are as open as possible with each other.

There are many excellent foster parents. Prospective adoptive and foster parents should be required to attend educational sessions on sexuality and to discuss their views on how it relates to children.

The repeat offender. Child sexual abuse occurs in a particular family. Father is the offender. Mother decides her children are more important than the marriage. The marriage is dissolved. Father begins a new relationship, sometimes with a woman who has daughters from a former marriage. Even when a complaint has previously been filed with the police, no one pays attention to the fate of the new stepdaughters and their mother. From our interviews, but also from recently publicized cases, we know that incest offenders are usually repeat offenders. City and state police confirm this observation.

The myth of "playing doctor." Rape by brothers or the boy next door is not taken seriously; it is called "innocent sexual contact occurring while children are playing." However, the expression "children playing" disguises five factors:

(1) The traditional status discrepancy between boys and girls still exists today, even in the so-called intellectual milieus.[3] In 1984, I spoke to six girls between eleven and eighteen years of age who had been raped by their brothers. In these families, the brother was considered the one who would pursue a "big career"; consequently, he received more allowance, had more freedom, was always trusted and was waited on by his sisters; (2) the hierarchy in the family; (3) the violence that an older child uses to force the younger child; (4) the morals and values that apply in the family; (5) the fact that, even today, many girls know very little about their own sexuality and connect this with marriage, pregnancy, motherhood, and being a housewife. They behave submissively toward boys and men, and they cherish the same ideals as their mothers when it comes to choosing a partner.

In 1983–84, I had a great deal of difficulty encouraging the police in a medium-sized city to listen to a girl who wanted to file a complaint against her brother who had raped her thirty times in a year and a half. She knew that this brother had also abused the sisters who were still living at home, and she was extremely worried about them. However, the police believed that the brother had a right to protection because he was a minor. Finally they agreed to file a report and the boy went to juvenile court. When a

---

3. See J. Meyer, *Sekse als organisatieprincipe* [Gender as an Organization Principle] (Amsterdam, 1983).

four-year-old girl was raped by an eleven-year-old boy, the police tried to reassure the girl's parents by playing down the incident: It was just a little healthy curiosity.

There is but one response to this myth of "playing doctor," the Universal Declaration of Human Rights:

Article 3: Everyone has the right to life, liberty and the security of person. Article 5: No one shall be subjected to torture or to cruel, inhuman, or degrading treatment of punishment.

The myth of "erotic games." Offenders sometimes confess to a small part of the truth and apologize for it. In doing so, they appear to be a model of integrity while getting a reduced sentence. When they go to a therapist, the therapist often believes what they say, and validates their excuses about their pathetic childhoods and their unhappy marriages. Following these sessions, the offender picks up at home where he left off. Many therapists do not consider incest a serious matter unless coitus or attempted coitus has taken place and they dismiss all other humiliating sexual acts as erotic games. They do not understand that what may be a game to an adult male is a deeply intrusive experience to a child. It is characteristic of the tenacity of the masculine norm that these perfectly well-meaning professionals consider a woman's sensations in her erogenous zones less important than the man's sexual act.

Escape, drugs, and prostitution. The children who report what has happened are the strongest; they survived under relatively favorable circumstances. Many others have disappeared: Boyfriends subsisting on the fringes of society aided them in their escape; they have been absorbed by youth gangs, they have learned to abuse drugs and alcohol; they slip into prostitution to get money. Sometimes one of these girls or women surfaces. Psychologists and social workers know little about the problems in incest and they call in self-help organizations "to help her work out her problem." Together with the survivor, we attempt to order the chaos, although this depends on her own willingness to work with us.

The confrontation with incest makes one powerless. Repression and minimization are the result, for those outside the family as well. The way to break loose is to use your energy to break through the taboo in yourself, to take your feelings of pain and powerlessness seriously and to work on a strategy to eliminate future child sexual abuse.

xual Abuse as a Power Issue During talks with caring professionals, priests, and ministers, I discovered that they continue to analyze the family within the system of parental love and child love, and to refer to it in terms of mutual support, obedience, and security. As the breadwinner, Father provides the finances and the contact with society, while Mother takes care of the household and raises the children. Father sees to it that the family religion is practiced faithfully, and Mother supports him in this. Father provides his wife and children with loving guidance. Mother is responsible for the emotional bonds, the atmosphere, and harmony in the family. She mediates between family members, smoothes over arguments, and is responsible for Father's emotional life.

In conservation, whenever I analyze the family structure in terms of power, giving a rundown of the power resources available, I notice a certain reticence and suspicion in others. Discussions on the power systems in society can be conducted on macro- and meso-levels, but this discussion is considered unacceptable on the micro level with respect to the family. Sexual violence, religious traumas, and power relations are taboo. The overwhelming emphasis on mutual love and solidarity obscures the power discrepancies that are present in authoritarian as well as anti-authoritarian families. In the latter category the axiom is: Do whatever turns you on. The strongest person, the person with the most power resources, can violate as many boundaries in this type of family as in authoritarian families. If this veiled power can be made visible, and the taboo on talking about power broken, there is a good chance that the less powerful will stand up for themselves and try to acquire more power resources. The dominant group would then have to give up some of its power.

Power figures are often aware that the erogenous zones are a significant part of one's identity. That is the reason these areas have been used to oppress people for centuries. History and current events give abundant examples of this. A substantial amount of torture involves injuring people sexually, either by using physical or mental violence.[4]

Plantation owners had the habit of abusing their female slaves; conquerors rape the women of a conquered people with the added intention of humiliating the men, and seizing their possessions. Women's ability to experience their own sexuality is taken from them by clitoridectomy (euphemistically called "female circumcision"); in our Western culture it is denied or humiliated by pornography and Freudian theories, which have been largely superseded by modern sciences.[5] In Christian religions Mary has no sexuality. She must bear a son while still a virgin. Patriarchal religions thus demonstrate that a woman is not allowed to have a will of her own. She serves only for reproduction. Women's sexuality is termed "dirty": Therefore women are forbidden from becoming involved in the official religion, or tribal rituals, or the altar, or the sacraments, or the sermon. Each patriarchal society has sexist jokes: A woman is always judged, ridiculed or complimented in terms of her body. She is labeled a seductress, identified with evil, Satan, the underworld, or death. Otherwise she is the unfailing angel who cares for one and all.

Sexual violence is a disorder of power. Rapists enjoy the power trip they get, as they admit in the film *Rape, Face to Face*, for example. Oppressed groups are accused of having sexual aberrations: Women are supposedly lustful; blacks in the U.S. have been falsely accused of raping white women; and German Nazis told similar nonsense about the Jews. Someone who has been sexually abused feels humiliated, less worthy, robbed of a part of herself, and oppressed in her will. That is the power figure's entire objective.[6]

---

4. Watching Sexual Violence (Pamphlet). See also *Martelen is mensenwerk* [Torture Is Manmade] (Amsterdam: Amnesty International, 1984); C. E. J. De Neef and S. J. De Ruiter, *Rapport sexueel, geweld tegen vrouwelijke vluchtelingen* [Report on Sexual Violence against Women Refugees and on the Nature and Impact of Sexual Violence Undergone by These Women Elsewhere] (The Hague: Ministry for Social Affairs and Employment, 1984).

---

5. Jeffrey M. Masson, *The Assault on Truth: Freud's Suppression of the Seduction Theory* (New York: Farrar, Strauss and Giroux, 1984).

---

6. See also M. Bullinga, *Het leger maakt een man van je* [The Army Makes a Man of You] Amsterdam: SUA Stichting Socialistische Uitgeverij, 1984).

A woman who has been raped by a male family member is imprisoned literally and figuratively: She lives in the same house, sometimes under the offender's authority, always under his power, because brothers are more important than sisters. She has been warned about strange men, but not about those in her own circle. This makes her defenseless. She feels that something is wrong, but knows at the same time that no one will believe her. This explains her confusion. She becomes entangled in a web of group loyalties, her own as well as those of other family members. Rarely does a family member choose her side, the powerless side, but even she is torn by her own doubts, because she has also learned to choose the side of the person with direct power. By making this choice, she places herself within the power he radiates, enjoying the resulting advantages, but this man, or his son, is now her rapist. The chaos grows. She is not permitted to express her feelings, to scream. She must remain silent. He determines whether the rape involves violence, pain, or pleasant feelings. She has no say. When her body responds, she does not want him to notice because she fears that it will make her even more defenseless. This is how she learns to separate reason and emotions, and goes through life as a person with a split identity. When the chaos is complete, her spirit can fall apart into little pieces. Her only certainty is his power over her. She is at risk of playing the role of the victim, repeatedly finding a new power figure to cling to who will oppress her again, so that her familiar, pathetic powerlessness will be validated. The goal of support groups, like those in the association, is to help women become aware of this so that they can protest; they can then use their energy positively.

Talking with Incest Survivors We could not foresee how the interviews would affect the incest survivors we interviewed. We chose not to include young girls in our study and limited the study to women over twenty who volunteered to participate. We observed that the interviews themselves had a therapeutic effect. I sometimes rewound the tape, so the woman could hear herself tell her own story. This had the same effect as reading the transcript of the interview later on. The survivors told me that this hit them hard. It was a shock to hear someone (her own, unrecognizable voice) tell her life story or read it in black and white. This was the first time they realized how terrible their experiences were. Women who had learned to repress every emotion broke down. They could no longer repress their anger and sorrow. Having people write down their experiences is a technique that is also common in contemporary psychotherapy, but the women we spoke to claimed that the therapists either never read their story or never used it in therapy. This makes them feel rejected all over again; it makes them afraid to expose their emotions a second time. We referred back to the woman's story when we talked to her again. In fact, we reviewed the entire story with her one more time. The woman has the opportunity to tell us: "This part doesn't quite say what I meant to say." She searches for the right words. Feelings are articulated. We are able to talk about them.

When we listened to the tape together, we paid attention to the intonation, slow or fast speech, sighs, silences, or laughter. We asked ourselves why there is so much laughter during the interviews. Together, we became aware that this laughter is a substitute for tears.

What she relates is so awful that you wanted to cry when you heard it. Why is she laughing? She herself says: "I laugh because I don't want to cry, am not allowed to cry or am afraid to cry." This kind of laughter has nothing to do with humor, which can have a liberating effect. It is not an attempt to make fun of herself, but the only form of emotional expression that is left to the oppressed human being. We recognize this phenomenon in other oppressed groups: the laughing, cheerful black, for instance. Women and children are not permitted to be angry, either. We say to children, "Oh, my, what a little temper!" with a disapproving note in our voice. An angry woman is called a screaming bitch; an angry man, on the other hand, gets the respect he demands. Some doctors still have a habit of calling overwrought mothers "hysterical dames".

During one of the follow-up sessions, a woman heard herself keep using the words "horrible, awful" and realized that she also uses these words to describe everything that happens to her in the present, although it is not nearly as oppressive. She realized that she interpreted the present undifferentiated from her past. When she was a child, she was helpless in the face of everything adults did to her. Now she is adult herself, and she can prevent herself from being repeatedly victimized, even though she is still oppressed as a woman. What happens to her now may be unpleasant and she may be angry about it, but the terms "horrible" and "awful" could seldom be applied today as they could in her childhood. This woman had not learned to laugh everything off, but had let herself be swept up in her initially-justified rage. She interpreted the present on the basis of her horrible past and projected that past onto everything that happened to her in the present.

The woman learns to step back from her experiences and gain some distance because she has the opportunity to relive her experiences together with someone. She learns that it is like any other book or tape: she can pick it up and read it or listen to it when she chooses to do so. In the past these events played through her mind like a never-ending tape. A random association suddenly made her feel threatened. Her past surrounded her in her dreams in the form of monsters or fire. Now she may think of her past when something unexpected reminds her of it, but she can think to herself, "That sounds like my story the way it's typed out, lying there in the drawer." A space has been created between her and her history, room that she can fill as she chooses. These women tell us after three months that their behavior is much more self-aware than before. "When my parents-in-law visit, I think, 'They'll just have to do things my way,' I'm not afraid of being confronted with my past anymore. It's easier for me to handle" (Ingrid).

We try to emphasize the positive aspects of her childhood. Susan says: "I became aware that there were good things, too, like in church. Because you asked about their attitude toward my handicapped brother I realized that it was really positive because of the church. That makes me feel good."

We also pay attention to the positive aspects of their present lives. As she got older, one woman kept discovering more and more of her father's facial features in her own face. She felt drawn to every mirror she saw so that she could see those hated features. She also started looking for other signs of him in her body and in her gestures. We took a piece of paper, divided it in two columns and made an inventory of everything that resembled Father and of everything that was good and uncontaminated. During this talk, we touched on clothing, makeup and hair, and discovered that she could decide to accentuate the "good" features and camouflage the "contaminated" ones. Two weeks later, I saw a completely different woman. She had received compliments about the sparkle in her eyes, she had styled her hair differently, and she had bought white boots, which focused attention on her small, slender feet. We had taken her problem seriously and helped her through the pain of her resemblance to her father. By listing the positive aspects, she was able to see that, as adults, we can choose an approach to life based on our incest experience or one based on something else. In the following sessions, this woman became aware that she still gave her father power over her because she still expected something from him. Accepting the painful fact that he will probably never apologize for what he did, that this man is not the father in the beautiful fairy tale about fatherhood, costs time and energy; nevertheless, it liberates her from his power so that the makeup, hairstyle, and boots will soon be superfluous as distraction mechanisms. They serve a temporary purpose.

Survivors sometimes have difficulty distinguishing between good and bad. Father did it and so it was good, but she experienced it as bad. What is good? What is bad? She imitates others to make it easier: Whatever they call good or bad, she does. Her own feelings are out of reach. When discussing the consequences of this strategy, it is important not to limit the new space that has been created by making decisions or interpreting things for her. One should never say, "Let me tell you why that is . . ."

Many girls are ashamed of their bodies. They move stiffly, are tense when they sit. They do not want to be touched, are later physically distant with their children, sometimes have problems making love.

Almost all of these women had to flee in order to escape the violence being done to them. Some of them escaped into a marriage with the first man who came along. Others escaped into drugs, prostitution, or alcohol. Many chose an educational institution away from home so they could get out of the house. Catholic girls had the option of entering a convent where they thought they would be safe. This escape forms the basis for their present problems. After our first few sessions a survivor becomes aware that she has a will of her own. All of the morals that rule in families ("You have to . . .") are turned into one question; "What do you want?" She then distinguishes between the morals that have been imposed on her and her own values. She becomes willing to take responsibility for her own choices and breaks free of her victim role. She can share her anger with others. This creates space in her mind and spirit that she can fill as she wishes. She can free herself from the offender's power over her.

Active listening is always asking, "What did you feel and what did you think then when this happened?" "What are you feeling now while you tell me this?" "What are you thinking as you talk about this?" "What would you like to achieve? What are your goals?" "What steps are you planning to undertake to achieve them?" "What options are available to you in order to achieve them?" "What consequences will this choice have for yourself, for others?" Summarize the responses and ask for clarification, "Could you be a little more specific?" "What do you see as your problem now?" "At which points did you feel that I wasn't really listening or didn't understand you?"

Talking with Children

What can be done in a case of suspected incest involving small children?

We never intervene independently but always work with a team of caring services professionals in a metropolitan or regional network. An intervention strategy is developed, depending on the age of the child. Because the options and problems are so complex, it is impossible to discuss this process in the space provided here.

When I am called in my capacity as ombudswoman for such a case, I operate within the code the child knows: you can trust the men within your own circle, but you must be careful with men outside the circle. I try to stay within the child's own world and use questions like the following: "Who are your playmates? When and where do you play? What games do you like? Where's Mommy? Where's the rest of the family, then? Are they allowed to play, too?"

We talk about taking a bath, going to bed, getting tucked in, cuddling, being read to aloud, and taking walks. We go into details, for example about the color of the bathroom tiles, the blankets, the pictures in the books read aloud to her. We talk in the child's vocabulary about reward and punishment. The child draws pictures of the parents or of her room.

It is possible that the child has been turned against Father, by Mother following a divorce, for example. How do we find out the truth if Father denies the allegation? By talking to the child again several days later using a different approach and different questions, I can determine whether the child is describing her experiences in her own words or whether she repeatedly does so in the same terms. If she is unable to tell anything about what happened in her own words, it's probable that she has memorized her story. However, if on various attempts, she continues to describe the same event in her own language, and if her responses correspond to the different approaches, then we can assume that she is telling the truth. It goes without saying that, during these sessions, the child must have a feeling of security, and feel that her interests are being looked after.

Talking with Adolescents

The child has been over-stimulated from an early age and sometimes has even had to fulfill the sexual duties of an adult woman as a toddler. With us, she is allowed to be a child, but we do not say, "She must repeat her childhood." She does not "have to" do anything. Because of her experiences, she often thinks many things are childish. She determines with what she feels comfortable. Sometimes she talks at length about what happened and then falls silent. If she does not return to the subject again, do not assume that it must not have been so bad after all. It could simply be embarrassment. Incest is unspeakable, for the child too. Children do not learn its name; they learn to keep silent about it. If it happens to come up—depending on the child's age—I point this out. For example, I ask: "What do you hate the most about his body?" The answer is always: his face, and in that face, his eyes that leer at her, his stare that undresses her, or his mouth with its mean little smile. I allow them to think about this. We go back in time, sometimes using a photo album. Some girls do not have even one happy memory. The sexual abuse overwhelmed their lives so completely that they can remember how sad and awful they felt in every photograph. The self-recrimination is sometimes the worst. I ask her how she feels about me as an incest survivor. The child explains that she does not blame me for anything, because "I was just a child at the time, and . . .," followed by all the arguments that excuse herself. "If you do not blame me for it, then why do you blame yourself?" Even the worst self-recrimination cannot stand up to this logic. In this way, I can allow her to be a whole person again. The album has served its purpose and, together, we bring back the moments when she resisted. In my questions, I emphasize her strength and will finally to break the silence.

The disordered family relationship remains a problem. Can she expect anything in the future from Mother or the others? Some of the girls don't want that any more. Others adjust their expectations to the reality of the power dynamics and the complex of interests: The warmth and affection she gets from her family from now on is icing on the cake. The pain of celebrating lonely birthdays and Christmases is tangible, but with every sad feeling, I call on her strength. How bad would the pain be, compared to the pain of her incest experience? She survived that. Family can be replaced with other relationships. She can build them by working on herself. How can she do that? We make plans, look at the options. Counseling incest survivors is a difficult and time-consuming task, which costs a great deal of energy and empathy, and requires expertise. Unfortunately, caring services are often too quick to apply family therapy in which the psycho-social development of the child is subordinated to the interests of Father and his model family.

The Relationship with Mother The survivor often has negative feelings about Mother. She needs room to express these feelings. Only then can she ask herself to what degree Mother deserves this anger. In order to achieve this, a process must be initiated in which she becomes aware of the traditional man and woman relationship. This can be a long process. It is essential to keep raising the subject of the survivor's relationship to Mother; a negative mother image is often closely related to the surivor's own negative self-image because Mother is her most important gender role model. In light of the initial aggression toward Mother, the counselor or therapist does not always have to be a woman. This choice should be left to the survivor. When the counselor is male, he will have to make a conscious effort not to validate this aggression and not to stay within the patriarchal system. Because Mother was not the offender, she need not be held responsible for what the offender did. The girl will begin to distinguish between the messages she has received and internalized about Mother from Father, and her own observations and reality. Together with her counselor, she can demythologize the image of Mother, a process that will do justice to her own emotions as well as to Mother as a person. An alliance with Mother makes the child strong.

Confronting the Offender and Parents

Incest can be reported to the police as long as it is not barred by the statute of limitations (twelve years in the Netherlands). The survivor may ask someone to accompany her, even during questioning. After her statement has been typed out, she has the right to read it carefully before signing it. Experience has taught us that this is necessary. She can indicate whether she wishes to press charges or is satisfied with filing a complaint. The criminal justice system has reached a point where her wishes are respected. Simply reporting the incest or filing a complaint can sometimes be beneficial to her sense of justice: The police should be aware when a crime has been committed. In each case, it is her choice. In this process, she must not be talked into or out of anything. Physical abuse is not a pre-condition for filing a complaint. Sexual assault or rape of a minor in itself can be sufficient. Reporting incest to the police or filing a complaint may be necessary as a preventive measure: Other girls at home are in danger. The victim often fears repercussions, but the police can offer her little protection. In reality, however, repercussions are the exception rather than the rule: The suspect only damages his own case. Still, we advise the woman to take a course in self-defense. Even if nothing should happen to her, it strengthens her self-confidence and makes her feel less afraid.

Just because the suspect confesses does not mean that he will not repeat the offense. Women in the association strongly advise talking to the offender, no matter what the circumstances. If he refuses, the threat of a conviction may force him to reconsider. Talking with the offender is not easy. Some excellent therapists in this area of expertise can help, but in our experience many therapists are easily misled by offenders. It is sometimes useful for a woman from the incest support group, whether she does this together with the victim or alone, to explain to the offender the damage he has done. A confrontation like this must be carefully planned in order to protect the survivor from renewed humiliation. She must be aware of her expectations and goals in such a confrontation. It sometimes fails. The variation in incest situations makes it impossible to give guidelines for conducting a conversation between victim and offender. Some women make a choice to confront him directly. If he denies nothing, things can go reasonably well. If there is a good chance that he will minimize the abuse, I ask the woman whether she is aware that she is still in his power. Does she need to validate her pain? She knows that already? Is that not enough? When a brother or other family member is the offender, it can be a great relief for the survivor finally to be able to talk with her parents about it. Here too, careful planning is necessary. We recommend that she take with her someone whom she trusts. In addition, we advise that the parents also have a counselor.

Mother needs some time to let this unacceptable news sink in and overcome the initial shock. When her husband is involved, this news can prove to be a relief, and give her the incentive she needs to file for divorce. In every case, no matter the age of the survivor, it is best to be as open as possible with all family members. Relationships can only benefit from a clear understanding of the situation between all people involved. Nevertheless, it is the incest survivor who must determine when she is ready to talk. When she is ready, she, her mother, and the offender must each have her or his own counselor. The interests of the various family members, their status and their power resources differ significantly so that the weakest person can feel threatened. Maximum security is guaranteed to all parties when each person has her or his own counselor. This will also enable the counselor to be more open and honest. This applies to a participating priest or minister as well.

Outsiders who are confronted with incest also need counseling or "intervision."[7] Incest is so impermissible and so shocking that no one can work through it without help. There is always the danger of repression or minimization. In the Dutch situation, the network of caring services in various disciplines working together with association ombudswomen provides good initial intervision. We hope to prevent these children from ending up as patients in the wards or isolation cells of psychiatric institutions. This is the worst thing that could happen to an incest survivor. This treatment is a confirmation of the isolation in which she found herself as a result of resisting suppression. In our self-help therapy, we can

---

7. *Intervision* is an interactive method of support and supervision used by Dutch counselors and therapists — Trans.

often help these women to stand on their own two feet reasonably well, but the wasted years sadden me. The extent of recovery is also dependent upon the seriousness of the trauma. No one can completely free herself from deeply wounding experiences, and the family can always continue to be a source of tensions.

The Situation Today The average age of women and children who report cases of incest to the association is gradually decreasing. Exact national statistics are not yet available.[8] Many children leave home and go to child protection and social services without reporting their cases to the police. Many children reach us via the children's hotline. The number of boys who are abused by their gender mates is increasing. In the Netherlands, male incest survivors have started their own group in the association. When their experiences have been recorded and analyzed, we will be able to review and refine our theories on power dynamics and sexual boundaries within the family. Girls who have contacted the association since this study was completed continue to validate every finding of the study. In churches, the patriarchal Bible is still read as God's word. In non-religious circles, a secular ideology substitutes for the religious one; the substitute is just as patriarchal as the religious ideology, but it can be more obscured and confusing because of its progressive myths, as we saw in Carol's interview. Men's sexuality is still unlimited. In the past, father and son could go unpunished for violating not only the family daughters but also the servant girls. Every girl is expected to put up with sexual harassment because "boys will be boys." Men in society imposed this norm on her. It is refreshing to hear that, along with groups against incest and sexual violence such as our own association and Women for the Prevention of Sexual Violence, male groups against sexual abuse are also being started. In the Netherlands, Men against Sexual Violence was established in 1984.[9] The factors that keep a girl silent today are the same factors we found while interviewing women over twenty. When a girl complains that she is being harshly treated, that she receives too little allowance, and that she is never allowed out of the house, we

8. See N. Draijer, 1988, Introduction, n. 1.

9. *Man-u-script* 1984, no. 10.

know that there could be more to it. In such cases, caring services professionals should ask direct questions about the behavior of the men and and the brothers in the family. Some doctors and agencies have added such questions to their standard question forms. Children are always relieved to find out that they can talk about these things. We need not fear that they will fantasize sexual assaults. Children do not imagine such things; with a little questioning, a professional can soon find out what is true and what is not. If the story of the powerless younger person is taken seriously at the outset, then the story of the powerful older person can be examined in its light.[10]

---

10. For additional literature on counseling incest survivors, see: Liz Kelly, *Surviving Sexual Violence* (Minneapolis: University of Minnesota Press, 1989); Suzanne Sgroi, *Handbook of Clinical Intervention in Child Sexual Abuse* (Lexington, Mass.: Lexington Books, 1982); Van Lichtenburcht et al., *Verder na incest, Hulpverlening bij het verwerken van incestervaringen* [Going on after incest: Caring Services and Working through Incest] (Baarn: Ambo), 1986).

Part Two
CHRISTIAN
INFLUENCES

5
The Impact of Christian Images

God Men constitute the dominant group in Christian society; for centuries, they have thus appropriated the right to define how God must be viewed, how the world was created, and how that world should be ordered according to God's will. From their position of power, they have determined that only men possess this ability. In doing so, they have looked after their own interests and reduced women to silence. They have issued laws, commandments, and bans that reinforce the world order they have conceived, as well as their own position of power, while rendering women powerless.

The God of Our Fathers Christian church fathers, theologians, and church leaders have become accustomed to referring to God exclusively as a father. Jesus used this father-image to express his relationship with God and to show how people can experience God as a close, loving, confidence-inspiring presence. Through the ages, men of the church have added various characteristics and features to this Father God that are typical of domineering fathers. They have determined that God can only be talked about in that particular way. God commands "that I rightly recognize the one true God; trust in him alone; submit myself to him alone in all humility and patience; expect all good from him alone and love, fear and honor him with my whole heart, so that I would forsake all creatures before I would do the smallest thing against his will."[1]

---

1. Orden van dienst/Catechismius voor de Gereformeerde Kerken in Nederland [Order of Services/Catechism of the Dutch Reformed churches in the Netherlands] (Leusden, 1981).

God the Almighty Father, the Lord God, Father, Lord, he who created all things; these are the terms used to speak of God in the officially authorized prayers and texts of Christian churches. This is the way God is seen within the patriarchal experience of Christianity. It is an image of God as a domineering and jealous father who does not tolerate disobedience and rivalry, but expects submissiveness and self-hatred. In Exodus 3:15, we can see how we are supposed to view this one-sided God: as men define Him. "The Lord God of your fathers, the God of Abraham, the God of Isaac, and the God of Jacob." We can add another long list of men to this: the God of Augustine, the God of Thomas, the God of Luther, and so on. The God of our fathers is God who allocates power to men to rule over women. The God of our mothers and their daughters who were rendered powerless has had little opportunity to be heard and to be named. Women are now occasionally allowed to participate in theological discussions. When they do so, they often elicit laughter or irritation from both men and women. God the Mother as a temporary alternative is dismissed as unrealistic before it has even been given a chance, because God is ultimately intended to be genderless and nonhuman. A telling quote from a minister says, "God the Mother, that's impossible. For me, that would be some dame who would steamroller right over everybody."

God's Will, Men's Law and Women's Role

Men not only claimed the right to define how we may imagine God, but they also presented themselves as the ones called by God to define His will. And so they claimed the power to issue laws which safeguarded and provided for the interests of men and protected their property. Exodus 20:17 is a good example of this: "Thou shalt not covet thy neighbor's house, thou shalt not covet thy neighbor's wife, nor his manservant, nor his maidservant, nor his ox, nor his ass, nor any thing that is thy neighbor's." No one could argue that, in this passage, "thy neighbor" might possibly refer to a woman. The neighbor in the passage is the owner or caretaker of everything included in the list of his possessions. His wife is one of these possessions.

The writings of Paul, and those attributed to him, are particularly notorious among women for the way in which they have been used in Christian Churches to reduce women to silence and to make them subordinate to men.

Ephesians 5:22–23: "Wives, submit yourselves unto your own husbands, as unto the Lord. For the husband is the head of the wife, even as Christ is the head of the church: and he is the saviour of the body." Christian women still hear this text in the marriage liturgy.

1 Corinthians 11:7–9: "For a man indeed ought not to cover *his* head, forasmuch as he is the image and glory of God: but the woman is the glory of the man. For the man is not of the woman; but the woman of the man. Neither was the man created for the woman; but the woman for the man."

1 Corinthians 14:34–35: "Let your women keep silence in the churches: for it is not permitted unto them to speak; but they are commanded to be under obedience, as also saith the law. And if they will learn any thing, let them ask their husbands at home: for it is a shame for women to speak in the church."

1 Timothy 2:11–15: "Let the woman learn in silence with all subjection. But I suffer not a woman to teach, nor to usurp authority over the man, but to be in silence. For Adam was first formed, then Eve. And Adam was not deceived, but the woman being deceived was in the transgression. Notwithstanding she shall be saved in childbearing, if they continue in faith and charity and holiness with sobriety."

Ecclesiastical Statements Contemporary leaders in the Roman Catholic Church still often cite these passages from Paul in order to explain the role of women according to "God's will". The following statements from Pope John Paul II and Mgr A. J. Simonis, then bishop of Rotterdam and presently archbishop of Utrecht, make this clear:

Pope John Paul II According to Genesis 4:1, the man is the one who "knows," and the woman, the wife, is the one who is known, as if everything that determines the actual depth of her femaleness was kept hidden by woman's specific determination through her own body and gender. In contrast, the man is the first who, after the Fall, felt shame for his nakedness; he is the first who said: "I was afraid, because I was naked; and I hid myself" (Gen. 3:10). (Later, we will return to the frame of mind of each of them after the loss of innocence. However, we must conclude here that, in the "knowing" to which Genesis 4:1 refers, *the mystery of femaleness is clearly present and fully revealed in motherhood as in the text: "She conceived and bare . . ."* The woman faces the man as mother, bearer of new human life that has been received in her, develops further in her, is born of her, and brought into the world. Thus the full mystery of the maleness of the man also reveals itself, that is to say, the procreative and "fatherly" meaning of his body.[2]

Bishop A. J. Simonis   Through Genesis, the man stands before us as the "radiance of God's glory", procreator of life in His name; the woman stands before us as the perfect answer to this, as the one who completes this gift, as the preserver of life. Catholic theological teachings on woman's specific, unique nature are not "myths", as is often claimed today, but the deepest interpretation of what is revealed to us by God's word.

Simonis summarizes: What must we conclude? That woman has her own nature with respect to man. Without declaring it absolute, one can say that there is such a thing as woman's natural nobility; this consists of the female nature's capacity for altruism, the capacity to serve in the most noble sense of the word.[3]

According to these writings of men in the church, women must be seen in these ways according to God's will.

— She is one of the man's possessions along with his house, his servant, his ox, and so on;
— She is submissive to the man, because he is her head;
— She is the reflection of man's glory and was created for his sake;
— She must remain silent in church, because she must stay in the background;
— She is not permitted to speak, because Adam was formed first and because it was not Adam who was deceived;
— She must bear children and continue in faith, then she will be saved;
— She is the one who will be known, while the man knows;

2. Pope John Paul II, *Male and Female in the Image of God* (Antwerp: Nieuwe Stad, 1981), p. 113; italics in original.

3. Bishop A. J. Simonis, "Thoughts on Woman's Place in Society and Church," speech to the Catholic Women's Guild, 1982.

— She is determined by her own body and gender, but Adam was the first to feel shame after the fall;

— She stands before the man as the bearer of new human life that she has received;

— She is the answer to the man as the "radiance of God's glory";

— She has her own nature and from that nature flows her capacity for altruism, her capacity to serve.

In this vision of men, God expects women to see themselves as having been created for men's desire, as men's property, as a reflection of their glory, and as the answer to men's demands of women. For these reasons women are expected to bear children, to be submissive, silent, subordinate, quiet, altruistic, and subservient. Only then do women live according to God's will and according to their own nature and ability. They will be determined by this as long as men, who see themselves as the "radiance of God's glory," are in charge.

Impact on Women   Using the survivors' responses to the questions about God and the will of God, we have shown the impact of the patriarchal approach to God and God's will on these women. Their responses clarify our view of the patriarchal approach's effect on all women, because these women's experiences in their childhoods can be seen as the ultimate consequences of a society that is legitimated and partially brought about by patriarchal Christianity. Because the incest survivors experienced the impact of this Christianity to a serious degree, they are able to articulate the impact clearly. They name the God of mothers and daughters who have been rendered powerless.

God as Experienced by These Daughters   During the interviews, we asked the question, "How do you view God, or what is your image of God?" The woman indicates in her answer how she imagines God—as a father, for example—and then names a characteristic that she attributes to God.

While analyzing the interviews, it became apparent that each woman had also described the effect this image of God had on her, and how it had influenced her behavior. When her ideas about God changed, so did her attitude and behavior toward the offender, other family members, and society. This became evident during the follow-up sessions. In order to make the information about God more accessible, the responses have been categorized on the following pages (196–205).

Survivors' Images of God   Under the heading "God's attitude and expectations," the only expectations included are those the incest survivors themselves mentioned in direct relation to God. The impact of the expectations which they experience as coming from God is far more drastic than that of the expectations which they experience as coming from the church or from people in the church. For example, many women had difficulty with the fact that women are looked down on in Christian churches. But when they had the feeling that God himself looked down on women, it was seen as rebelling against God if they didn't accept it or resisted.

God as a person is always seen as male, and predominantly as a father (11 times). God is seen as the ideal father (3 times), as opposed to the woman's own father. God is identified with the woman's own father (6 times): "That was all jumbled together"; "Father wanted to be worshiped, too"; "Father knew how God punished, he heard that directly from God"; "My father could have been God"; "Father was a kind of god"; "God resembled my father."

In addition, God was defined as: a man (5 times), big man; creator (4 times), ruler; judge; love (2 times); good; he; spirit; shepherd; friend (2 times); Grandpa, God and Jesus are seen as identical three times.

Not one time is God given female names. When we occasionally asked for one, the idea was immediately dismissed due to the woman's experience with her own mother. "God the Mother, no, I can't see that. Mothers are so powerless."

The Patriarchal Image of God as Destructive of Women   God is omniscient, omnipotent, and all-seeing; at the same time, God is good, just, strict and protective. What God wants, happens; God is almighty (more powerful than the woman's own father).

God expects the survivor to love her fellow human being more than herself, to honor her father and mother, and to pray often. Then God will take care of her. A woman had to remain silent, and if she was struck on one cheek, she had to turn the other cheek. Someone who has wronged her has to be forgiven unconditionally. Crying about or resisting sexual abuse by Father is seen as rebellion against Father ("defying Father"), therefore sinful, and as rebellion against or defying God. God rewards good behavior. Sin is punished with hell, but also results in things going badly during this life. Unchastity or lewdness is considered a great sin. There is either a lot of emphasis on this, or it is not mentioned at all. Sex before or outside marriage, which isn't intended for procreation, is so sinful that talking about it is taboo.

The women we interviewed were sexually abused by father, brother, uncle, or grandfather, and sometimes by more than one. When they dared to ask the offender questions about it, they were told that all fathers do that, that it was good for them, or that they themselves had given cause because they were seductive and evil, just like Eve. They could not talk to Mother about it because she would not understand, or because she was too weak. Father also used these arguments to prevent the daughters from broaching the subject with Mother. Brothers did not need to use these arguments. Incest survivors who were abused by their brothers did not dare talk about it because they were afraid they would be blamed, or knew that their parents would not believe them. "Go ahead and scream. They won't believe you, anyway," said Susan's brother. Another woman told us, "I knew that I'd be blamed for it."

These sexual abuse survivors increasingly tried to meet the expectations God had of women, which they learned from various educators (school, church, and family). They hoped to come into God's favor so that God would end the sexual abuse. They loved their neighbors, and did so increasingly at their own expense. They honored their fathers and mothers, despite the sexual abuse by their fathers. They granted the offender forgiveness, although he never gave them cause to do so. (None of the offenders asked for forgiveness and most of them denied the abuse, or blackmailed the survivors.) "If I ever told what I know about you . . .," Mary Beth's brother still threatens when he wants to silence her. Sometimes the survivors turned the other cheek, as they were expected to do. Turning the other cheek does not mean that the girls allowed "another side of themselves" to be seen when the offenders' behaviour gave them cause. Instead, it means that they bore the abuse with even more resignation.

The next step was to do penance for the offenders and to pray even more. When the incest still continued, they began to doubt

God as Experienced by These Daughters

Age	Offender and religious milieu	Survivor's image of God	God's characteristics	God's attitude and expectations	Feelings toward God	Attitudes toward God	Impact on incest survivor
50	Grandpa Dutch Reformed and Free Evangelist	God the Father (Grandpa's images, own deceased father, and God the Father jumbled together).	Looks down on women, always sees you, sees everything. Protective. Almighty. Strict.	Women must keep quiet, be good to Mother. Didn't intervene, doesn't understand you.	Confusion. Anger. Despair. Doubt.	Tries to find things wrong. Is wary.	Undergoes incest due to great feeling of responsibility toward Mother. Doubts God and herself, has guilt feelings.

She no longer believes in a higher power, and now feels guilty primarily toward herself because of the incest experience.

Age	Offender and religious milieu	Survivor's image of God	God's characteristics	God's attitude and expectations	Feelings toward God	Attitudes toward God	Impact on incest survivor
29	Father Roman Catholic	God the Father	Has terrible almightiness, resembles own father (who wanted to be worshipped too).	Love your neighbor. Honor your father and your mother.	Confusion. Guilt (because she can no longer pray to God the Father). Anger.		Can no longer pray. Her faith is destroyed. Left Catholic church.

In the past she found inspiration in the image of the innocent child, or the image of the twelve-year-old Jesus, in order to be able to resist her father's behavior at home. These images still inspire her today to fight injustice.

27	Father Dutch Reformed	Strict father, sort of judge.	Judgmental. Strict. Watching. Almighty.	You must forgive. You must obey your parents. Women must obey and serve men.	Anger. Guilt.		You always feel bad and guilty.

She now wants nothing to do with the church, does not know what to believe anymore.

44	Father Roman Catholic	God the Father, Creator	Knew all, saw all, could make it all right. God's will—incest?	Didn't help. You must forgive. You must honor your father and your mother, love your neighbor.	Unrest. Doubt. Guilt. Responsibility.	Blames him for not intervening. All wrong. Completely dependent.	Difficulty with God the Father. Did her best, kept hoping God would intervene. No sense of own strength, no longer prays.

She still has difficulty with God. "But I sometimes think, too, that I'm my own God." She can stand up for herself, now, and for others, and help to break the taboo on incest.

37	Father Dutch Reformed	Like a father is supposed to be. God is love (fragmented pieces).	Nice, old, with a big warm heart and beard. He's where good love is.	People may not separate what he has joined together.	Security.		Mother had problems with divorce. Arguing in a love relationship means that that love is not good.

Father saw God as a rival. He asked Mother to put her faith aside in order to prove to him that she loved him more than God. Survivor now experiences God as a big black hole, that is to say, it could be anything.

Age	Offender and religious milieu	Survivor's image of God	God's characteristics	God's attitude and expectations	Feelings toward God	Attitudes toward God	Impact on incest survivor
26	Brother Roman Catholic	A "he." Creator.	He can always see you. Sees all. Knows all. Everything happened the way he wanted. He has the whole world in his hands. He made everything.	Love your neighbor, more than yourself. You must forgive.	Fear. Impossible to understand. Confusion.	Someone like that can only be a "he." The more you go to church, the closer you are to God. You can only pray. Wanted to prove it was wrong.	There was nothing He did not know about. You have no rights whatsoever, are responsible for everything. Bothered her for a long time.

The last few years, she feels that she has an increasingly peaceful feeling about herself. She now wants to name God as the good in people, the good in herself.

| 56 | Brother Roman Catholic | (In dream: a man). God is love. Sort of a father. | Loved children. His power is greater than others. He can make or break a person. | Puts his arms around her. You're not allowed to enjoy life. You sleep and eat to stay alive. | Confusion. Revulsion. Fear. Guilt. Penance. | Many questions. People must serve Him and make great sacrifices for later. | Something to hold on to at a difficult moment. Long and intense fear of death and hell. Chronic sleeping problems. |

During the interview she had a great deal of difficulty with God, and had many questions. "Why does there always have to be one more powerful than the rest?" Her fear has largely disappeared because she no longer believes in God, but her purpose in life is also gone. She would like to believe in a God who loves people but finds the reality very different. Later, she said, "I've decided to only believe in myself for a while and to trust only myself. Later on, I'll see what life has planned for me."

28	Father Roman Catholic	In any case, a man. Creator.	He could do anything, protected everybody, created everybody. Punishes with hell, rewards with heaven.	He did nothing. You must do everything for others and never think of yourself. When you are struck on one cheek, you must turn the other.	Doubt. Fear.	Questions: "Where is God?"	Doubts herself. Was she so bad that she had to go through all this? You must allow yourself to be hurt and do nothing, ask for even more. That is sacrifice.

She has left the Roman Catholic faith, "Because I think it's only words, cold words with no meaning."

36	Father Dutch Reformed (strict)	The Lord Jesus. Someone to be afraid of. Punishing God.	Cures sick. Punishes immediately or much later. Own father heard from Lord Jesus how trespasses in family must be punished. His will be done. Forgives trespasses.	Did not intervene. What Father did was what fathers were supposed to do. She was not allowed to cry, because that was rebelling against father and that was bad. She must be very good. She was bad, unwanted, but God-given, guilty of neighbor's and cousin's suicide. She was not allowed to be sad even about a	Fear. Doubt. Guilt. Disgust. Disappointment. Confusion.	Kept praying that rape by her father and husband would stop. Continued to experience God in this way.	Longstanding and intense fear of dying and hell. She was repeatedly told that all of the misery that befell her was supposed to, was her own fault, and punishment because she was bad. Doubted herself as a result. Was able to put an

Age	Offender and religious milieu	Survivor's image of God	God's characteristics	God's attitude and expectations	Feelings toward God	Attitudes toward God	Impact on incest survivor
				girlfriend's death (who was safe in Jesus' arms). She would end up in hell. When you are struck on one cheek, you must turn the other.			end to her own rape when her three-year-old daughter was about to be raped.

She learned to articulate her feelings about this sadistic God. That helped her to develop her resistance toward her father and ex-husband.

Age	Offender and religious milieu	Survivor's image of God	God's characteristics	God's attitude and expectations	Feelings toward God	Attitudes toward God	Impact on incest survivor
32	Three brothers. Extremely strict Dutch Reformed.	A man.	He runs everything. He knows all, sees all.	God wants women to have a lot of children. He lets it all happen.	Always guilty.	Women are always responsible. "He knows I'm going to die, so I won't do it, I'm not going to give him the satisfaction."	That man doesn't exist, what a lot of nonsense. He is just someone invented to keep you in line.

She now believes in a good atmosphere and in the good in people. She has no need of a hereafter.

	brother. Roman Catholic.	above you, with a beard. "My father could have been God." God and Jesus are the same.	stands up there watching and keeps an eye on things. He could intervene. He has power.	it.	Guilt. A feeling that someone is always watching you. Confusion. Fear.	endlessly that it would stop. He saw that she was sometimes catty and perhaps gave Father cause. God found her difficult because she did not live according to the rules.	unfeeling, shut herself off, and saw it as God's punishment. Is afraid to say anything negative about God when girlfriends ask questions about God. Will do anything for others and so forgets herself

She is now trying to free herself of the images of God described above. This is difficult. She has distanced herself from the Catholic church little by little. She has joined the Dutch Humanist League.

57	Father. Roman Catholic.	God the Father.	Merciful. Loving. Almighty. Omnipresent. All-seeing eye. More powerful than Jesus.	Allowed this to happen.	Loneliness. Fear. Disappointment. Guilt. Confusion. Doubt. Split. Contradictory. Mortal sin. Penance. Willing to sacrifice.	Prayed for change, confession sometimes four times in a week, or took no communion, a daily requirement as a child. Lay awake nights if she missed confession. Difficulty with Our Father. Questions: "Is it my fault? Should I make more sacrifices?"	Problems with faith. Is willing to sacrifice for everyone. Felt forced to do penance for her father, and thus sacrificed entire life; became a nun. Has not been able to pray for some time. Was outwardly religious for some time but inwardly rebellious. Doubts God and herself.

She lives now in a feeling of vacuum toward God. She hopes for happiness from experiencing God in a different way.

Age	Offender and religious milieu	Survivor's image of God	God's characteristics	God's attitude and expectations	Feelings toward God	Attitudes toward God	Impact on incest survivor
31	Brother. Roman Catholic.	A big man. God and Jesus are the same.	Sees all. On the cross. Watching. Much patience, but at a certain point, it is gone.	Watches you from above. The woman is beneath the man. You must love your neighbor more than you love yourself.	Guilt. Disbelief. Doubt.	Own father did not fulfil the image of God's substitute. As long as I pray, everything will be all right.	Faith suppressed her energy. Feared bearing responsibility.

She is now learning to believe in herself. She is hesitant about setting aside her belief in God, angels, hell, or heaven.

Age	Offender and religious milieu	Survivor's image of God	God's characteristics	God's attitude and expectations	Feelings toward God	Attitudes toward God	Impact on incest survivor
31	Father. Father antireligious, mother formerly Dutch Reformed.	Father said: "God, that's nonsense, people simply invented it." Father is a sort of God.	Socialism and father's family served as a kind of religion. We were dogmatic progressives. Everything else was bad.	Church people could not be trusted. They take refuge in capitalism, cause wars, and are opposed to peace.	Confusion. Disbelief. Guilt because she couldn't stop it sooner.	Criticism: not practicing what they preach; you could not be yourself; Socialists were not very good at seeing the role of women.	She thinks of others before herself. Being there for others is the only worth you have left.

In this family, Father had the same role as was customary in Christian families, although it was not sanctioned or discussed. In progressive circles, this role is rarely discussed because these men do not believe that they discriminate. The woman no longer believes in big political parties but in people who are close. She hopes she will be able to change things together with others.

Roman Catholic.		...human characteristics. Grants forgiveness, saw all, knew all, was strict, but just (resembled own father).	...will be okay. Those who don't believe in him can't be happy. You must be good to others, sacrifice yourself for them, honor your father and mother.	between her faithful side and her critical side, the latter won.	Confusion. Unhappiness. Disbelief.	for her life before sixteen, certainly for sex. Image of ideal woman made her easy prey. She felt bad afterwards. She no longer wanted to pray, but kept asking for forgiveness.

Now faith is living a certain way based on her own strength and intuition. She feels close to humanism, but does not want to join the league. Leaving the church and traditional faith was liberating. Getting back her self-esteem is important. She never again wants to be subordinated to a set of rules.

31	Uncle. Two different Dutch Reformed Churches.	God the Father.	Gray figure. Dominant. Almighty. Far away. Judging. Supervising.	You must be good to others and have children. Divorce is bad. The man is the head of the family. You must forgive.	She and her mother rejected this image of God and had no alternative.	Fear. Guilt. Need to forgive her offender. Confusion. Loneliness.	Minimizing what happened in order to grant forgiveness. Great feeling of responsibility for others, forgets herself. Lack of confidence in others, feels guilty about this.

Grandfather on mother's side talked about God a lot and passed on the images and ideas described above. Mother did not believe strongly in God but she did believe in "poor," sacrificing Jesus and his role as a victim. Jesus was therefore experienced as something close by. Grandpa thought that people were bad. Not going to church was bad too. The incest survivor now says "The church is a reflection of society. What people get out of Bible stories is so oppressive to women."

Age	Offender and religious milieu	Survivor's image of God	God's characteristics	God's attitude and expectations	Feelings toward God	Attitudes toward God	Impact on incest survivor
34	Brother Dutch Reformed/nonreligious.	For herself, God has to do with goodness. That image was overshadowed by images of God from her upbringing and particularly from the church.	A thundering God, with pointing finger. Grants mercy, grants forgiveness. Almighty, threatening.	People are evil by nature. Nothing good can come from people of their own efforts. You must resign yourself. Tempered joy is the best. Women must be subservient to men.	Confusion. Doubt. Guilt. Fear. Anger. Depression. Rage.	You never did it right because we are bad by nature. Not knowing if penance helps or if God forgave. You could have good intentions and still do it wrong. Maybe people who were good did it out of narcissism.	Experiencing faith as destructive and as serious business. There was little happiness in it. It made you depressed. It gave her suicidal tendencies and thoughts. Has left that behind her. Wrote a prayer about God in her own experience.

She now believes that every person has a piece of God in herself or himself. That's what life is all about. By experiencing God in this way, God and people can come closer together. That gives them strength. Then there is not damnation alone.

Age	Offender and religious milieu	Survivor's image of God	God's characteristics	God's attitude and expectations	Feelings toward God	Attitudes toward God	Impact on incest survivor
37	Brother. Dutch Reformed.	(Her own image of God) Friend, Father.	Loving, old, wise, bearded, ideal father (everything her father was not). Strict for those who don't want to believe.	Always listened.		I had a right to exist.	This image of God was suppressed by the image described below. The negative image cropped up in times of crisis.

		(Images of God imposed from outside)					
		Middle-aged man, ruler.	God of Revenge. Distant. Kept an eye on things. Participated in war. Allowed his son to be crucified.	You must be perfect, pray a lot, have a lot of faith. Then it will be okay. Obedience is subservience to men. If your faith is good, you go to heaven; otherwise you go to hell.	Depressed. Abandoned. Suffocated. Strangled. Afraid.	Imperfect, thus lost. Thought only in guilt and sin. Learned to repress emotions. Lost her own image of God temporarily.	Left the church, but has not left the faith.

She no longer wants to go down on her knees before God out of fear. She now objects to God being portrayed as male. She now sees God as one with the oppressed, that is supportive in liberating yourself from norms and values imposed from without.

| 30 | Father. Two different Dutch Reformed Churches. | A shepherd. Your friend. Something. Father of us all (her own father is called "not real father"). | Good. Not a bogeyman. Does not make everything right that people do wrong. He watches over us. Can intervene if he wants to. | People do not have to go to church. If you are good you will go to heaven. You must forgive. | Comfort. | When you are in trouble, you can go to him. Problems have a reason. The church is an institution invented by people, not by God. | Does not believe in church; they let an unwed mother fend for herself. Faith is important, however. No problems with God. |

She asked forgiveness for the incest and received it. She has done nothing wrong in the eyes of God and has no guilt feelings about it. You must forgive, so she forgave Father, but she has only recently become furious with him. She thinks you find strength in yourself when you are acknowledged by others. Then you are happy with yourself.

themselves: They assumed that they had given cause for the abuse. They had no rights whatsoever, and they were simply bad. For this reason God did not intervene, and let the incest happen to them. It was also possible that God had reasons for it, that it was good for something. Therefore, they simply had to learn to accept it, and to forgive the offenders.

In trying to meet God's expectations and do penance, God was on the side of the sexual abusers. The image of the patriarchal God, his characteristics and his expectations of people—but especially of women—strengthens the power of the offenders; the victims are rendered powerless and deprived of all rights. Moreover, they feel responsible for the abuse that has befallen them, which they are powerless to stop. These women's image of God is propagated in the patriarchal way of experiencing Christianity and has been internalized by these women in part as a result of the offenders' influence. From this image of God, men derive the ability to humiliate and sexually abuse girls, and to blame their victims for it. The survivors' innermost feelings were systematically denied and negated by this image of God. The destructive impact of incest in combination with this oppressive image of God is expressed in the fear and confusion aroused by this image. God is good, almighty, all-seeing, and just—and allows this to happen. Consequently, these women doubted themselves, and experienced God as terrifying. They were afraid of God's almightiness in combination with the divine all-seeing eye. They recognized these characteristics in their own fathers who committed incest. They saw adversity and unjust treatment, no matter what the source, as a confirmation of their guilt and as proof of their own evil. They thought that they must resign themselves to this, because God wanted it this way.

All of these women went through periods in which they had self-destructive urges, and at the same time experienced a deep fear of God, of hell, and of death. "But that fear of hell does have its upside," one of these women says, "It keeps me from committing suicide."

Patriarchy as Destructive of Women   These incest survivors have acquired from their Christian upbringing an image of God that strengthens the abusers' power over them, and makes the women themselves powerless and deprived of all rights. They have internalized the image of God that was propagated by their oppressors and rapists. The patriarchal experience of Christianity is destructive to women. Men derive from it the ability to humiliate and sexually abuse girls and women, as well as the ability to blame them for the abuse. Consequently, the innermost feelings of these women were systematically denied, negated, or raped.

In concluding this, we are not claiming that Christian churches have propagated this patriarchal image of God in order to encourage men to sexually abuse girls in their families. However, we do show the impact such an image of God can have, which has been invented and taught over the centuries in Christian churches by men.

Thoughts on the patriarchal image of God   On the basis of the image of God as defined by these incest survivors we should like to demonstrate that it is possible to look at God from various viewpoints. People who have power dominate others, and wish to maintain that status quo, profit by a God who legitimates the exercise of power, the domination of others. Moreover, they profit by a God who possesses these characteristics himself in divine measure. God is thus the ultimate in power, almighty. Power can only be maintained by constantly keeping an eye on everything. That is what the powerful do, and God does that, too. He is all-seeing. People who want to dominate always know what is best for themselves, but especially for others; in this manner they are able to maintain their power. God knows more than all human beings together; God is omniscient. People who question the earthly power of the powerful or stand up against those in power, are a threat. Rebellion is therefore seen as evil; rebellion against God is the greatest evil. That evil can best be fought by punishing the rebels, and by calling the powerful who punish good and just. God, who punishes those who rebel, is good and just. He parallels exactly those in power. This is how God is created and made equal to those who wish to dominate others.

If God is good and just, then the oppressed and the humiliated should be considered best able to articulate what God should be like. If they have no safe place, then they should be able to experience security with God. If they are raped and negated, then they should be able to find a positive strength in God in order to survive and to prevent it from recurring. Women experience this security and strength when they can call the God of the oppressor by name and in doing so realize on whose side this God stands. Then they can learn to let this God go. When this space is created, they experience something of God or of a strength or force, close by and within themselves. If God is good and just then God gives the oppressed and negated courage and strength to stand up, and She/He stands up with them. Then God does not inspire the oppressed to bear patiently man-made, unjust suffering so that they will later be rewarded in heaven. Then God does not ask survivors to sacrifice so that the incest offenders fare well. It is more in keeping with this God's wishes to expend time and energy on holding the offenders responsible for what they have done, as well as those who have helped to cause this incest and to keep it secret.

Creating a Liberating Space for God-Talk We conducted a number of follow-up sessions with several women who had severe problems with the old, imposed image of God. We also conducted therapy sessions upon request. During these sessions, we learned to use various methods that proved to be effective. An example of such a method is demonstrated below.

With the one exception, all the survivors had left the church of their childhood. They rejected everything that had to do with religion and God. They indicated that they did not want to talk about it anymore; they were afraid to express their anger toward God, and at the same time kept mentioning God in the conversation. Through questions and comments, we sometimes succeeded in getting them to express their feelings.

For example, we asked; "What do you think about when you think of God? When do you think of God? Why? How do you feel when you think about it? Why do you get angry? Do you think that is all right? Are you angry with God too? Why not? Why do you think that is not allowed? Who told you that? You ask what I think about it? Well, when I think about what you have gone through, I . . . What do you think about that? Who taught you to see God in this way? You don't want to have anything more to do with God? The next time you feel that God has let you down again, will you write down how you feel about God? Do you feel able to do that?" Nell wrote the following:

"God is the Father in heaven who does everything for His children because He loves them. That's what some people say. Well, I'm going to tell God exactly what I think of Him.

God gave me a mother who didn't want me. She always told me I ruined her life.

God gave me a father who raped and abused me for 30 years.

God gave me a husband who constantly abused me and my children.

God gave my little girl a father who wanted to rape her when she was three and a-half.

Well thank you very much, God, that you wanted to give me all of this and that you loved me so very much. But God, I need nothing more from you, do you hear me? I want absolutely nothing from you; just leave me alone, please.

Let me live my own life, goddammit.

Goddammit, let me decide for myself what I want and stop trying to push your way into my life all the time.

I want you to get out of my life forever.

But you won't do that will you, you idiot? You keep letting people tell me that I should think of God for once—well, I don't want to think of you. When do you ever think of me?

I don't think you're a father, I think you're a sadist who's out to pester some people and humiliate us.

Well just leave me and my children alone for a while. Please give me the time to finally find out who and what I really am.

Because, thanks to you I haven't been able to do that—even after 36 years.

So just leave me the hell alone and get out of my life because I don't want you anymore. I don't need you."

We found that it is vital for these women to have the room to express their rage and sorrow about God. Even more crucial is the response. One reaction given to her oppressive image of God and the problems she still has with it is: "Well, God isn't like that, you're looking at this all wrong. That's a false image of God you're describing." This response does not take her seriously and it gives her no room to liberate herself from her oppressive image of God. "This God" should not be the subject of these discussions. It is more pleasant for the priest or minister, because it takes a great deal of resilience and restraint to talk about God in the way that

incest survivors need to talk about their oppressive image of God.
When the minister or priest starts talking about "this God" during
such a conversation, he or she creates a safe distance from his or
her own experience of God, and then he or she cannot feel how
threatening it is for a woman like Nell to express her rage and
sorrow about God in her experience. For *her*, God is not "this
God," which people are not supposed to struggle with. For her, it
is her only image of God. And that's why she still has so many
problems with it.

When giving women the space they need to express their
feelings about God, it is tempting for the priest or minister to fill up
that space with his or her own image of God. However, we feel it is
crucial that, precisely at this moment, these women be given the
room to start seeking their own image of God, one with which they
can be comfortable; a God whom they can love after their suffering
with their whole soul, whole strength, and whole mind.

We observed that Nell's attitude toward God changed after
several sessions. Because her view of God changed, she was able to
oppose her father.

"What I say to my father now, I never would have had the
courage to say if I hadn't had the feeling that God is behind me. My
father sees that, too. He tells the family that I've changed
completely. He also says that if I'd had this much self-confidence
before, he would have treated me totally differently. So he's still
trying to act like it was all my fault. Before, I would have fallen for
that. Then I would have felt like it was all my fault. Now I tell him
that he always knows how to twist things around. But if he ever
shows up at my door again, I'll have him carted off by the police. I
can do that now, because I look at God differently. If that hadn't
happened, I wouldn't have dared to stand up to my father. Now I
have the feeling that God was abused too. Now I almost feel sorry
for God. No, that's not the right word. But he was abused pretty
badly too. That's for sure."

When incest survivors are given the room to express their
feelings about the image of God others have imposed on them, a
space is created in which they can think and feel about God in a
way that liberates them. This makes them more resistant in their
lives. The space that is created when they liberate themselves from
their oppressive images of God should be left open. Women have
the right to seek the God whom they can love.

Jesus Prior to the study, and during the construction of the interview guide, we assumed that incest survivors had found inspiration in passages from the Gospel. We suspected that there would be some criticism of the way in which it was experienced and taught in many Christian churches, but anticipated that the stories about Jesus himself would have given these women strength, courage, and hope in their situations. We expected that some passages might have helped them to end the incest or to break their silence. One of the passages we had in mind was the expulsion of the moneychangers from the temple (Mark 11:15–19).[4] We also had other passages in mind, such as those in which Jesus treats and speaks of women with respect, as in the widow and the unscrupulous judge (Luke 18:1–8), the faith of the Canaanite woman (Matthew 15:21-28), the healing of the crippled woman (Luke 13:10–17), Jesus speaking with the Samaritan woman at the well (John 4:1–42) and the resurrection and appearance to Mary Magdalene (John 20:1–18). During the interviews, we asked these incest survivors, "How did you see Jesus?"

Survivors' Images of Jesus
During the period these women experienced incest, they primarily experienced Jesus as loving, good, human, and close. He was closer than God, more pleasant, less judgmental, less strict, and less powerful. They could also ask him for forgiveness. In addition, he was a goody-goody, pathetic and a victim, but at the same time, a strong hero. This was evidenced, for example, in his actions against the Pharisees, and when he expelled the moneychangers from the temple. He also provided security, particularly to children. Joan and Nell's fathers, who sexually abused their daughters, crushed their belief in Jesus that had offered them security. Even Amy's father, who was non-religious and a non-offender, did this. The friendlier and more human images of Jesus and God were often communicated by the mother, aunt, or grandmother.

The text, "Suffer the little children to come unto me," or visual illustrations of Jesus surrounded by children, were inspiring to Anne, Nell, Amy, and Ingrid. They gathered from this that Jesus was good to children. That quality in him especially appealed to

---

4. See also Annie Imbens and Louise Muller, "Vrouwen zijn het wachten beu" [Women Are Tired of Waiting], *De Bazuin* 64, no. 37 (1981): pp. 6–7.

them because they seldom encountered it in their own lives. Several of the incest survivors told us that, as children, they had been sad about Jesus' crucifixion; they did not understand why he had not come down from the cross, or why God, his Father, allowed him to be crucified. The combination of the way they often experienced Jesus (as loving, good, close by, and providing security) with this torturous death (often explained as God's will in order to redeem the sins of humankind) gave these survivors a terrifying image of God: the image of a sadistic father, someone hungry for power.

"God and my father were a lot alike," says Joan. Jesus said to his Father, "Thy will be done," when he died on the cross in accordance with God's will; because of this, Nell's guilt feelings intensified when she cried because she wanted her father to stop abusing her. She thought; "My father's right to see this as rebellion against God." The twelve-year-old Jesus in the temple (Luke 2:4–52) is mentioned four times. We observed, however, that this story was experienced very differently each time, which is clarified when we place these experiences in the context of the respective interviews. Ellen feels it is mean of Jesus to allow his mother to search for him so anxiously. Her reaction is in keeping with her great sense of responsibility toward her mother. Joan experienced this text as a ray of hope in her situation. She explains: "I knew that I would do it sometime too—leave my parents and go my own way. This passage finally gave me the courage to turn my father in to the police when the situation at home became intolerable for everyone." Judith thought it was an inspiring story, but also told us that, for her, Jesus never grew any older than that twelve-year-old kid. Anne thought it was too bad that there was no more information about the period when he was between twelve and thirty years old.

In the statements of these incest survivors on the subject of Jesus and women, we observe that, in their view, Jesus is good to women and stands up for them. But the view they have of the women themselves who play a role in these stories is negative: "Jesus stood up for the woman who was going to be stoned. He saved her from death, but he said, 'Go and sin no more.' The woman in the story was a sinner" (Ellen). "Jesus healed women, but those women were bad, diseased, or possessed by the devil" (Margaret). "In the Bible, the woman is the seductress. Jesus is compared to Buddha, Muhammad, and so on, but he was put on this earth through a line of whores," according to Susan. "Jesus granted his forgiveness for everything Mary Magdalene had done. She was a woman with a past, unpopular, and she was allowed to wash the feet of Jesus" (Mary Beth). Amy refers to the whore who anointed the feet of Jesus and says: "He allowed her to do that, even though the others complained."

These images of women don't evoke positive self-images in these girls. The images do not stimulate them toward developing into strong, self-confident women. The self-confidence of sexually abused girls is seriously undermined. This was exacerbated by the interpretation of the gospel passages discussed earlier. None of the women we interviewed could tell us anything about Mary Magdalene as the first witness of the resurrection, not even when we asked about it. Why are these women not familiar with this passage? When and how is this passage now used in preaching and liturgy?

Two of the women interviewed were inspired by the passage on Mary and Martha (Luke 10:38–42). Christine gathered from this that Jesus thought a good discussion was more important than housework. Ellen says that this passage was always interpreted negatively. According to this interpretation, Mary was allowed to talk to Jesus, but she had to finish her housework first. Still, this passage made her feel good. She had her own secret interpretation of it: "Jesus talked with Mary. He thought she was worth talking to." Lisa cannot remember anything about Jesus. Barbara doesn't complete her sentence about Jesus, but says that is why she left the Catholic faith. As a child, she was impressed by the priests' vestments and the gold in the the church. We wondered: What is the impact of the colorful vestments made of silk and other costly materials, and of the abundance of gold used in churches, on passing down the story of Jesus?

Jesus submissive to his Father   Jesus was attentive to children and offered them security and protection. This same Jesus was tortured, and died on the cross. If this death on the cross is seen as the will of God for the sins of humankind, it does not offer sexually abused girls a liberating perspective, but a terrifying one. This is particularly true when we remember that this Jesus also said to his father, "Thy will be done." In this case, Jesus is the model of a good and gentle person who allowed himself to be hurt with the approval of his father and did not rebel against it, but remained submissive to the will of his father.

Jesus is good to women; he stands up for them. But women themselves are sinners, diseased and weak. Women cannot save themselves. They need Jesus. Jesus is the hero who saves weak and sinful women in need, and grants them forgiveness in spite of their evilness.[5]

Mary We have often heard Protestants say to Catholics: "Women may not be able to become priests in your faith, but the Catholic church is more woman-friendly because of your devotion to Mary." Protestant women have often added: "We're constantly being bombarded with quotes on women from Paul's writings." We asked the incest survivors about their image of Mary. The responses of the Catholic and the non-Catholic women are examined separately due to their different characters.

Seven women with a non-Catholic upbringing give responses about Mary. Nell says that she is the only woman mentioned in the Bible with any regularity. That is all she can remember about her. Three non-Catholic women, one of whom had the anti-religious upbringing, say nothing at all about Mary.

Seven women with a Catholic upbringing also respond. One says, "Means nothing to me" (Lisa). Two say nothing about Mary. Thus, interest in Mary, or the presence of memories about Mary are about the same for Catholic and for non-Catholic incest survivors. There is, however, a marked difference in the nature of these two groups' responses on the subject of Mary.

Non-Catholic Survivors' Image of Mary
Mary was referred to negatively in non-Catholic milieus. This became clear in the interviews. Mary was primarily spoken of in the context of

---

5. For additional information on images of God, see: Jann A. Clanton, *In Whose Image? God and Gender* (New York: Crossroad, 1990); Robert Coles, *The Spiritual Life of Children* (Boston: Houghton Mifflin, 1990); Ari L. Goldman, *The Search for God at Harvard* (New York: Random House, 1991); I. Carter Heyward, *Touching Our Strength: The Erotic as Power and the Love of God* (San Francisco: Harper and Row, 1989); J. Pohier, *God in Fragments* (London: Scan Press, 1987); Anna-Marie Rizzuto, *The Birth of the Living God: A Psychoanalytic Study* (Chicago: University of Chicago Press, 1981); Edward Schillebeeckx, *God Is New Every Moment: Conversations with Huub Oosterhuis and Piet Hoogeveen* (San Francisco: Harper and Row, 1983).

some event or other person. Ellen remembers that the emphasis was more on Joseph in her church. She adds, "He was so sweet in accepting the blame." Here, Mary is used to show what a good man Joseph was. He accepted the blame. But who was to blame in this context, and for what? Was Mary found guilty because she was pregnant and bore a son who became the basis and source of inspiration for Christianity? Christine sees the view that women should serve in more earthly ways and men in more spiritual ways as resulting from the idea that God and Jesus represent the head or mind of the church, while Mary and other women represent the body.

Susan says that Mary was considered only in her capacity as the woman through whom Jesus was brought into this world. Ingrid had heard about Mary in connection with stories about the resurrection and the birth of Christ. Susan indicates that she was not permitted to view Mary in the same way as the Catholics: "That would be worshiping a human being." Mary, a woman, the mother of Jesus, cannot be divine, whereas Jesus, her son, a man, was supposed to be viewed as divine.

Tina often heard the story of the wedding at Cana (John 2:1–11). In Tina's view, Jesus put Mary in her place at the wedding.

The non-Catholic women give the image of Mary as guilty, materially subservient, portraying the body of the church, a human female creature who brought forth Jesus. Jesus put her in her place when he grew up. According to these women, Mary is honored differently and incorrectly by the Catholics.

Catholic Survivors' Image of Mary

Mary was the ideal mother, as she was honored in the Roman Catholic church. She was a woman who was "gentle, a good listener, nurturing" (Judith); "exemplary, pure" (Barbara); "loving, beautiful, fragile, caring, sweet" (Theresa). She was the divine symbol of the good woman, who asked nothing and gave everything (Mary Beth). Her statue was decorated with extra flowers. Hers was the "immaculate conception," (understood as pregnancy without intercourse). This made Anne think that it would be beautiful if she were to become pregnant by her brother. Cathy had immense problems with Mary's immaculate conception. She experienced her own incest as contradictory to the religious community's strong Mary worship. Judith tells how Mary provided, and continues to provide, an ideal to grasp. It is this image of Mary that her father manages to distort shortly before his death. In their childhoods, Barbara and Mary Beth thought Mary was important or inspiring. Mary Beth adds that she now considers an independent woman who can take care of herself inspiring.

These Catholic women's images of Mary can be viewed as the result of Catholic, celibate men's theological teaching to and about women. These men presented their fantasies about the ideal woman in their teachings about Mary: a woman who bears priests (the followers of Christ), and who does so without a hint of sexuality; the ever-serving mother who asks nothing and gives everything, and who can be laughed at for her stupidity when she opens her mouth. Because she has again been unable to understand what the priests are talking about, for they as men have claimed the sole right to teach spiritual values. Women cannot be blamed for that. Mary, the ideal woman, had that tendency, too.

In the accepted interpretation of the story of the wedding at Cana, it is also said that Mary did not understand what Jesus was talking about.

Bible passages have nearly always been read within the context of the sexist prejudice that a mortal woman who appears in the passage would be too dumb to understand the intentions of her divine son Jesus and within the context of the prejudice that Jesus was born as a divine person and therefore never had any doubts during his life. Reading the texts on Jesus' life within this context leads to the conclusion that Jesus is a divine hero, and that women are insignificant in comparison. Whereas, when reading these passages, you could ask yourself instead, whether Jesus responded with humanity and integrity to human, everyday situations, and whether women are really as stupid as men claim.

When we examine the wedding at Cana in this light, we ask ourselves why Jesus reacted so irritably: "Woman, what have I to do with thee? Mine hour is not yet come," to his mother's comment "They have no wine" (John 2:3–3). This reaction is familiar to contemporary mothers with adult sons. In a comparable situation, sons might say, "Look, don't bug me, okay? I'll make my move when I'm ready." When these sons make a decision at a fork in the road, they want encouragement, yet it irritates them that they still need it as adults. In hearing this story, these mothers also recognize the way in which Mary creates the conditions to ease her son's first step on his road in life. She takes the measures that lay within her power. She acts boldly and uses her influence. She goes to the servants and tells them: "Whatsoever he saith unto you, do it." In this way, Mary encourages Jesus to assume his responsibilities and to hesitate no longer in doing so. When Jesus then instructs the servants to "Fill the waterpots with water," they fill them to the brim (John 2:7). When he tells them: "Draw out now, and bear unto the governor of the feast," they also do this (2:8–9).

In this reading, Mary emerges as a wise and independent woman who used her capabilities to her son's advantage. Women today can learn to use their abilities in order to end their second-rate position in the church and in society, for themselves, for their sisters, mothers, and daughters.

Context and Image of Mary   Protestant and Catholic churches perpetuate images of Mary that are negative toward women, and have a negative impact on them. In Protestant churches, this is clearer because statements about Mary are formulated in negative terms. The Catholic church honors the image of Mary as the loving, gentle, ideal woman, and mother; an image that makes women powerless and gives them a feeling of inadequacy. When we refrain from reading the texts about her within the sexist context, we see Mary as an inspiring woman.

Women in the Bible   Girls who have experienced incest and a Christian upbringing, know that they are seductive, sinful, and evil, while they are told to be sweet, subservient, and obedient. Women and girls are supposed to behave in this way. When these survivors, who are sweet, obedient, and subservient to men or boys, are sexually abused by them, they are blamed for the abuse because they are seductive—that's just the way women are. They are responsible for the misconduct of their abusers, due to their seductiveness. "I knew that I should be stoned," Ellen says. She has to be punished for Grandpa's misconduct.

When survivors resisted, they are also bad because they are disobedient, rebelling against men and the natural order created by God, in which women are intended to be subservient to men, and children obedient to fathers. The offenders also used Bible passages about women to legitimate the sinfulness and guilt of women. Incest survivors often mentioned the biblical image of women in reply to the question, "What aspects of religion did you experience as oppressive?" These women repeatedly brought up this negative image of women. We collected and categorized these responses. We first show the general image of women throughout the Bible, followed by the image of women in the Old Testament (or as feminists prefer to call it, the "First" Testament) and in the New Testament.

General Images

Women were mostly whores, as in the family tree of Jesus. They were bad, mean, weak, and sneaky. They betrayed their husbands and God. For Ellen, these stories constantly confirmed how bad she was, and she went through life with her head bowed. She hated the biblical patriarchs, old and horrible, who kept adding new young girls to their possessions and slept with them. There were some strong biblical women, but they were not real women because they did not fulfill the norms that applied to women: being a mother, loving, radiant, and nurturing. Everything that had to do with sexuality was dirty, except when men did it. Then it was called "begetting sons."

Joan thinks that her father had very "Christian" ideas about women. A woman was supposed to be submissive, willing, and subservient. Karen thinks that women in the Bible were mainly sinful and bad. Margaret sees women as always bad, diseased, or possessed by the devil. Susan thinks that the woman is always the one to blame in the Bible. She is still having problems with this. She knows that Jesus came into the world from a long line of whores. According to Mary Beth, the women in the New Testament were obedient and wise, and the men were aggressive. Amy thinks that women in the Bible were subordinate or insignificant. The passage on marriage laws (Deut. 22:13–30) terrified her. This says that a girl who is married off by her father, and turns out not to be a virgin, must be stoned by the men of her town.

Women from the First Testament

Eve: Eight of the women we interviewed mentioned Eve. "She was a seductress; that's why she had to bear children in affliction" (Ellen). "She was the symbol of sinful women" (Karen). "She instigates the man to do evil. It is always the woman who is the symbol of evil and weakness" (Margaret). "She was the first woman on earth and she was bad. She seduced Adam" (Barbara). "My father said that all women were the same as the first woman, Eve. She brought him into temptation, too, unconsciously" (Nell). "The fact that the woman is always to blame can be traced back to Eve seducing Adam. Humankind brought it all down upon itself through the Fall" (Lisa). "She ate from the apple and seduced Adam. That's how she ruined paradise. That's why she has to bear children in pain" (Tina). "She was a very bad woman. But Adam let himself be persuaded by her. He was no saint, either" (Ingrid).

Lot's wife: "She turned into a pillar of salt" (Nell).

Sarah: "She deceived everybody, was treated badly by Abraham, like Hagar" (Ellen). "Abraham's wrinkled old wife, she laughed at God when he said that she would have a child. The result was son Isaac" (Tina).

Hagar: "The story of Hagar and Ishmael was beautiful" (Carol).

Potiphar's wife: "Deceitful—she seduces Joseph" (Ellen).

Miriam: "Miriam took care of her brother Moses with the result that his life was saved" (Tina).

Jael, Heber's wife: "One of the most horrible stories in the Bible. She slept with a man and put a 'nail of the tent' through his head in order to win the victory" (Susan).

Bathsheba (and David): "David spies on Bathsheba while she is bathing. Disgusting. When David is old, a young girl has to keep him warm in bed" (Ellen). "Bathsheba was bad, but God had his reasons for that" (Susan).

Tamar: "Tamar was bad, but God had his reasons for that" (Susan).

Esther: "Esther was a quiet girl who became a beautiful queen and saved the people of Israel from death" (Tina).

Ruth: "It was said of Ruth that it was her own fault that she was in trouble. She never should have left the good country. That's why she shouldn't complain. She had to give her body in order to get protection, or to get a son for her former husband. She was obedient. That was emphasized in the sermons" (Ellen). "That was humiliating, that she had to lie at the feet of that man" (Christine). "Ruth's loyalty to Naomi was beautiful" (Carol). "She didn't let her mother-in-law down, but gave up everything and followed her. She started to love God. The result was that Boaz, who also loved God, married her, and saw to it that she and Naomi no longer had any worries" (Tina). "They went to another country. They had no men so they had to work for a living and they went to glean the fields for ears of corn. The boss saw that and gave her work. Later on, she married him" (Ingrid).

Deborah: "She fought in the wars and didn't fit the norms that applied to women" (Ellen).

Women from the New Testament

Mary and Elizabeth: "Mary is seen as a young girl who seeks support from an older woman" (Mary Beth).

The wife of Herod: "She saw to it that John was beheaded" (Judith).

Mary and Martha: "That was an inspiring story. Mary wanted to know everything. The interpretation was always negative. Mary was allowed to talk to Jesus, but she had to get her work finished first" (Ellen). "Jesus told Martha that what Mary was doing was more important than housework. I used this reason when I had to break off a discussion in order to help with the housework" (Christine). "They fought about the housework. Jesus said that it was more important to listen to Him than to do housework" (Tina). The only women Tina knew were ones who did housework. The men sat on the church council. Mary was so thankful to Jesus that she gave him her most expensive perfume and poured it over him. She dried his feet with her hair. Jesus was pleased with this.

The Samaritan Woman: "It was a beautiful story, but she was sinful because she went with so many men" (Ellen). "She confessed to

Jesus that she had sinned because she had had more than one man. Jesus forgave her" (Tina).

The Adulterous Woman: "Jesus stood up for her, but said, "Sin no more" (Ellen). "This woman was forgiven for sinning. My mother thought that was wrong. She would have rather had her taken out of the Bible" (Nell). "She had committed adultery. Jesus told her she must not do that anymore, but she could not be killed, like the others wanted" (Tina). "She had to be stoned because she had committed lewd acts" (Ingrid).

The woman who had an issue of blood: "She was bad; she was menstruating and touched Jesus. She called attention to her menstruation. The minister preached about that in church. I was embarrassed because menstruation was dirty, something to be ashamed of. In Leviticus it was called unclean" (Ellen).

The Wife of Pontius Pilate: "She had little influence in the choice to crucify Jesus or not" (Judith).

Mary Magdalene: "That was a true sinner. She had to fall on her knees before Jesus. Only he could grant her forgiveness" (Ellen). "She was a bad woman in the eyes of the others. She was loving and caring for Jesus. She anointed his feet with oil when he was tired. She went on, even though Peter and the others protested" (Judith). "That was strange of Jesus, to approve of her pouring that expensive oil over his feet" (Anne). "She washed Jesus' feet and was a whore. Mother made us skip over that passage" (Nell). "She was bad, but God has his reasons for that" (Susan). "She was important. She must have been a strong woman to stand under the cross" (Amy). "She found the body of Jesus when he was dead" (Tina).

Image of the woman as a whore: The Whore of Babylon. Ellen has heard this passage so many times that it still echoes inside her. "That whore who anoints Jesus with ointment. The others complained about it. He let her do it" (Amy). "No names, but the idea that there were women who did something with men that they weren't supposed to. They sometimes asked money for doing it. It was bad, dirty, sinful, shocking" (Tina). "There's a story about a prostitute, too" (Ingrid).

Biblical Images in Patriarchal Culture All of the women with Christian upbringings had or have problems with these Biblical images of women. Bible stories originated in a patriarchal culture; they have an oppressive impact on women when they are passed on as the Word of God, which supposedly gives people timeless instructions regarding how they must live. Because the Bible originated in a patriarchal culture, its laws and instructions ignore women's interests.

Men's interests are protected in one of the Ten Commandments: "Thou shalt not covet thy neighbor's house, thou shalt not covet thy neighbor's wife, nor his manservant, nor his maidservant, nor his ox, or his ass, nor any thing that is thy neighbor's" (Exod. 20:17). In this text, the wife is named and categorized with the possessions of the "neighbor": that is, the man. In such a case, rape or sexual abuse is not seen as a crime against the woman who has undergone this violence, but as a violation of the man's possessions. In Judges, a father is free to offer his virgin daughter (for whom the father can get the full bridal price when he marries her off) to be raped in order to protect his houseguest against sexual violence. The fact that this daughter is a virgin makes his deed well respected in the eyes of men. He was willing to pay a high price to protect his guest. When the men refuse this offer, the guest seizes his own concubine, thrusts her outside, and allows her to be abused all night (Judg. 19:24–30).

When we read this text as "the word of God," meaning:"What is written in the Bible is good because God has willed it," we give men the right to view women as their possessions and do with them as they wish. Men who want to keep women subordinate to them can read and interpret the Bible in such a way that demonstrates their right. They abuse the Bible using God to legitimate their misconduct toward women and girls. Many of the survivors say that their incest experience, combined with their Christian upbringing, caused them to believe they had no rights. They had or have the feeling that they were sexually abused because they were bad and seductive by nature. They made a connection between their guilt feelings and the image of women that is communicated in the church through biblical stories.

Incest survivors have experienced the negative impact of patriarchal teachings intensely. They are able to articulate this impact clearly. In these stories many women recognize their own experiences of humiliation and denial in Christian churches and families. Incest survivors who have the courage to break the silence strengthen the unified voice of many women to demand an end to this humiliation and denial of women in Christian churches.

The interviews allowed us to see the impact of patriarchal exegesis and teachings on sexually abused women. The sexist image of women they communicate contributes to causing and legitimating incest, as well as to the survivors' guilt feelings.[6]

Women Saints Generally speaking, Catholic women know relatively few biblical women. They are familiar with stories about female saints. In the Roman Catholic church, stories about saints serve to present models to emulate. Saints practiced the morals preached by the church in their own lives. Women saints provided examples for Catholic women to follow. We asked the women which saints they knew, and the impact of their stories. These saints are mentioned: Lidwina of Schiedam (3 times); Bernadette (3 times); Maria Goretti (twice); Theresa of Lisieux (once).

Judith thought that stories about the saints were exciting. She thought it was marvelous that Theresa of Lisieux, Maria Goretti, and Lidwina were willing to give up so much for God. Her mother was deeply devoted to Lidwina and chose the name Lidwina as the confirmation name for both Judith and her sister. Now, Judith has difficulty with the fact that Mother gave her this woman as a role model in her formative years: a saint who, following a fall on the ice, lay on her bed for the remainder of her life. She sees a lot of resemblance between Lidwina's way of dealing with things and her mother's. In addition, she thinks that saints have no opinions

---

6. For additional information on women in the Bible, see: Karen Armstrong, *The Gospel according to Woman: Christianity's Creation of the Sex War in the West* (New York: Doubleday, 1987); Sharon Pace Jeansonne, *The Women of Genesis: From Sarah to Potiphar's Wife* (Minneapolis: Fortress, 1990); Elizabeth Schüssler Fiorenza, *In Memory of Her: A Feminist Theological Reconstruction of Christian Origins* (New York: Crossroad, 1983); F. Van Dijk, "Een sterke vrouw, wie zal haar vinden?" [Who Can Find a Virtuous Woman?] in *Leer mij de vrouwen kennen* [Teach me about women], ed. H. Lam and S. Strikwerda (The Hague: Boekencentrum B. V., 1981); "Bijbellezen in feministisch perspectief" [Reading the Bible from a Feminist Perspective] in *Vrouw en Woord* [Woman and the Word], no. 6 (1982).

of their own and are awfully self-sacrificing, all to the increasing honor and glory of God.

Lisa took Lidwina as her confirmation name. She was very impressed by the courage and patience this saint was able to muster in order to bear her suffering. At the time, she tried to emulate her.

Cathy saw Lidwina's life as a tangible example. She now laughs at the sugar-coated stories, but at the time wanted to be just like her. She compares her own suffering to Lidwina's suffering. She saw her own suffering as her cross. She also remembers Bernadette.

Mary Beth mentions Maria Goretti, a girl who was seduced by a young man and refused to do what he wanted, and Bernadette.

Anne thought the stories of Bernadette were beautiful. She later saw Hannie Schaft[7] as a martyr.

Two of the women are particularly relevant to the religion-incest theme: Maria Goretti and Lidwina.

Maria Goretti

Maria Goretti was a young girl who lived next door to a boy who tried to rape her. She was home alone. Everyone else was at work in the fields. Maria tried to fight him off with all her might because she wanted to preserve her chastity. She fought him to the death: He murdered her by stabbing her repeatedly with a knife. Maria Goretti was canonized a saint in the 1950s. This story makes it clear that a girl has to be willing to pay for her chastity with her life.

In a schoolbook we found another variation on the Maria Goretti story.[8] The book's introduction states that this reading material is intended for girls from twelve to fifteen years of age: "We may be certain of the students' interest in this reading material as it has

---

7. Hannie Schaft was a member of the Dutch resistance who was captured and executed by the Nazis during World War II.

8. M. Hugolina and G. J. Ten Dam, *Het Klokkenspel; Leesstof vor oudere meisjes van onze katholieke scholen* [The Carillon: Readings for Older Girls in Our Catholic Schools] (Helmond: Helmond, 1952).

been carefully chosen to correspond to the girl's psyche in the stage of development related to this age group."

Highspirited Margaret van Leuven lived in the thirteenth century. She was hardworking and obliging. One evening, eight robbers attacked the inn where she worked. The inkeeper and his wife were killed immediately but highspirited Margaret was not. Finally the robbers decided to kill her, too, because she would be able to identify them. However, they gave her a chance to save her life: If she would sin with them, they would let her go. But Margaret refused. "Never," she cried, "I would rather die." Then the murderers killed her, "all the more savagely because of her refusal".

The moral of both stories is that it is better for a girl to die than to sin by allowing herself to be raped.

Lidwina of Schiedam   The title above Lidwina's story, which we reprint from the same schoolbook, is "A valiant girl."

She was born in one of the small, old streets in the heart of Schiedam and grew up like any other child. One day when she was fifteen years old, she went skating with her girlfriends, fell on the ice, and was brought home. She had a broken rib. Normally this would have healed within a reasonable amount of time: It is a common accident and quickly mends. Man did what he could, but God willed otherwise. God had chosen Lidwina to be ill, to do nothing else but be ill and, in doing so, to do penance for the sins of the world, and to become an example to all those who came after her. That is why Lidwina did not heal, no matter what the doctors trying to help her undertook. On the contrary, her illnesses multiplied. She could not tolerate light, slept very little, was almost completely paralyzed, took little food, suffered from excruciating headaches: Her entire body was one gaping wound.

So she lay, year after year, flat on her impoverished bed in the little house on Long Church Street. No one could help her. One of the doctors who was treating her had a sharper eye than his colleagues. He observed that something extraordinary was at hand, something more powerful than medicine, and wiser than all the sciences. He walked through the streets of Schiedam deep in thought, "What I would not give if God had bestowed such a daughter upon me!" He understood that Lidwina was a privileged, chosen soul. "Thy will be done!" How many times Lidwina must have said this little prayer during her childhood! This was the time for her to prove that she had been in earnest. She succeeded—not all at once, mind you! Lidwina was a young girl who was not pleased at being ill. In the beginning, it cost her a great deal of effort to keep her patience, but she gradually learned to submit, all the more because God helped her. No one is tested beyond his strength. Lidwina suffered, but when she thought of what Christ himself endured for us, how he was beaten, belittled, whipped, insulted, laughed at, and crucified, then her suffering disappeared soundlessly into nothingness. God tested her. God helped her to endure this testing. There was her Guardian Angel, who appeared to her, not once, but several times. Her tortured body lay there prostrate, but the angel swept her soul to heavenly pastures, where all was beauty and joy, where lilies and roses blossomed in untold measure or rather, she visited the Holy Land, she saw the places that had been blessed with the presence of the Divine Master; she beheld Rome; she abided in Heaven amid the Angels and Saints while the Holy Mary came to her and adorned her with a crown of roses. These comforting visions were so indescribably lovely that she once exclaimed, "Were I able to get back my health by praying a single Hail Mary, I would not utter it!" Lidwina lived this way for thirty-eight years. In human eyes she was a poor creature, and no one understood how she tolerated it so long; in God's eyes she was a valiant soul, who fully submitted herself to His Holy Will. To everything mortal comes an end. Lidwina's suffering worsened, until it became unbearable. For years, she took no food other than the Holy Communion, which was brought to her regularly. This, together with the heavenly comfort of her visions, kept her alive. One day, when the Guardian Angel again took her to the heavenly fields, he showed her a rose bush, full of blossoms and buds. And he spoke: "When the last bud blossoms, then your hour will come." Lidwina understood from his words that the moment of her salvation was nigh. She prepared herself, praying and suffering. Some time later, she saw the rose bush again: The single remaining bud had burst open! Easter of 1433 dawned. The legend tells us that, on that joyous morning, Jesus Himself entered her abode, accompanied by His Holy Mother and a host of saints. A wondrous glow filled the impoverished little house. Lidwina saw that a table stood at the head of her bed, covered with a shining white cloth; on it stood a vase, a cross, and a wax candle. The Savior is said to have anointed her Himself with the Holy Oil to strengthen her in her final struggle. Outside, the bells were rung in joyful commemoration of the Resurrection of Our Lord. There was joy in the people's hearts everywhere. What joy could equal that which filled Lidwina when she lay alone again and everyone had departed? Her days were numbered. Her suffering became more intense. One day—it was Tuesday—her little nephew, who sat with her, could no longer watch and ran away sobbing to warn her confessor. They hurried back together . . . and found Lidwina dead! She had died in solitude. Her arms, which she had not been able to move during her illness, lay crossed on her breast. Her face, which had been riddled with wounds, was unblemished and reflected perfection. The Will of the Lord was done (Aug. A. Boudens).

Lidwina was canonized in 1890.

We found another story about Lidwina. The story was entitled, "A Girl Who Was Courageous in Illness."[9] It tells how Lidwina fell on the ice: "She was busy at home all week long. She had to help her mother in the large family. There were eight little brothers at home. Little wonder Lidwina did not take her time once she had her skates on!" The language lesson about Lidwina ends with a Dutch exercise for two words which sound alike but have different spellings and meanings. The two words are "lijden" and "leiden." The exercise reads as follows:

'Lijden' and 'leiden'
'Lijden' with 'ij' means: to suffer from pain, to suffer from hunger, to suffer from thirst, to suffer from poverty, to suffer from cold.
'Leiden' with 'ei' means: to guide, to lead, to bring someone to a place.
Fill in the correct vowels: Lidwina l_____ (suffered) a great deal of pain due to her fall. She also l_____ (suffered) from the cold when she was on the ice. She would never again be able to l_____ (lead) her little brother through the living room. The doctor could not cure her. He had deep sympathy for her in her l_____ (suffering). The pastor came to visit her. Under his l_____ (guidance), Lidwina learned patience in her l_____ (suffering). She trusted him completely. He provided her with excellent spiritual l_____ (guidance).

The moral of the Lidwina stories is that people must be happy in their suffering, because God wants people to suffer as penance for human sins. A girl who is valiant is happy in her suffering.

---

9. H. J. A. Nijkamp, *Taal in nieuwe banen* [New Directions in Language: A New Language Method for Roman Catholic Elementary Schools, Fifth Grade] (Amsterdam: J. F. Duwaer & Zonen, 1957).

Dorothee Soelle identifies three theses that recur in all sadistic theologies: First, God is the almighty ruler of the world, who controls all suffering; second, God is just and does nothing without a reason; and third, all suffering is penance for sin.

She sees the adoration of the executioner as the ultimate consequence of theological sadism.[10] The story of Lidwina has the characteristics identified by Soelle and adds that a person must be happy with this suffering which comes from God.

Analysis of the Lidwina stories   These texts tell us that Lidwina was responsible for caring for eight brothers. We wonder whether these brothers needed so much help that they themselves could not help with the housework. After caring so long for her brothers, we wonder how Lidwina felt when she received care and a great deal of attention following her fall on the ice. We do not know whether she had opportunities to find relief from her family duties and to receive some attention herself prior to her fall. One of the doctors observed that something extraordinary was happening, "something that was more powerful than medicine, and wiser than all the sciences." He came to the conclusion that Lidwina's suffering had to do with God's will. We reach the same conclusion when we buy into this doctor's delusions of superiority. What is observed in Lidwina surpasses the doctor's power and wisdom. His knowledge and methods fail. He is male and a doctor. A female patient cannot be wiser and more powerful than this male doctor. He cannot ascribe his lack of insight and the failure of the means at his disposal to the girl's refusal to get well. Lidwina may have had her own reasons for not getting well. If she recovered, she would once again be made responsible for her brothers. Both Lidwina's behavior and her illness surpass the doctor's wisdom. Because he believes in his delusions of superiority, that a female patient could not be wiser than a male doctor, he does not seek an answer to his failure in Lidwina herself. He looks higher up for an answer. Only God is more powerful than men. The power of God is on the same continuum as the power of men. Men are powerful; God is more powerful. Someone with power is accustomed to his will being law. When something happens against his will, he attributes it to someone more powerful than himself. It must also

10. Dorothee Soelle, *Suffering* (Philadelphia: Fortress, 1979).

be someone he can acknowledge as having more power without having to lose face. In that case, God is the best solution. In our analysis, we also wonder what was the pastor's role, who gave her "spiritual guidance". In this story, the extent of the pastor's "spiritual guidance" as he sees it, is encouraging Lidwina to be happy in her illness and attributing her illness to the will of God. Lidwina's illness can perhaps be more appropriately attributed to the inability of her environment to offer her a humane existence.

Women Saints and Suffering

The combination of experiencing sexual abuse and identifying with stories about saints such as Maria Goretti and Lidwina of Schiedam is destructive to these girls' psyche. The saints serve as role models for the faithful trying to live Christian lives. Girls are in effect told that they must be prepared to pay for their chastity with their life. They must be willing to be stabbed to death for it. Then they will be courageous, holy, and good. Incest survivors had not done that. They had submitted to sexual abuse. They are still alive, so according to these moralizing stories, they are bad girls. Incest survivors experience sexual abuse and everything connected with it as suffering. We know from the interviews that they prayed for it to stop. Spiritually, they continued to struggle against this suffering caused by other people. In the story of Lidwina, her resistance to suffering is seen as not accepting God's will. The moral of these stories makes incest survivors believe they are entirely bad. They do not fight to the death; they refuse to accept the suffering willed by God; they rebel against it. Praying for the suffering to end is going against God's will, according to the story of Lidwina.

Difficulties with working through incest Women today who are still plagued by the mental violence of these images of ideal Christian women often have nowhere to turn. Psychiatric professionals generally consider them silly to be still upset about something so minor. It was ridiculous that they had believed these stories at the time; they should certainly have recovered from them by now. Priests and ministers explain how these stories should be viewed: as hagiographies (made-up stories about saints that are invented in order to illustrate how people should live). This is another example of harmful mental violence against women being minimized.

Mary Magdalene a Whore? Almost without exception, the Christian images we have examined have had a negative impact on the women we interviewed. Images of biblical women have been especially disturbing to both Catholic and Protestant women. This negative impact has primarily been caused by the patriarchal interpretation given to Bible passages. This patriarchal interpretation legitimates the second-rate position women occupy in the church and in society. It has portrayed women as weaker, more stupid, and more evil than men. In contrast, a feminist interpretation of biblical texts acknowledges that the Bible originated in a patriarchal culture, that it was written, selected, translated, and transmitted by men with a patriarchal mentality. When women keep this in mind while reading the Bible, and examine these stories in light of their own experiences and insights, these passages can have an inspiring effect on them. Women who are Christians and feminists recognize their own reality. They must find new ways of dealing with it.

In the following paragraphs, I (A. Imbens) offer a feminist, narrative interpretation of the Bible passages that refer to Mary Magdalene. I chose her as my subject because a great majority of the incest survivors labeled her as a whore and a sinner, whereas I personally find her an inspiring and fascinating woman. Through my work with women's groups in the past years, I know that both women and men generally think of a whore or a sinner when Mary Magdalene is mentioned.

Mary's negative image is so strong that several women objected when I suggested discussing "The resurrection and appearance to Mary Magdalene" (John 20:1–18) during a retreat shortly before Easter. They said that they experienced this passage as negative because Mary Magdalene was a sinner. Jesus may have forgiven her, they said, but they could not use this text about a fallen woman for inspiration during an Easter retreat. A participant in a Bible class I recently conducted reacted similarly when I suggested reading about Mary Magdalene. She said; "I think we should keep it positive. Why read about a sinner like her when you claim there are inspiring stories about women in the Bible?" After some discussion, the group decided to investigate who Mary Magdalene really was by examining the Bible texts about her. We spent two evenings on this project. The first evening, we wrote down everything we knew about Mary Magdalene from sermons, school, and our upbringing. Everyone believed that she was the sinner who anointed the feet of Jesus with ointment (Luke 7:36–50). We then read the resurrection story (John 20:1–18), and discussed it in small groups while answering preformulated questions. During the discussion in the full group that followed, participants asked: What are angels? What's an "appearance"? Why didn't Mary Magdalene recognize Jesus at first? What does Jesus mean when he says "Touch me not"?

I have incorporated answers to these questions in the following letter, which I wrote "in Mary Magdalene's name" to the women taking the course. Their response was so positive that I have included the letter here. Several women later told me that they had asked others what they knew about Mary Magdalene. Everyone responded in the same way: "Wasn't that the sinner who anointed Jesus' feet with ointment?" Mary Magdalene's letter follows.

My dear sisters and brothers,
I have been asked to write to you about my experiences at the tomb. First I would like to say I'm pleased that you haven't allowed yourselves to be discouraged by the negative stories that have been told about me in Christian churches, but instead are conducting your own search for the truth about me. Let me begin my story by stating that I am not the same woman who anointed the feet of Jesus with ointment (Luke 7:36-50). This woman's name is never given in the Bible—the only information given about her is that she was "a woman in the city, which was a sinner." In the following chapter (Luke 8:1–3), Luke gives a description of the people who followed Jesus. In this description I am named as one of his followers: "Mary called Magdalene out of whom went seven devils."

Why is a man like Peter remembered for more than his shortcomings while I am blamed for the sins of some unknown woman, and I am identified with them in the church through the ages? Look up my name in any church book. You won't see me named as a witness but as penitent or as a sinner. In Matthew 14:31, Jesus says to Peter, "O thou of little faith, wherefore didst thou doubt?" Yet Peter is never called "Peter the man of little faith," or "Peter the Doubter." I never come across the epithet "Peter the Denier," although Peter denies Jesus three times (Matthew 26:69–75).

Here is my own story of my own "connectedness"[11] *with Jesus. From the moment of our first meeting he meant a good deal to me. For years I had been plagued by what we in those days called "evil spirits" (Luke 8:1–3). This still occurs in your own time. You must understand that I have always had very little self-confidence. I tried to hide it but I always paid too much attention to what other people said and did. I tried to make everyone happy and meet everyone else's expectations. I wasn't interested in who I really was and what I really wanted. I'd never learned to pay any attention to that. I increasingly doubted myself, and was inwardly torn by the various expectations others had of me. No matter how hard I tried, I always had the feeling it wasn't good enough. That made me even more afraid, afraid of the people with whom I associated, and especially afraid of God.*

I was cured of this through my encounters with Jesus. Our talks together had a liberating effect on me. I learned to believe in myself. This made me stronger, less dependent, and less afraid of others. It also made me see God in a new light. It was all interrelated. God was less someone who was always watching me and observing my shortcomings. God became someone close to me, whom I trusted, and someone who was happy every time I stood on my own two feet more solidly. As Rabbi Hacohen writes in his book Touching Heaven Touching Earth:[12] *"One of the disciples of the Ba'al Shem Tov once asked him why it is that a person who is faithful to his Creator and knows that He is close by still sometimes experiences a feeling of distance and loneliness. 'The cause is clear', the Ba'al Shem Tov answered. 'It is the same in this world. Watch how a father teaches his child to walk. First he lets the child stand while holding it. Then he stands facing the child with outspread arms because the child may fall when it takes its first steps. The child walks forward awkwardly between its father's arms and keeps trying to get closer to him. But the closer the child gets the more the father moves backward and he continues to do so until the child has learned to walk without his help.'"*

Jesus encouraged and inspired me particularly to be faithful to my innermost feelings. I thought his ideas and the way he treated people was so inspiring that I supported his work. I had some money, which I used to stimulate his work. I followed Jesus, together with a number of other women who had also had similar experiences (Luke 8:3). We were his

---

11. See Hayward, *Touching Our Strength.*

---

12. Rabbi S. Hacohen, *Met één been op de grond, Chassidische humor en Wijsheid* [Touching Heaven, Touching Earth: Hassidic Humor and Wit] (Tel Aviv and Amstelveen Amphora Books, 1976).

disciples. We even called Jesus "Master." That was exceptional because it was unusual for women to receive religious instruction in those times. This was reserved only for men, but Jesus never paid any attention to those discriminatory rules.

It was difficult for me to accept that during his life Jesus met such little understanding from scribes and other powerful men in the Jewish community. Those who subsisted in the lower classes of society and had much to endure would have done anything for him. How misunderstood he was. His suffering and his death affected me deeply. But it was unavoidable. Jesus too saw it as the consequence of his actions and didn't attempt to escape it. The only thing I could do was have faith in him and be with him as long as I could.[13]

The night before I went to the tomb, in the early morning I had slept very little. I was restless. I couldn't accept that everything was over after his death. That he was lost to us now. Several times he had said that he would survive death. He had said it with such conviction that I truly believed it. In our times we believed that, after death people go to a place inhabited by spirits, a place where no one else can enter: not those left behind, not even God. So in some way I was convinced that Jesus had not been lost to us after his death, but I was groping in the dark, in other words, I had no insight into what that meant, not exactly. This is the meaning of the symbolic words "It was yet dark . . ." (John 20:1). On the way to the tomb I kept thinking of Jesus. I wanted to see him to talk to him. I wanted to know what he meant when he said that he would rise from the dead. I went to look for him and thought that my best chance of meeting him would be at the place where we had left him: in his tomb. I wondered whether I would be able to roll away the heavy stone all by myself. I knew that it was much too heavy for me to move, but, to my surprise, I discovered that it had already been removed, "the stone taken away" (John

---

13. After reading the first edition of this book, Jewish author Maartje Van Tijn wrote to me [A. Imbens] in connection with the preceding paragraph that I had "no doubt unintentionally and without thinking" included in that paragraph "anti-Semitic ideas and sentiments." I contacted Van Tijn, and as a result she formulated this new paragraph, which supplements and clarifies the original: *I, Mary Magdelene have always understood why Jesus met with such little understanding from the powerful men in the Jewish community. They were friends of the Romans, the collaborators, the Jews who were "on the wrong side."*

Because in the days of Jesus (and before, and for centuries afterwards), the Land of Israel was occupied by the Romans. Those who subsisted . . . (as original) . . . did not attempt to escape it. He knew that the authorities considered him a "subversive element" because he disrupted the ruling social order. He was seen as a threat to the authorities: the military, the civilian Roman occupation forces, and the Jews who collaborated with them. That is why they persecuted him. The only thing I could do was have faith in him and be with him as long as I could.

20:1). *When I glanced into the tomb, I saw that Jesus was no longer there. I ran quickly to Peter and the other disciples to tell them that Jesus was gone (John 20:2). They wanted to see for themselves. When they had seen that Jesus was no longer in the tomb, they went back home (John 20:3–10).*

I wanted to find out more. I could not accept that Jesus had disappeared. I wanted so much to talk with him again. While I stood there and looked again into the tomb, I began to understand. I asked myself why I was crying, and what I wanted. I realized that I would not find him in the tomb in the place of the dead (John 20:11–13). So I turned around, turned my back to the tomb. I turned to the place of the living. It's hard for me to describe what happened next and it's hard for people who have never experienced anything like that to understand. I was thinking of Jesus with all my heart and mind. I didn't want to give him up. I didn't want to accept that his life had ended with his death. He himself had said it would not be so. All at once, it was as if someone was standing before me. It didn't even cross my mind that this had anything to do with Jesus. I wanted to reach Jesus. That was all I could think of. I didn't want him to remain with the dead. I asked this figure in front of me, who for just a split second made me think of the gardener, where I could find Jesus (John 20:14–15). Then I heard his familiar voice call my name. I turned to him and recognized Jesus my beloved Master (John 20:16). I had not found him in the tomb, the place of the dead, nor when I had turned away from the tomb toward the place of the living. I found him only when I had turned away from those two places and reached out to him with all my thoughts, love, hope, and longing. At first, I wanted to hold on to him in the place where I was. I could not let him go. But Jesus asked me not to touch him, not to cling to him, but to let him go so that he could be with his Father, be with God (John 20:17). He asked me to go to the disciples to tell them what I had seen and he gave me a message for them. He made it clear to me that after his death, he was with God, whom he saw as a beloved and trusted Father. He said that God is a trusted Father to us, too, who is waiting for us after our death (John 20:17). I had gone to the tomb in the dark, groping in the dark. Meanwhile day had broken and I saw everything in a clear light. I went to his other disciples and told them what I had seen (John 20:18).

When the church in your time says that it is continuing the line of Peter, and passing on what Peter witnessed, I ask myself on what grounds the church has based that policy. Moreover I wonder what impact that policy has had on the women of your time?

With sisterly greetings

Mary Magdalene

6
Religious Themes

One of the questions we asked in our interviews with the incest survivors was "What do you associate with these words?" One of the words was "forgiveness." We decided to explore this theme as a result of conversations we had with priests and ministers relating to our research. We observed that they often spoke of forgiveness and reconciliation. We also became aware that the minister or priest felt that his task would be successfully completed only when the woman learned to forgive her offender and was reconciled with him.

orgiveness We re-examined the interviews to determine what role this theme played in each woman's situation. Charlotte told us that a pastor told her that it was extremely important that she maintain a good relationship with her uncle, after she had told him that her uncle had abused her, and how this had affected her life. Ellen was repeatedly told that she must stop ignoring her grandfather and should go to family gatherings in which he was included. When Mary Beth told her mother what her brother had done to her, she said, "Will you forgive him? Please work things out between the two of you. I'll pray that it all works out."

Women's Responses   "It's a loaded word" (Ingrid). "Mostly negative things: awful, terrible" (Ellen). "Aggression" (Karen). "Sadness, anger" (Christine). "Nothing positive" (Susan). "Not knowing what to do, negative and aggressive feelings, and discontent" (Cathy). "Negative" (Charlotte). "Not daring to get angry, getting depressed" (Amy). "Feeling guilty and depressed, and not knowing why" (Tina).

Forgiveness is seen as an obligation that others unconditionally impose upon the person who has been wronged—even when the offender denies the deed, blackmails the victim, continues to abuse the victim, and shows no sorrow or regret. You must forgive, "seventy times seventy times," you must make the first move. It is evil not to be able to forgive. Nell's father demanded that she ask for forgiveness because she cried when he sexually abused her. Forgiveness is forced upon her.

Several survivors now feel that there are certain conditions that should be met prior to granting forgiveness. "You must forgive yourself and take your own feelings seriously" (Joan). "The offender has to admit what he's done" (Christine). "He has to show that he's sorry" (Karen and Theresa). "First, he has to pay for what he's done and she must receive justice" (Charlotte). "It needs to be be talked through" (Tina).

Most of these women have difficulty forgiving the offender. "He knew exactly what he was doing" (Ellen). "No way" (Karen). Judith hated her father but is now able to forgive him, adding, "For the most part, at least." Christine wants to forgive but says, "It's unacceptable." She thinks she might be able forgive him for her own good in order to be able to let him go. Anne wants to forgive her dead brother so he can rest in peace, but she cannot. Susan thinks forgiveness is unproductive when it is granted to avoid being punished. Lisa is full of hatred and anger. Cathy wonders how you can forgive when you cannot even explain what has been done to you. Amy is afraid to blame her brother for what he did to her. Five of the women interviewed think that they will never forgive their offender or that he will never be forgiven. Margaret and Amy say that they were never aware that they themselves had been forgiven.

The forgiveness theme is a difficult one for these incest survivors. They feel that they are supposed to forgive the offender. That proves impossible when the offender denies any wrongdoing or gives the victim no indication that he regrets his actions. Victims are often told by those in their immediate surroundings, as well as by their priests or ministers, that they are obligated to forgive the offenders unconditionally. This in turn only burdens the victims with new feelings of guilt. Those who try to forgive the offender, and suppress the anger and hate that they feel toward him become depressed. Because their families and friends do not allow them to express the negative feelings they harbor for the offender, victims eventually direct these feelings inward toward themselves.

Approaches to Pastoral Counseling

We do not feel that it suffices to show how destructive the wrong approach to forgiveness can be for these women. That is why we have chosen to show how we tried to approach the theme of forgiveness in such a way that the survivor was not burdened with new guilt feelings. We did not believe that the woman should learn to forgive the offender. We broached the subject in an initial conversation only in order to discover which aspects regarding her experience and her faith were bothering her most. We did this by suggesting a number of themes in the interview questions. When we received the impression that she had difficulty with forgiveness, we asked whether this was correct and whether she wished to discuss it more fully. For example, Lisa remarked, "Why would you want to forgive someone who ruined your whole life?" We asked a series of questions and allowed her to formulate an answer she could feel comfortable with, an answer with which she could do justice to herself and the offender. What do you feel when you think of him? What do you think of those feelings? Why would you forgive him? Can you forgive him? Can you explain why? Do you want to forgive him? What do you want to achieve? Do you think he deserves to be forgiven? Why?

The survivor usually asked for our viewpoint. We feel that someone who has experienced incest has a right to her anger toward the offender, toward his behavior, and his attitude. The offender has no right to ask the victim to grant him forgiveness until he has admitted his gross misconduct toward her, and has acknowledged the consequences of his actions. As long as this has not taken place, we feel that a woman who has experienced incest should not be burdened with new guilt feelings because she cannot forgive the offender. On the contrary, she has the right to accuse the offender who has done her this injustice, and to express her anger about it. We can think of no reason a woman should be made to cover up this violation with "Christian" love. When she is given enough room to deal with forgiveness in such a way that she can make her own peace with it, she will not be burdened by new guilt feelings. In this way, she need not violate herself again in order to meet the expectations of others.

Love Thy Neighbor   All of the women interviewed showed themselves to be capable of great empathy and understanding with regard to others' feelings and problems. In their upbringing, they were discouraged from taking themselves and their own feelings and problems seriously. We asked, "What do you associate with the text, 'Thou shalt love thy neighbor . . .'?" Next we asked "Were you also aware that the following words are 'as thyself'?"

Women's Reponses

Not one incest survivor had learned that it was important to love yourself as well. On the contrary, you had to love others. "It was wrong to stand up for yourself" (Ellen). Joan tells us that she had no control over her own fate because she was constantly told that you must love your neighbors. No one ever told her that "as thyself" was part of the text. Anne learned that you must love your neighbor more than yourself. You were supposed to devote your life to others. Everyone learned that it was important to love others and, in doing so, to forget yourself. Now they are discovering that you are allowed to love yourself and that this fundamental love allows you to learn to love others.

Issues for Pastoral Counseling

We saw how difficult it was for these women to stand up for themselves, out of self-respect to force others to take their feelings into consideration. This is a characteristic that many women share. Women and girls receive little stimulation to love themselves as they love their neighbors. Such behavior in women is considered egotistical. In a family relationship, it is assumed that the woman "loves" her husband and children so much that she is willing to sacrifice her own identity. She is expected to efface herself and cater to the desires and needs of the others, husband and children.

Girls are prepared for this future role in their upbringing. They are taught to accommodate the wishes of fathers and brothers. Mother also counts on her daughter to assist her in serving and accommodating the male members of the family. Boys' self-respect is vigorously stimulated and frequently overrated. In this way, boys learn to overestimate themselves and develop a contemptuous attitude toward others, especially girls and women. It is considered normal that they should love themselves more than another. They are not expected to be sensitive to the feelings and needs of their female housemates. They need to learn to love their neighbor as they love themselves. They must learn to stop loving themselves at others' expense.

Because girls learn to sacrifice and to underestimate themselves, they learn to love others at their own expense. Thus boys often have the upper hand in relationships. Girls are trained to take a back seat to boys. Boys and girls are brought up in such a way that men's power over women remains intact. Because girls and women from a Christian background are constantly told that they must be subservient and sacrificing, they associate the text "Thou shalt love thy neighbor as thyself" primarily with loving the other. They have been taught that this can happen at their own expense. This is the way women should be. This differing interpretation of "thy neighbor" and "thyself" is conducive to the sexual abuse of girls within families with Christian backgrounds. The offender thinks primarily of himself, the survivor primarily of the other.

If Christian theology is directed at human liberation, it must address this problem of men and women if we wish to eradicate abuse and exploitation of women. In a conversation with a biblical scholar, Jesus discusses the text: "Thou shalt love the Lord thy God with all thy heart, and with all thy soul, and with all thy strength, and with all thy mind; and thy neighbor as thyself" (Luke 10:25–37); the scholar asks him, "And who is my neighbor?". He apparently knew who he himself was. It is the question still asked by an élite, controlling group in Christianity today: "Who is my neighbor?" Do teachers of modern Christianity and leaders of Christian churches see women as their neighbors? Why is there so little room for women to express themselves on the subject of who they are or would like to be? When we are told to "love thy neighbor", do we realize that we have learned to love our neighbor at our own expense, at the expense of our self-confidence and our self-respect? We know that this is bad for ourselves and our neighbor. When we are told "Thou shalt love thy neighbor as thyself," we must ask, "Who is this 'self'?"

Sources of strength and Courage

From the start, we observed that the incest survivors found the subjects of religion and incest depressing. The question "What aspects of religion did you experience as liberating?" also frequently elicited negative reactions. We felt it was important to end the interviews with a liberating and upbeat aspect in their lives, so we always closed with the question: "Where do you get your strength and courage in life?"

Women's Responses The sources of strength and courage identified by these incest survivors can be divided into three categories: first, strength and courage from inner resources, whether related to God or not; second, strength and encouragement given by others; and third, pleasure and satisfaction experienced from earthly things such as nature, work, and so on.

Sixteen women receive strength from within themselves. Charlotte says that her inner strength made her decide to talk about her experience. She also recognizes two forces within herself. One says "You must talk about it." The other force minimizes what happened. According to Charlotte, the latter is reinforced by caring professionals. Five of the women relate their inner strength to God. Amy derives her strength from her experience of God as something alive within us all, showing us that we must each make our own way in life. This brings God and people closer together. It gives strength: There is an alternative to damnation. Theresa does not believe that her inner strength has anything to do with faith or prayer. Ten women receive encouragement from other women: women in a club or organization to which they belong; friends; girlfriends from childhood; a girlfriend's mother; a superior at work; women's studies; consciousness-raising groups; the women's center.

These women sometimes found support and understanding from an aunt or grandmother. Joan cites the story of the twelve-year-old Jesus and the image of the innocent child as a source of strength in resisting unjust treatment. Christine gets her strength from other people with the same ideals; Nell and Susan from their children; Barbara from someone who believes in her; Cathy and Theresa from a therapist; Carol from people with whom she hopes to be able to change things. Amy gets her strength from the warmth and friendship of others; Tina from people; Ingrid from people who value her.

Pleasure and satisfaction are gained from: study and work; ideals to fight for; doing something yourself and not having to wait for God (Margaret); hard work, being proud (Nell); work and pleasant surroundings, ambience (Susan); a jubilant feeling (Lisa);

her own creativity (Cathy); a personal letter, the sun, nature, the place she lives, a good shower, her job (Theresa); nature and little things, music (Amy); her work and the pieces she writes (Ingrid).

This question drew few responses relating strength to the faith in which these women were brought up. Most of the women relate strength primarily to something within themselves, the encouragement of other women, and the things that make life pleasant. These answers are particularly conspicuous when one realizes that the theme of the interview was religion.

Issues for Pastoral Counseling
In the counseling sessions, we saw how much courage and strength of spirit the women had. They are strong women, each of whom keeps fighting to learn to live with her humiliating experience and to build a humane life for herself and her children. Furthermore, they have a sense of responsibility for others. These interviews left us with the sense that people have a certain inner core, which cannot be destroyed from the outside. The core has to do with the essence of every human being. It is this core that keeps these women going, in spite of the humiliation they have endured. From our conversations with these women, we have found the strength and courage to denounce sexism in Christian churches.

During our conversations on this subject, we recognized the danger of focusing attention on the strength of spirit which these women have. We know that priests, ministers, and theologians are quick to presume that their suffering has perhaps served a purpose, and that God may have meant it to be this way. We disagree because this condones suffering inflicted upon young girls on someone else's initiative. It is wrong to try to find a purpose in suffering inflicted by others' free will. This suffering is senseless and cannot be made purposeful by attributing it to God, or by presuming that a woman has been made strong by her incest experience. When we assume that this suffering has had a purpose and that God must have had a reason, then we see God as a sadist, a power-monger: more powerful and more sadistic than the rapists who violate their own family members.[1] When we presume that women draw strength from their incest experiences, we ignore the destructive effect that incest has had on them. Only the strongest

---

1. Dorothee Soelle, *Suffering* (Philadelphia: Fortress, 1979).

women manage with intense effort and under favorable conditions to build a humane existence. These are the survivors. They are the ones who give voice to their experiences and thus protest this injustice in order to put an end to it.

Marriage Rites among Protestants In the article seeking feminist theologians, one key question was: "Do words contained in the marriage service perhaps lead a man to gratify his sexual desires by using the girls in his immediate or extended family?" We will examine the marriage services of the Dutch Reformed and the Roman Catholic churches.[2] How is marriage viewed? Which behavior is prescribed for women and men? Who holds the power in the family as a result? We will examine older services, because they were in use when the incest survivors' parents married. We will also examine texts that have been officially approved by the churches in recent years.

Dutch Reformed Service (1925)
Dutch Reformed churches have three marriage services from which couples can choose. The oldest dates from about 1925, the next is from about 1956, and the newest was approved by the General Synod in April of 1982.

Legitimacy of Marriage. According to the words of the service, the Word of God tells us how honorable the state of matrimony is. Married people are blessed and guided by God; in contrast, whoremongers and adulterers are judged and punished. Human beings are created in God's likeness. The writings in Genesis and the words of Saint Paul are used to demonstrate that God instituted marriage. The text of the Wedding at Cana is interpreted as follows: "This is why the Lord Jesus Christ so highly honored this estate with his presence, gifts, and miraculous signs at Cana in Galilee, in order to affirm that the estate of matrimony should be held in honor by all."

---

2. These are English translations of the Dutch texts, which have been officially approved by the churches indicated. The translator and the author considered supplementing these texts with the official English language versions, but considering that these texts have been officially approved by the respective churches, we do not anticipate significant differences between the language used in the Dutch and English language services.

This statement is based on a specific interpretation of marriage and Bible passages are used out of context to support it. For example, "And the Lord God said, It is not good that the man should be alone; I will make him an help meet for him" (Gen. 2:18) is supplemented by a specific interpretation of the role of women in the family—that of the housewife: "Because he who created Adam's housewife brought and gave his housewife to him Himself, herewith demonstrates that He still to this day brings to every man his housewife as if by his own Hand."

The word "help" in "help meet" from Genesis 2:18 ("helper" in the Revised Standard Version, 1952, and the New Revised Standard Version, 1989; "helpmate" in The Jerusalem Bible, 1971; "help" in the Dutch and other versions) can be interpreted in three ways:[3] First, as a help who is superior to the man Adam, "Because thou hast been my help, therefore in the shadow of thy wings will I rejoice" [Psalm 63:7]. "Thou art my help and my deliverer; O Lord, make no tarrying" [Psalm 70:56]; second, as a help who is equal to the man Adam; and third, as a help who is inferior to the man Adam.

The interpretation of "help meet" in these marriage vows is that of a help(er) (the housewife) who is inferior to the man. This inferiority of the woman to the man becomes even clearer when we examine the goal of marriage. It is important to recognize that men have divinely legitimated this inferiority by using Bible passages and supplemental interpretations to establish their patriarchal view of marriage.

These same passages and supplemental interpretations can just as easily be used to demonstrate that men are inferior human beings. They have been assigned an help meet (help, helper, helpmate) by God (Gen. 2:19), a help who is their superior or a help who liberates them (Psalm 63:7). We can add, "Because He, who gave Eve a workman, who will eat his bread by the sweat of his brow, herewith demonstrates that He still to this day brings to every woman her workman as if by his own Hand." Here we show the imperfection of the man in exactly the same way as the women's inferiority is shown and divinely legitimated in these marriage services.

---

3. Also see, Phyllis Trible, "Eve and Adam: Genesis 2–3 Reread," in *Womanspirit Rising: A Feminist Reader in Religion*, ed. C. P. Christ and J. Plaskow (San Francisco: Harper and Row, 1978), p. 75.

Goal of marriage

1. A man and woman are joined by sincere love and faith, supporting each other in all things pertaining to this and eternal life.
2. The children are to be brought up in the "faithful knowledge and fear of God: to His honor and their joy" for the continuation of the human race.
3. The holy estate of matrimony is reserved for those who "have reached their years and do not have the gift of abstinence". Sexuality is exclusively reserved for married people. It is not clear whether abstinence is more highly regarded than sexuality.
4. The relationship between husband and wife is arranged according "to God's word".

The husband.   The husband is the head of the wife; leads her with wisdom; educates, comforts, and protects her; shall love his housewife as his own body; shall not become bitter towards her; shall live with her wisely; shall honor the womanly vessel as the weaker; shall eat bread by the sweat of his brow; shall labor faithfully and industriously in his divine profession, in order to support his family and share with the needy.

The wife.   The wife shall know how to keep the Word of God with regard to her husband; shall love, honor and obey him as her lord in all things right and just; must be obedient to her husband, as the body to the head and the church to Christ; shall follow the example of the women saints who were obedient to their husbands; shall be helpful to her husband in good and just things; shall care well for her household; shall be modest, virtuous, and without worldly grandeur; shall long for a gentle and tranquil spirit; shall set a good example of modesty for others.

The relationship between husband and wife is compared with the relationship between Christ and the church, whereby the man represents Christ and the woman represents the church. In this comparison, one of the three images (of marriage at that time) that Paul used in his letter to the Ephesians to express the relationship of Christ with the faithful church, is used as divine legitimation of the patriarchical relationships in matrimony. The three comparisons that Paul makes are: the faithful church is like a building, in which Christ is the cornerstone and the apostles and prophets the foundation (Eph. 2:19–22); the church is as one body with Christ as head (Eph. 4:11–16); the relationship between Christ and the church is like the marriage between husband and wife (Eph. 5:22–33 or Eph. 5:21–33).

In this marriage service two reasons are given that the wife should be obedient to her husband: First, Adam was created first, and then Eve as Adam's help meet; and second, after the "Fall," God spoke to Eve and in her person to the entire female gender: "And thy desire shall be to thy husband, and he shall rule over thee." (Gen. 3:16, King James Version). This notion of desire is reflected in other translations: "Your yearning shall be for your husband, yet he will lord it over you" (The Jerusalem Bible, 1971); "And your craving will be for your husband, and he will dominate you" (New World Translation of the Holy Scriptures, 1984); "Yet your desire shall be for your husband, and he shall rule over you" (New Revised Standard Version). To this is added that this command of God may not be transgressed, but must be obeyed.

In this second reason women should therefore be obedient to their husbands in marriage because God wills it. It will be evident that what is meant here is "because men determine that God wills it". The validity of the second reason is thus suspect.

But to what extent is the first reason for the wife's obedience plausible? Adam was created first, and then Eve as Adam's help. We have seen that the word "help" can be interpreted in three ways. Therefore, the wife's submissiveness cannot be derived from the word "help." Nor can it be derived from the creation of Adam as the first human being. In the story of the creation, there is a progression from low to high. The conclusion that Adam, who was created earlier, has a higher place in the order of things than Eve, is then incorrect. It would be more obvious to conclude the opposite. Eve was created last, after Adam; she is the crown, the climax of creation. We are not using this observation as an argument for a role reversal. We are merely showing that the rulership of men over women on the grounds that the man was created earlier, is not the obvious conclusion that can be drawn from the story of creation. The opposite is true.

Questions to the bridegroom and bride.   The man is asked whether he promises that he will never leave his wife, and will love and faithfully support her as befits a faithful and God-fearing man. The questions asked of the woman are approximately the same, but in a different sequence. Only the woman is told "to be obedient to him". She is addressed as "pious and faithful housewife" instead of "faithful and God-fearing man". Matthew 19:1–12 in which some Pharisees ask Jesus: "Is it lawful for a man to put away his wife for every cause?" is used to demonstrate the strength of the bond of matrimony.

Dutch Reformed Service (1956)

Legitimacy of marriage.   Matrimony is seen as "an ordinance of God," meant as a union for life. Genesis 2:18 and 2:24 are cited to demonstrate that matrimony is God's will. Matthew 19:5–7 is quoted to show that matrimony is indissoluble, and Ephesians. 5:22–33 is again used to compare the joining of man and wife in matrimony to the relationship of Christ with the church (as in the Marriage Service of 1925). Married people can be assured of God's help.

Goal of marriage.   No significant changes were made to the text of 1925. Again, the text states that the relationship between husband and wife is arranged according "to God's Word."

The husband.   The husband shall love his wife (as Christ loves his church, Eph. 5:25); shall sanctify his wife (as Christ the church); shall be the head of his wife; shall serve her in love, guide and protect her; shall faithfully and devotedly perform his labor to support the family; is the head of the family, which is a part of a greater community; has responsibilities to society, and to the needs of the church and community.

The wife.   The wife shall know that God has bound her to her husband (as the church to Christ); shall love her husband and follow him in all things which are right and just (as the flock loves and follows its Lord); shall care well for her family; shall keep her family in the fear of God: Those who are entrusted to her care shall be thankful for this to God and praise him.

Questions to the bridegroom and bride.   The bridegroom is asked to guide and protect his wife in love. The bride is asked to obey and help her husband in love. Several prayers follow.

Dutch Reformed Service (1982)   In this service, matrimony is seen as an opportunity given by God: the joining of two people for life. There is no discussion of the relationship between husband and wife according to God's will. Instead: "Together they will seek the will of God regarding his wishes for their life. Together they will perform their task and care for their family; show their children the way in life with the Lord and His Church; accept their place in the community as man and wife." This is followed by: "Their union with each other is like to the bond between Christ and his flock. Therefore, bride and bridegroom, will you love each other as Christ loved his church?" In the remaining text, the same is expected of both husband and wife. There are no references to Bible passages, but the likeness of marriage to Christ and His Church is clearly taken from Ephesians 5.

Protestant Rites as a Group   The texts of the first as well as the second service are based on unbalanced power relationships between women and men in marriage. In both services, Bible passages and various additions and interpretations are used to claim that marriage has been instituted by God. The husband is considered the head of the wife, her guide and protector, the breadwinner in the family. In both services, the wife must obey her husband, follow him, and care for the household. In the first service, the words "in all things that are right and just" follow the passage on the wife's obedience to the husband; in the second, this phrase corresponds to her following the husband. The addition of the words "in all things that are right and just" would seem to ensure that women in marriage are not totally abandoned to male whims and power abuse. But who determines what is right and just in a relationship in which the power is not equally distributed?

This brings us back to the question: Do words contained in the marriage service perhaps lead a man to gratify his sexual desires by using the girls in his immediate or extended family? In the case of the Dutch Reformed churches, the answer is yes. The texts that were officially used up to 1982 cause and legitimate unbalanced power relationships between men and women in the family. Research needs to be conducted on the nature and frequency of use of the new marriage service, which is clearly an improvement on the other services. We have no information regarding how often the new service is used. Furthermore, we do not know what ministers preach alongside the new text. In light of the past texts, questions arise concerning the comparison of marriage to Christ and his church. The comparison from Ephesians 5:22–33 plays an important role in legitimating the unequal distribution of power in relationships between men and women in the family.[4]

Figure 5.1.

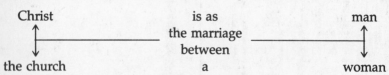

When this text is used to legitimate hierarchical relationships in matrimony, the man is put on the same plane as Christ, who is considered divine. The woman is put on the same plane as the church, which consists of humans. The relation between man and woman in marriage is made parallel to the relation between God and human beings. Through this text and this interpretation, men/husbands receive the God-given right to rule over women/wives. Men/husbands can therefore exercise as much power in the family as they think right and just. Women/wives have no opportunity to set limits to the power and will of the man/husband. They are completely subject to the whims of their men/husbands. Men/husbands, unhindered by women/wives, who have been rendered powerless, can do whatever they like. Girls in Christian families are brought up in such a way that they learn to be submissive to men (fathers and brothers). The image of the ideal woman portrayed in these marriage services is used to teach girls about ideal womanhood. Girls are thus easily made prey to sexual abuse by male members of the immediate or extended family. They learn not to resist power abuse by men and boys. Sexual abuse of girls in the family is the ultimate consequence of male domination of women legitimated by the church. The survivors we interviewed confirm this in their statements that Father was authoritarian and that he determined what took place

---

4. See Rosemary Radford Ruether, *Mary—The Feminine Face of the Church* (Philadelphia: Westminster Press, 1977), p. 24.

in the family. Mother was expected to organize everything according to his wishes. The girls were stimulated by father and mother to be obedient and accommodating in their behavior toward their father and brothers.

riage Rites ng Roman Catholics We will examine a marriage service from a missal used in 1947, and the marriage service drafted by the National Liturgy Council in 1981.[5]

Roman Catholic Rite (1947)   The text from this old missal is examined because it influenced the Roman Catholic mothers of girls who were sexually abused. This text was replaced in the 1960s.

After the blessing of the couple, the question the bridegroom is asked: "Wilt thou, . . . here and now, take to be your lawfully wedded housewife, according to the tradition of our Mother the Holy Church?" The bride is asked the same question, except the word housewife in the text is replaced by the word man. In this text, there is also mention of the blessing of one ring. The prayer that accompanies this reads: "Bless, Lord, this ring, which we bless in Your name, that she who will wear it will stay immaculately faithful to her bridegroom, will forever persevere in Your peace and Your will, and live forever in everlasting love. Through Christ our Lord. Amen." This ring is put on "the ring finger of the left hand of the bride" by the bridegroom, while the priest once again prays aloud. The marriage ceremony concludes with a prayer, which proclaims that God has ordained the reproduction of the human race through matrimony.

This is followed by the Mass for the bridegroom and bride. Ephesians 5:22–32 is used for the Epistle reading. When we compare the introduction of this epistle with the Willibrordus translation,[6] we see that the Willibrordus text begins: "Be obedient

---

5. *Missaal bevattende alle missen van het missale Romanum* [Missal Containing All Masses from the *Missale Romanum*], ed. G. Van Deun (Den Bosch: G. Mosmans-Zoon, 1947), and *Marriage* (Het Huwelijk), National Liturgy Council, Hilversum, September 8, 1981.

---

6. The Willibrordus translation is the official Dutch translation of the Roman Catholic Bible. — Trans.

to each other in the fear of Christ" (5:21), and is followed by; "The wives to their husbands as to the Lord" (5:22). The Nederlandse Bijbel Genootschap[7] translation begins; "Wives, be obedient to thy husband as to the Lord" (5:22). The epistle in this missal begins: "Brothers, the wife must be obedient to her husband, as to the Lord". In this text, the husbands are addressed and told that wives must be obedient to them. The women/wives themselves are not addressed at all. Instead, their inferiority is announced to men, while they themselves are ignored. After the epistle, the text is read: "Thy housewife shall be as a fruitful vine by the sides of thine house: thy children as olive plants round about thy table" (Psalm 128:3). Matthew 19:3–6 is used as the Gospel text, which concludes with the words: "What therefore God hath joined together, let not man put asunder."

One of the subsequent prayers explains the wife's place in marriage (according to the story of Creation), and the value God places on matrimony (He has thus illustrated the union of Christ with His Church and the union between husband and wife. God has not taken this away in spite of the punishment for Original Sin and the punishment of the Flood). Then God is asked to look with mercy upon His "female servant, who, in entering this marriage, fervently wished to be protected by God". What is desired of her reads as follows:

May she carry the yoke of love and peace. May she live in matrimony faithfully and chastely in Christ and always follow in the footsteps of the women saints. May she live as long and stay as faithful as Sarah. May the worker of sin find nothing in her that is his. May she stay devoted to the faith and to Thy commandments. May she, bound to one man, flee from any improper intercourse with others. May she strengthen her weakness through a regular life. May she be serious through modesty, virtuous through chastity, experienced in heavenly things. May she be fruitful in offspring, of tempered innocence. May she rest in the peace of the faithful in the heavenly kingdom.

Another prayer for both husband and wife follows this: May they both see the children of their children into the third and fourth generations, and attain a desirable old age.

---

7. Nederlandse Bijbel Genootschap [Netherlands Bible Association] is an ecumenical group that includes Roman Catholics — Trans.

What ideas about men underlie the writing of this prayer for the "female servant"? Did the authors of this prayer think that men are so perfect that similar prayers need not be said about them? Or did they think that what is expected of women cannot be expected of men? The priest concludes with the blessing of the couple, saying: "The God of Abraham, the God of Isaac and the God of Jacob be with you and fill you with his blessing, that you may see the children of your children into the third and fourth generations and afterward possess eternal life without end, through the aid of our Lord Jesus Christ, who as God with God the Father and the Holy Ghost lives and rules . . ." May our children learn that, for centuries, the God of the mothers of their mothers has been treated as nonexistent, and that it began with Sarah.

The question: Is there a connection between this Roman Catholic marriage service and the sexual abuse of girls in the family? can only be answered in the affirmative. The notion that the wife must be subordinate to the husband provides men with ample room to concern themselves solely with satisfying their own needs in the family, without paying attention to the needs of others. When we told a married Roman Catholic woman about this study, she replied; "Is there really a connection between religion and incest? I find that very hard to believe. Or is it because religion tells the husband that he's the boss in the family? It's becoming more and more clear to me how devastating this is for women. Sometimes there's just no place a woman can go . . . you're completely boxed in. I'm realizing more and more that it all starts with the church. My husband thinks that I am letting myself be influenced by other women. But that isn't true. I just know it inside, and it makes me feel terrible. But I'm afraid that men will never give up the power they have."

During this study, we often received similar reactions from women who had no experience with sexual abuse as a child. The texts of the marriage services show that the power of men over women in the family is legitimated by Christian churches. This results in power abuse, which has negative effects of varying degrees on many Christian women married to men who put into practice the theoretical ideas on which these marriage services are based. This power of men over women, which receives its legitimacy from the Christian churches, is the most important factor in the sexual abuse of girls in the family.

National Liturgy Council Service (1981) The Catholic marriage service text has undergone many changes in comparison to that of 1947.[8] The National Liturgy Council suggests using three readings during the marriage ceremony. Fifteen readings are offered from which to choose each of the three selections.

We have the following comments on the texts offered for the first reading:

The first reading selection is Genesis 1:26–28, 31. Man and woman are presented as equals in this text.

The second text is from the book of Tobit (7:9c-10, 11c-17). Tobias, invited by Sarah's father Raguel to his table, tells his host that he will neither eat nor drink until his request has been granted and the host promises to give him his daughter Sarah. Sarah is given to Tobias, because he fears God. This is done with the words: "The God of Abraham, the God of Isaac and the God of Jacob be with thee, join thee, and grant thee his blessing." Sarah's fate is decided by her father and her future husband; she is never consulted. Here, the woman has no voice.

The third text is from the Song of Solomon (2:8–10, 14, 16a; 8:6–7a). The images in this text appeal to both women and men.

The fourth text originates from the Book of Ecclesiasticus (26:1–4, 13–16). The first passage has been translated directly from the Dutch *Book of Marriage Services*. For comparison, the second passage has been taken from Ecclesiasticus in the English "John Brown" Bible, 1813.[9]

A good wife makes her husband happy; the number of his days will be doubled. A staunch wife is the joy of her husband, she allows him to live out the years of his life in peace. With a good wife, men are well-endowed: those who fear the Lord receive her as their reward. Rich or poor, they will be glad of heart and cheerful of face. . . . A graceful wife gladdens her

---

8. Only the sections of the marriage service relevant to this study will receive treatment here.

---

9. Het huwelijk [Book of Marriage Services, National Liturgy Nationale Raad voor Liturgie, Hilversum, Gooi en Sticht, 1981. Council]. The full citation of the "John Brown" Bible from the title page is *The Holy Bible with Analysis, Explanatory Notes, Evangelical reflections, Etc.*, by the Late Rev. John Brown, Minister of the Gospel at Haddington (East Lothian, Scotland), printed and published by Brightly and Childs at Bungay, 1813 — Trans.

husband, her dignity gives him new strength. An unassuming wife is a gift from the Lord: She who is well-trained will be highly praised. A modest wife is a great blessing and nothing outweighs her self-control. Like the sun rising in the high heavens of the Lord, so is the beauty of a good wife, the jewel of her family.

Blessed is the man that hath a virtuous wife, for the number of his days shall be double. A virtuous woman rejoiceth her husband, and he shall fulfil the years of his life in peace. A good wife is a good portion, which shall be given in portion of them that fear the Lord. Whether a man be rich or poor, if he have a good heart toward the Lord, he shall at all times rejoice with a cheerful countenance. . . . . The grace of a wife delighteth her husband, and her discretion will fatten his bones. A silent and loving woman is a gift of the Lord: and there is nothing so much worth as a mind well instructed. A shame-faced and faithful woman is a double grace, and her continent mind cannot be valued. As the sun when it ariseth in the high heaven: so is the beauty of a good wife in the ordering of her house.

In reading this text, we see yet another example of the way in which women in Christian churches are constantly told how they should behave. The image of the ideal woman, which has been invented and used by men to control women, cannot be attained and is not worth attaining. A woman who attempts to achieve this ideal in her marriage becomes merely a shell of a woman, fashioned from male dream images and adolescent desires. This "ideal woman," invented by men, is a being without a soul, a puppet on a string.

The wife.   A good, staunch wife is happy whether she is rich or poor; always has a cheerful face; is graceful; has dignity; knows her place; is modest; has a chaste character; has strong self-control; has the beauty of a good wife.

What she offers to her husband.   The number of the husband's days is doubled; joy; he will live out his life in peace; he is well-endowed; she is given to him as a reward for fearing God; she gladdens him; she gives him strength; she is a gift of the Lord, a great blessing, like the rising sun, the jewel of the family.

A woman who tries to meet these expectations learns to suppress her own feelings and to concentrate on the feelings of her husband. She will always feel guilty, because she can never live up to everyone's expectations. Or she will become depressed and feel divided, because she has learned to fit this image and she becomes empty inside, cold, and full of sorrow. She "gives him strength" at her own expense.

For the second marriage service reading, the couple may choose from five texts, all taken from Paul, and all dealing with love. One of the texts is Ephesians 5 (2a, 21–33 or 2a, 25–33). This text, in which the husband in the marriage is given power over women, has already been discussed. In the new Catholic marriage service, the section on the wife's obedience to her husband and the respect that a wife should have for her husband has merely been placed between parentheses.

Questions and prayers. The questions asked of the bride and bridegroom are identical to the questions asked in the marriage rite of 1947. Prayer for the bridegroom and bride (*silent prayer*).

A partial quote reads: "Thou, who hath made Man in the image of his God, and gave the man a woman as his inseparable help meet"; "God, Thou hath made the bond between man and wife a Holy Mystery, as great as the love of Christ for His bride, the Church. . . . God, through Thee the wife is joined to her husband. Grace Thee this bond, which has existed since Creation, with Thy blessing, a blessing that has remained with us even after the punishment for the original sin and the flood. God, look with mercy upon her, Thy servant_____. She asks for Thy aid in her marriage through Thy blessing: Let love and peace radiate from her and make her in the image of the great women whose examples are set down for us in the Holy Scripture. Bless her, that she may possess the full trust of her husband, that he may recognize her as his equal companion for life, that he give her the honor she deserves, and love her as Christ loves His bride, the Church." The rest of the prayer addresses the bride and bridegroom. Once again in this prayer, the bride is told how she should be as a wife; the bridegroom is not.

There are several improvements in these texts. From the fifteen available readings, it is possible to choose three that avoid traditional role-stereotyping and patronizing attitudes toward women. Nevertheless, texts remain that are unsuitable for use in a church that regards women as equal, independent, thinking human beings—not as an extension of their husbands and existing for the benefit of their husbands. Therefore, use of the texts from Tobit and Ecclesiasticus (from the Apocrypha) cannot be justified. The text from Ephesians is equally unsuitable to marriage ceremonies because of the hierarchical relationships contained in the text, which strengthen the hierarchical and sexist interpretation of matrimony.

The marriage vow, which is identical for bride and groom, is an improvement on the 1947 vows, but the silent prayer that follows is denigrating to women. Women are confronted with an ideal image to which they are expected to conform, and men are not.

Marriage rvices and ual Abuse Reference to Paul's letter to the Ephesians (5:22–33) is included in all of the marriage services analyzed for this study. The comparison contained in this text is also used in the newest marriage service of the Dutch Reformed Churches. According to the 1925 and 1956 services, matrimony is thus arranged "according to God's word." The relationship between husband and wife, as dictated by Paul, is hierarchical. The husband is compared to Christ, whom we regard as divine; the wife with the church, which consists of humans. The husband is seen as the head, the wife as the body, which is controlled by the head—her husband. Therefore, according to the old Dutch Reformed service, the wife must be subservient and obedient to her husband, in all that is right and just.

We read in the Roman Catholic texts, such as Ephesians 5:24 (NBG translation), that the wife must be obedient to the husband *in all things*. The 1982 Dutch Reformed marriage service states the comparison taken from Paul thus: "Their joining together is like to the bond between Christ and his church." This is acceptable only when the accompanying sermon makes clear that this likening has been wrongly used to make women subordinate to men. This comparison cannot be used in marriage ceremonies while the effects on women, men, and children are ignored.[10]

Sexually abused girls are brought up by mothers who, according to the official guidelines of the churches, were told in

---

10. Also see, Dorothee Soelle, *Fantasie en gehoorzaamheid* [Fantasy and Obedience] Baarn: Ten Have, 1979).

their marriage ceremonies that they must obey their husbands. Mothers who allowed their daughters to be abused were obedient to their husbands in all things. The survivors often have more contempt for their mothers than for the offenders. They considered their mothers responsible for their sexual abuse by the offender. Those who were abused by their fathers thought it was because their mothers were not adequately performing their sexual marital obligations. Those who were abused by their brothers found their mothers primarily responsible for not having protected them from abuse. Mary Beth said that she became easy prey for her brother chiefly due to the way her mother brought her up: "To me, my mother represents all the values and norms that the church imposes on women. We girls were stimulated by her—in a friendly, but compelling way—to be considerate of our brothers' wishes and to wait on them." She also told us that her father represented the "law making" power in the family and her mother the "law enforcement" power. She saw her father as a hard but fair judge and admired him for it. On the other hand, she had absolutely no respect for the behavior of her mother, who made sure that the father's decrees were carried out. In this family, the mother and father fulfilled the roles in Paul's letter that are imposed on women and men according to the church's explanation. She was obedient to him. He called the shots. But the mother is blamed for not protecting her daughter against incest.

We found that in the families of the women we interviewed, all of the fathers and mothers demonstrated similar behavior. Even Ingrid's father, who was an agnostic, behaved according to these norms, which have been preached by patriarchical Christianity for centuries.

Father's behavior   Father determines the laws and rules to be followed in the family. He does not need to enforce them. He sees to it that Mother executes and enforces his laws and rules. He does not permit any criticism of his laws, or of the patriarchical system, which gives him his power in the family, church, and society. Discussion is not tolerated. When his laws are questioned, his reaction is forbidding, surly, obstinate, taciturn, or uncontrollably angry. He makes sure that he is unapproachable. He considers it the mother's responsibility and task to see to it that everything is smoothly organized. She and the other family members must not bother him with details.

The father's behavior is legitimated in the older marriage service texts. In all of those services, he is appointed the head of the family, and women are expected to obey him. Even in modern services, he is not asked to be a joy to his wife and to radiate happiness, rich or poor. Saintliness, chastity, and modesty are not expected of men, but they are expected of women.

Mother's behavior

Mother maintains the patriarchical order in the family, which preserves the power of men over women. In this patriarchical structure, many virtues are attributed to the ideal woman, which are impossible for anyone to live up to. She must be like Mary and the saints, virgin-like and joyful in her suffering. But in essence, women are weak, seductive, sinful, and untrustworthy. It is therefore good for her that she is obedient to her husband and that her husband protects her from her own weaknesses. Obedient wives do not ask their husbands critical questions, do not complain, and do not show their emotions.

Mothers try to raise their daughters to be ideal women, who learn to meet the expectations and requirements men have of women. Daughters who rebel are considered troublesome and unfeminine. Mother tries to break her daughter's rebellion by ridiculing her when she acts "unfeminine", and by rewarding and encouraging her when she acts "feminine", that is, accommodating toward the male members of the family. Girls are stimulated by their mothers to conform to what men expect of women and what is said in the marriage services. A mother who has conformed to these expectations herself teaches her daughter:

— to repress her feelings, desires, and natural talents (which are not appropriate to her role), and to make these subservient to the feelings, desires and talents of men, specifically fathers and brothers;

— to see herself as subservient and inferior to men;

— to feel responsible for the well-being of her male partner;

— to feel guilty for the mistakes and shortcomings of her male partner.

It is no wonder that sexually abused women who have had this Christian upbringing find it difficult to accept their mothers' viewpoint. Mothers who have tried to live up to the image of the ideal woman propagated by Christian churches raise their daughters to be easy prey for incest offenders. A mother who fulfills the task she has been charged with is condemned by her daughter for doing so, while those who impose the task remain free of blame.

Dominant groups have so much power that they can pressure their subordinates to implement their unpleasant policies. Mary Daly describes this pattern and illustrates it by using the example of the Chinese practice of binding girls' feet.[11] Through this practice, the feet of little girls were transformed into small stumps on which they could only hobble around. Mothers, or other close female relatives, were responsible for carrying out this practice. Women were charged with ensuring that, from a very young age, girls were made dependent upon men. In the patriarchal Chinese culture, mothers and other women carried out this physical mutilation of the girls. In our Christian culture, obedient mothers carry out the psychological and spiritual mutilation of their daughters.

A mother who carries out the task with which she is charged is condemned, hated, and regarded with contempt by the survivor, her daughter. Mother knows that her daughter will have a difficult time in a society dominated by the patriarchal mentality if she has not learned to adapt to that male-dominated system. Mother constantly makes compromises in the family in order to keep everyone happy. She is also responsible for maintaining good relations within the family. Because children must learn the (male/female) hierarchical system as a part of their upbringing, she glosses over her sons' domineering and disruptive behavior. "Boys will be boys," she laughs. Many of the women we interviewed indicated that their mothers and grandmothers are proud of their brothers, and invent excuses for their behavior. This is particularly true of brothers who have committed sexual abuse. "He's the son and heir"; "He's a war baby"; "At least he still goes to church"; "Girls are more trouble than boys." Boys learn to get their own

---

11. Mary Daly, *Gyn/Ecology: The Metaethics of Radical Feminism* (Boston: Beacon Press, 1978; London: The Women's Press, 1979), pp. 134–52.

way with girls and to dominate them. When girls had a problem with their brothers' domineering behavior, they were told that they mustn't carry on, or that they should "be above" all that. Sisters learn not to offer any resistance to their brothers' domineering behavior. Girls learn to resign themselves to getting inferior treatment, and to accommodate themselves to men's wills. Mothers fulfill the ideal of the perfect woman preached by the church when they are servile toward fathers, and raise their sons and daughters to conform to the system. Their sons, husbands, and many church leaders idolize them, their daughters despise them.

Marital Instruction and Sexuality We came into the possession of a library of books from the estate of a Roman Catholic priest. In these books, we found a good deal of educational material on marriage, love, and birth control. There was also a series consisting of two books entitled: *Sexual Behavior in Practice* and *Fertile and Infertile Days in Marriage*. The first book is attributed to Professor Herbert Henderson; the second does not list an author. The books' publication years are unknown, but must have been after 1954, as one of the books cites a text written in that year.

In the introduction to *Fertile and Infertile Days in Marriage*, the author says that he felt no need to base his work on a particular philosophy. He advises people who wonder whether the rhythm method of birth control goes against their religious beliefs to seek advice from their priests or ministers. He then indicates that, according to the pastoral letter of the General Synod of the Dutch Reformed Church in 1952, the rhythm method can be recommended. Regarding the Roman Catholic position, he says that, in marriage instruction for Catholic couples, the rhythm method is considered a possible solution when a marriage is in trouble—for example, when a pregnancy or an addition to the family would cause insurmountable problems. Included in this book are "ten commandments for happier sexual togetherness". He actually gives eight "commandments" for the husband and eleven "commandments" for the wife:

Commandments for the husband

1. Be more attentive to your wife, even when you do not wish to commit coitus with her. Bring flowers for her occasionally. Let

her know that you appreciate her good care. Tell her sometimes that she looks nice when she is wearing new or different clothes. If you can afford it, allow her to have something new, and tell her that it makes you happy.

2. Prepare your wife for coitus. Don't start intercourse abruptly, but fondle her first; caress her breasts softly; kiss her behind her ears, in short try to find her "sensitive spots." You will find that this will give you satisfaction as well.

3. Do not turn away from your wife directly after coitus, but interest yourself in her a little longer. Women do not return to reality afterwards as quickly as men do. Allow her to stay a while in the ecstasy you have given her.

4. You can deeply insult some women by falling asleep immediately after the act of intercourse.

5. Try to cast off your (false) modesty toward your wife.

6. Do not let the sun rise on your wrath; if you have quarreled, make up with each other before you go to sleep.

7. Respect your wife's feelings, especially with regard to religion.

8. Don't blow little things out of proportion and don't bring up things that are over and done with.

Commandments for the wife

1. Be a wife to your husband and do not reject his sexual advances, but try to get closer to him.

2. Keep yourself clean, wash regularly, take care that you do not leave used sanitary pads lying around for him to see. Keep your clothing clean, especially your underclothes.

3. Make yourself pretty for your husband; keep trying to please him; occasionally wear something that is meant only for him, something that titillates his senses.

4. If your husband likes to see you in the nude, occasionally show yourself to him nude.

5. Cast off your (false) modesty toward him.

6. Do not bother your husband with trifles.

7. Try to be understanding of his bad moods and, without pressuring him to do so, allow him to talk about them, so that he can tell you what is bothering him.

8. Above all, never go on pouting over something he has done to you.

9. Try to suppress rising anger; anger generates anger.
10. Do not lose your dignity in your husband's eyes; spare him long speeches and endless, annoying crying binges.
11. Try to find out what he enjoys sexually and adapt yourself to it, without compromising yourself too much.

Images of Husband and Wife in these "ten commandments"

The husband desires coitus; prepares his wife for it; should interest himself in her for a while afterward; shouldn't fall asleep immediately afterward. Four of the eight commandments for husbands concern how he can satisfy his desire for coitus so that his wife also gets some enjoyment out of it. She must know that finding and caressing her sensitive areas gives him satisfaction. He is cared for by his wife and rewards her for it with flowers. He manages the money and allows her to have something new; his wife should know that this makes him happy. He is asked to *try* to cast off his (false) modesty toward his wife. The wife is told, "Cast off your (false) modesty toward him". The husband is expected not to stay angry too long and to make up the quarrels he makes. The wife must try to suppress her rising anger, because anger generates anger. But does his rage and his quarreling not cause anger? The wife must *above all* never pout over something he has done to her. Does this mean that wives must sit helplessly and pout, instead of quarreling and becoming angry? That is forbidden, as well. She must try to be understanding when he is in a bad mood. What about her bad moods? Are they included in her "trifles" with which she should not bother him? She must not lose her dignity in her husband's eyes through long speeches and annoying crying binges. When she has learned to repress her rising anger, and has learned not to sit and pout, and finds a release for her dissatisfaction by crying, that, too, is annoying to him. This kind of "commandment" limits the wife in every direction. Her sexuality is completely subordinate to that of her husband. She must not reject his sexual advances; must keep herself clean; make herself pretty for him; please him, and occasionally wear something that titillates his senses; show herself nude when it pleases him; and try to find out what he enjoys sexually and adapt herself to it without compromising herself too much. Apparently, the author realizes that a wife compromises herself by entering into this type of relationship with her husband.

Why do husbands not receive advice about their underwear and physical hygiene?

In his introduction, the author says that he felt no need to base his work on a particular philosophy. He does not realize that he is blind to the one-sided patriarchical thinking that has been and still is considered normal. As a result of his patriarchal way of looking at the world, his "ten commandments" are based on the feelings, needs, and wants of men. In his view, husbands are primarily seen as beings who are only out to have coitus with their wives, and who allow that to dominate all of their thinking and relations with their wives.

In this book, we also encountered the remark: "Conceiving a child is not something that is done rationally: It is the result of emotional circumstances that are governed by impulse instead of rational motives." Only men can reason in this way, men who have the power to make others responsible and to saddle them with the consequences of their one-sided reasoning on the subject of sexuality between man/husband and woman/wife.

Regarding brother–sister incest, we read on pages 82 and 83 of the same book: "The worst form of inbreeding is caused by pairing brothers and sisters, or parents and children." An example is cited of a woman who is married to a man who is sterile. Because she still wants to become a mother, she seeks intercourse with her unmarried brother. Her brother declines her proposal to make her pregnant, but he agrees to sex for mutual satisfaction. The woman sees to it that she becomes pregnant without her brother's knowledge. According to this example, the brother did not know about, and was therefore not responsible for, making his married sister pregnant.

Eve as Helpmate and Accused Whether the authors of texts on marriage and sexuality are Christian or not, the woman/wife—man/husband images are identical. The woman/wife exists for the man/husband; she serves the man/husband and his sexual needs. She is the servile help who exists solely for his sake. When a wrong such as incest is described, it is ascribed to the woman. As long as men dominate women, men have the power to use women in order to satisfy their needs and wants, to fulfill their wishes, and to make the women responsible for the consequences of (the men's) own behavior. The eternal Adam who needs a help meet and lays all blames on Eve. If Eve can see through this, she can teach Adam that he must also have regard for her needs and wants, and that she does not have to be/feel responsible for his behavior.

7

The Impact of
Religion

We asked the survivors: "What aspects of religion did
you experience as liberating?" Responses to this
question were often long silences and surprised looks. These were
frequently followed by a flood of words describing the problems
this woman had experienced with her church and her faith.

Eight women responded negatively to the question regarding
liberating aspects of religion. Joan, Christine, and Anne each
experienced problems with her church and the way her church
propagated the faith; Margaret felt that it was suffocating; Mary
Beth found it an unbearable burden; Amy said that it was very
depressing and triggered thoughts of suicide. Karen and Barbara
gave no response to the question. Charlotte said there was nothing
liberating about it.

The following aspects were considered liberating: the Bible
passage about Martha and Mary (Ellen and Christine); the
twelve-year-old Jesus in the temple (Joan and Judith); belief in God
in a way that they themselves experienced as positive (Cathy,
Amy, and Tina); that you could confess (Lisa and Theresa, but
incest was not confessed); belonging to a group (Carol); the bond
together, the peacefulness and quiet, the harmony of being
together (Ingrid); the choir (Theresa); the joy at the children's
church service (Christine and Nell [who attended with a girlfriend
but was later severely punished for doing so]); Sunday school
(Ingrid); Grandmother's children's Bible (Nell); the children's Bible
she bought herself, and praying in times of trouble and of joy
(Ingrid); respect for poor people with many children (Susan); the

atmosphere of harmony among the religious (Cathy); the biblical passage Romans 8 (Ellen); and the story of Esther (Susan).

The eight women who responded negatively to this question are significant. Their appreciation is primarily for the moments when they experienced warmth, affection, and togetherness in connection with their faith. As we saw earlier in the responses to the question "Where do you get your courage and strength?," we see here, too, that these women did not experience religion as a source of strength, encouragement, or rebellion against oppressive situations.

Oppressive Aspects   Following the question regarding the liberating aspects of faith came the question: "What aspects of religion did you experience as oppressive?" We deliberately posed the question in this way so that the women interviewed could give their own interpretation of religion or faith. Their answers show that their idea of faith consists primarily of what is written in the Bible; what was preached in the church; and what was said about faith at home and at school.

Responses   We have categorized the responses according to the following themes: women, God, values, Bible and church. When more than one theme applies, the responses appear under the corresponding themes.

Women   Women in the Bible were bad and mean, and all of them had something wrong with them (Ellen); were sinners (Karen); were supposed to be subservient to men (Christine and Mary Beth); were humiliated (Margaret); were portrayed as the symbol of evil and weakness. Woman is serpent, witch, and Eve (Margaret). She is guilty, and this can be traced back to Eve who tempted Adam (Susan). Women are seen in a negative light (Charlotte). As a woman, you had to be servile, inferior to men and sacrifice your own needs and desires; you had to suppress talents that weren't appropriate to your role (Mary Beth). As a woman, you didn't exist, you were unimportant, insignificant (Tina); you were to be seen and not heard (Barbara). The pastor blamed a woman if her husband drank (Ingrid).

God God is stern, he always makes you feel like a sinner
(Karen). He sees everything that happens and doesn't make it stop
in spite of all our praying (Lisa). God is almighty and merciful,
knows "this" (the incest), allows it to happen, and makes you do
penance for it. In doing so, he generates conflicting feelings and
makes it impossible for me to pray the Our Father (Cathy). He is
threatening and you can only do something good through his
mercy (Amy).

Values

— Honor thy father and mother (Joan).
— Love thy neighbor (Joan).
— Do not sin (Karen).
— Don't have any opinions of your own (Judith).
— Sacrifice your own needs and desires to the greater honor and
   glory of God (Judith).
— Don't be obstinate (Judith).
— As a woman, be secondary (Judith).
— Be obedient to the man (Judith).
— Have no say in matters (Anne).
— Be dependent upon the church (Anne).
— Don't think (Anne).
— Believe, even if you do so out of fear (Margaret).
— Because you're a girl: don't climb trees, don't do what you
   want, do the housework, don't run, walk quietly, be seen and
   not heard, be quiet (Barbara).
— Not doing anything fun (Nell).
— Not celebrating your birthday (Nell).
— Don't be sad, even if you're sad because someone has died
   (because that's not allowed either) (Nell).
— Be happy when someone dies (Nell).
— Reading aloud from the Bible constantly (Nell).
— Do not leave the church, because you will be damned (Susan).
— Go to church every Sunday (Lisa).
— Pray for hours on your knees (Lisa).
— Don't do unchaste things (Cathy).
— Don't have any opinions of your own (Cathy).
— Don't ask any questions (Cathy).

— Be good, even though it represses all of your energy (Theresa).
— Don't use your imagination (Theresa).
— Always pray to God (Theresa).
— Identify with the offender (Charlotte).
— Suppress your emotions (Carol).
— Not being yourself (Carol).
— Because you're a woman: being inferior to a man, being servile, sacrificing your own needs and wants. Suppressing talents which are not appropriate to your role (Mary Beth).
— Believe in God (Mary Beth).
— Not being happy and carefree (Amy).
— Walking heavily (Amy).
— Keeping your faith separate from the rest of your life, like incest (Ingrid).

Bible   Nine survivors mention Bible passages that they experienced as repressive. This particularly applies to the way in which women are portrayed in the Bible. Margaret also cites the passage about the angels who rejoice for the sinner who converts in the last minutes of his life. Such a person is welcomed in exultation in spite of the fact that he has led a life of sinful pleasure.

The Church and Its Lessons

— The church is hard, intolerant, and sexist (Ellen).
— It covers things up; people are afraid of it; it does not practice what it preaches; it gives people no say in matters; and keeps people dependent (Anne).
— We believed out of fear (Margaret).
— If you leave the church, you are damned (Susan).
— You must go to church every day (Lisa).
— You are not entitled to your own opinions and you must not ask questions (Cathy).
— It makes people believe that they are bad. It is suffocating and hypocritical (Amy).
— Children of unwed mothers are not allowed to be baptized. There's an elaborate show for the outside world: folk dancing, trumpet playing, singing and the occasional testimony to faith. Among the insiders, there's a lot of cursing and beer drinking at parties (Ingrid).

Breaking the Silence   In categorizing the responses to the oppressive aspects of religion, a picture emerges that corresponds to the total picture of the interviews when viewed as a whole. Significantly, there are numerous references to the negative images of women in the Bible, faith, church, and family. The statements on what one must do and how one was supposed to do it, what one could not do, and what was sinful, demonstrate a suffocating environment. It is tempting to those who are responsible for perpetuating these values to escape responsibility by claiming that these statements are one-sided, and negative, and that they have little in common with the original teachings of Christ. We share this opinion. These statements are one-sided, but they are the end result of what is taught to women and children in Christian churches. The incest survivors demonstrate the extreme negative impact these teachings have had on them. What they tell us is not in keeping with the life and the teachings of Christ, but this is because of the accompanying teachings they have received from the church. Women were and are supposed to be silent in many Christian churches when men preach the Word. Today, when women are allowed to speak, they must curry favor with men and the church, and repeat what men have asserted for centuries about men, women, and God. In this way, men repress women, which causes them suffering. Now that women are breaking this enforced silence, and are daring to speak out in their own words, they are holding a mirror before Christian churches in which this one-sided patriarchal teaching can be clearly seen. The incest survivors hold up this mirror by letting us see the impact of these church teachings on them.[1]

These survivors experienced their Christian upbringing primarily as oppressive. They experienced this oppression in the way women and girls were viewed; the values; and in the hard, intolerant, and hypocritical attitude of the church in which they are not entitled to their own opinions.

To those who are responsible for perpetuating the silence, or censured speech, of women, we offer two of Christ's teachings:

---

1. See, Dorothee Soelle *Fantasie en gehoorzaamheid* [Fantasy and Obedience] (Baarn, Ten Have, 1979), esp. her treatment of the hermeneutics of the Word of the Bible, unrelated to its effects and history.

Woe unto you also ye lawyers! for ye lade men with burdens grievous to be borne and ye yourselves touch not the burdens with one of your fingers (Luke 11:46).

Woe unto you lawyers! for ye have taken away the key of knowledge: ye entered not in yourselves and them that were entering in ye hindered (Luke 11:52).

The Correlation between Religion and Incest At the end of each interview, we asked: "What connection do you see between your religious upbringing and the sexual abuse you experienced?" These women were already talking about their religious upbringing in the course of the interview, so it was relatively easy for them to describe the correlation as they saw it.

These incest survivors indicated that their religious upbringing had contributed to causing the incest, to the conspiracy of silence surrounding it, and caused problems in working through the incest experience.

Through our interview with Carol, who was raised in an anti-religious background, and our conversations with other women who were not raised in religious backgrounds, we know that we cannot determine whether sexual abuse or the difficulties in working through it are more serious in Christian milieus or in non-Christian milieus. We can, however, show which factors played a role in causing incest in Christian milieus, and which factors played a role in working through it. Women raised in Christian backgrounds have the trauma of their incest experience as well as the trauma of their religious upbringing. Carol is burdened with her leftist, socialist upbringing. Women in both categories have difficulty with the ideology that was preached in their upbringing, which was at odds with the practice, and with their own experience.

In their responses, these women demonstrate numerous factors that made it possible for them to become incest victims. They indicate the impact of experiencing incest within a Christian upbringing. These consequences are related to gender roles; ideas regarding children, the ideal family, and the way Christians should behave; and the image of God.

Images of Women

— A woman is supposed to be humble, sacrificing, dutiful, loving, and have a sunny disposition (Ellen); subservient (Joan, Judith); willing and servile (Joan) and obedient to her husband (Karen, Judith).

— Women are sinners (Karen); temptresses (Nell, Charlotte); inferior and devious (Charlotte) and insignificant (Tina). They are kept under wraps, only to be brought out the moment there is any evildoing (Margaret). They are always the ones to blame (Susan).

— They are the possessions of men, objects without feelings, without a will of their own: "If they say no, they mean yes (Carol). The image of the ideal woman makes them easy prey for incest (Mary Beth). Religion and theology perpetuate the unjust system in which roles are imposed upon women, and they are then blamed for everything (Susan).

Images of Men

— Men commit incest because they are given a "Christian" view of women by the church. There is a discrepancy between the way men believe, what they preach, and how they translate their belief into actions (Joan).

— Father alludes to the image of the sinful woman as provided by the church. He believes that women should be obedient to men, and he does whatever he wants (Karen).

— The man is the head of the family and makes the decisions; women and girls must be subservient to him (Judith).

— Although Father committed incest, the farce of the model family was upheld to the outside world because of Father's position in the church (Christine).

— Christianity is male-oriented. Men are little boys who have to have their own way. There is no room for discussion. They are allowed to be brusque and say, "This is what I want." The family says that you mustn't wash dirty linen in public. That provides the offender with security (Charlotte).

— Men see women as possessions and as objects without feelings or wills of their own. Socialism and communism are typical male cultures. The sexual revolution in leftist circles was primarily advantageous to men. They don't discuss the ideology behind it, but ridicule the churches where women have no say (Carol).

Children

— Children must honor their father and mother (Joan).
— They must be obedient and loving, honor their father and mother and do what they are told. They must not talk back or be obstinate (Judith).
— You weren't allowed to cry when your father abused you, that was rebelling against Father and against God (Nell).
— In church, at school, and in the prayer books, you were taught that you had to honor your Father and Mother (Lisa).

Family

— To the outside world, the farce of the ideal family was upheld because of Father's position (Christine).
— In the Roman Catholic church, the family is sacred. The family is the only place sexuality is permitted. Father had his way in the family and said that it was not to be discussed outside the family, because that would be the end of the family (Cathy).
— In the Dutch Reformed congregation, you're not allowed to wash the dirty family linen in public. You must take care of it within the privacy of your home (Charlotte).
— Gender roles, even in a socialist family, are predetermined (Carol).

Christian Duties

— You must love your neighbor. Not much attention was paid to standing up for yourself (Ellen).
— You must always be the first to forgive and you must do so seventy times seventy times (Judith).
— You must always serve, serve God. Sexuality before and outside of marriage is bad (Margaret).
— Faith and standing up for yourself are conflicting concepts (Theresa).
— You must sacrifice your own needs and wants, you mustn't resist, mustn't stand up for yourself, must serve God, mustn't be your own person with your own ego (Amy).
— You must forgive (Ingrid).

God

— She never saw any indication that God existed (Barbara).

— She prayed to God that it would stop, but He didn't intervene. That meant that the incest was God's will and must be good for something, or must be punishment for her badness (Nell).

— Father said that God saw the incest and that it was good for her. She prayed that God would intervene, but because nothing happened, she thought that it must have some purpose, that God was punishing her because she had provoked it. Later on, she closed her mind to everything, and she saw that, too, as punishment from God (Lisa).

— You could receive God's forgiveness for the incest by being very good afterward (Mary Beth).

— God created people. People must serve Him. He determines what happens in your life. You are not allowed to be your own person with your own ego. That is why the incest happened (Amy).

— She does not let her belief in God be taken away from her (Tina).

The Cover of Christian Silence   One of the most striking characteristics is the over-developed feeling of responsibility these women have for their parents', brothers', and sisters' well-being. They take care that the family's public image is not disturbed. They let themselves be sexually abused, and they keep silent about it. They adhere to the norms prescribed for girls with a Christian upbringing, and are thus easy prey for sexual abuse by male family members; they are blamed for this transgression, and learn that they must forgive unconditionally and endlessly. Their silence is forced, because the family will otherwise collapse, as Cathy's father said. It is more difficult to talk about incest than to commit the act itself, because talking about it is washing one's dirty linen in public. The offenders are protected. The offender and the family place the responsibility for the consequences of incest on the victim. She is at fault when the family becomes the subject of discussion due to incest, because she has broken the conspiracy of silence.

The Problem of Christian Guilt   Judith excused her father, and felt that the responsibility for his behavior lay with herself or her mother. She thought that her behavior provoked the incest and that her mother was not adequately fulfilling her wifely sexual duties. Christine says that religion played a strange role. Father felt guilty and bad. Mother glossed over a lot of things. Anne believes that the consequences of incest would have been less serious had she not been brought up in such a strictly dogmatic faith. Issues would have been more out in the open, talked about. She felt guilty for a long time, because she was no longer "immaculate"— no longer a virgin. This gave her the feeling that she had no rights whatsoever. Margaret indicates that, because of religious attitudes toward sex, she has had much more difficulty with her sexual abuse by her brother. It has left her deathly afraid of everything. She thought that they would both go to hell, but she has never been able to talk about it until now. Barbara thought that she was bad, and for this reason had to go through all of this. Nell thought that she was bad and that incest was her punishment from God, or that he meant the incest to have a special purpose. Lisa thought that God had a special purpose, too, or was punishing her because she had provoked it herself. Lisa did not talk to anyone about it, because she did not want to be responsible for breaking up the family. The ideal of the model woman did not anger Mary Beth, but it made her easy prey for incest, leaving her afterward with the feeling that she was bad. Amy has only recently been able to feel anger about her incest experience. Ingrid felt guilty when she became pregnant by her father, because "it" then became visible.

Ten survivors say that they were plagued by guilt feelings. They thought that they had provoked it, that they were bad, and were therefore being punished by God. Because of their Christian upbringing and the powerful positions of their offenders, girls are not only easy prey for sexual abuse, but also scapegoats. Male family members in Christian milieus are in a position to abuse sexually girls within the family, blame them for their own violent crime, and make them responsible for the consequences of their deeds. We believe that the myth of the sinful woman, which is still propagated by Christian churches, not only brings out male domination over women, but intensifies it. We see this as a form of psychological or mental rape, which facilitates the physical rape of girls and women and makes the impact more serious. Feelings of sinfulness and guilt, which women are talked into, undermine their self-confidence. Self-confidence and self-respect are needed to be able to build defenses against dominant men.

Did Christianity Cause the Incest?

Gender roles and the position of the survivors from Christian milieus were identical to those in the anti-religious family. The anti-religious father accuses the churches of repressing women, but he determines the norms in his own family; the inferior position of women is not open to discussion. We were grateful for this interview when we discovered that "progressive" nonreligious people often commented that they could understand why it occurs more often in religious backgrounds. This "progressive" reaction is characteristic of all milieus. In all of the milieus represented in our interviews, men and women could imagine that sexual abuse occurred in another milieu, but they were convinced that the situation was different in their own context. A Catholic man responded, "It doesn't exist in the circles I move in. I'm sure of that." When we asked what circles he moved in, he replied; "Well, in discussion groups, and I go to parish functions." Two women from Dutch Reformed churches could imagine that incest occurred in the milieu of one of the interviewers: "Well, yes, you're Catholic, aren't you? I can understand that something like that could happen in such a strict religious milieu, but that could never happen in our Dutch Reformed congregations."

Through counseling and through the conversations we conducted alongside the interviews for this study in the Netherlands, we know that incest occurs often. In 1984, clinical psychologist Nel Draijer estimated that five to fifteen percent of the girls in the Netherlands are sexually abused within the family. When we present information on our study, we are no longer surprised when one out of six to ten women tells us that she was sexually abused as a young girl. This means that there are also many offenders, but because offenders often abuse more than one girl, there are fewer offenders than victims.

Knowing that this abuse occurs so frequently, we should ask ourselves: What is structurally wrong with our society? What causes and perpetuates these structural flaws? Through this study, we have found a provisional answer with regard to causes and their impact on women in Christian milieus. The values, norms, and images in our patriarchal society have influenced Christianity, and Christianity has provided the patriarchal mentality with a divine legitimacy. Christianity has increasingly identified itself with the patriarchal mentality, so that in time, a person could hardly be a Christian without a patriarchal mentality. In this patriarchal mentality, the basic premise is that women are inferior to men and that women should therefore obey men. Anti-religious men also subscribe to this "Christian" view.

The patriarchal deterioration of Christianity began with Paul. (Theologians call him the first "real" theologian.) Paul's writings that are included in the Bible show a chronological line from equality between women and men in Galatians 3:28 to misogyny in 1 Timothy 2:8–15.[2] It is rather extraordinary that a misogynistic passage such as 1 Timothy 2:8–15 is included in the New Testament, while texts such as the Acts of Thecla and Paul, and the Teachings of the Twelve Apostles are not. Thecla lived in the time of Paul according to the Acts. She was inspired by him to preach the Gospel.[3] These Acts serve as proof that women could be priests, because Paul himself had appointed women apostles.[4] The Acts were declared apocryphal several times by Tertullian among others who wanted to keep women out of clerical office.

Passages from Paul have been misused for centuries to keep women out of clerical office and to enforce silence upon them. Christian churches have been violating fundamental human rights in this way for centuries, particularly women's right to freedom of opinion. They have chosen the side of the dominant group in society: domineering men. The result is that they have legitimated and stimulated the denial of and contempt for women by propagating this morality to men and women. Christian churches did not propagate this morality with the intent to stimulate men to

2. Also see, G. Bouwman, *De vrouwelijke waarden in de theologie van Paulus* [Feminine Values in the Theology of Paul] (Averbode: Altiora, 1981), pp. 154–55.

3. See, for example, A. Imbens, *Thekla en de kerk* [Thekla and the Church] Protestantse Stichting tot Bevordering van het Bibliotheekwezen en de Lectuur-voorlichting, 1984).

4. R. Beurmanjer and M. de Groot, *Twee emmers water halen* [Two Jars of Water] (Haarlem: Uitgeversmaatschappij, Holland, 1982, pp. 27–41.

abuse sexually girls in their (immediate) family, but sexual abuse of girls *is* the ultimate consequence of a church-propagated morality which devalues women and makes them inferior to men.

We see the stories and the statements of the incest survivors as an indictment of society and the churches for permitting the suffering of these and other women. We hope that Christian churches will have the courage to acknowledge their part in this. It is the first step toward taking measures to alleviate this suffering and to prevent it in the future.

8

An Approach to Pastoral Counseling for Incest Survivors

When a priest or minister is approached by an incest survivor, various factors can interfere with the subsequent counseling. In this section, I identify and describe a number of these factors using statements made by the women we interviewed and from the conversations we conducted during follow-up counseling.

Problems in Pastoral Counseling When the minister or priest with whom a woman wants to talk about her incest experience personally knows the woman's family and offender, he or she may feel a need to deny the incident or to play it down and blame the victim. In her interview, Judith related how an assistant priest responded at the time: "I realize that teenagers sometimes fantasize, but what you've told me is incredible. It's absolutely impossible that your father, who's done so much for the church, could do something like that. I mean, some teenagers tend to get carried away by their imaginations, but there's no way what you're telling me could be true. You've really got to get some help; this is out of hand. Your father does so much for the church. He would never do anything against the law." The priest refused even to consider the possibility that her father would commit such an act, because he did so much for the church. He then accused the girl of having wild and dangerous fantasies.

Anne's chaplain knew her family and tried to play down the events. When she indicated how deeply troubled she was by what had happened, he told her that, theologically speaking, there was absolutely no problem with innocent little sex games between a brother and sister. He refused to take the victim seriously, or her feelings about being abused. He protected the offender and the other members of the family and left the survivor standing in the cold.

A second problem is the concept that men have a right to sexuality and that married women have a duty to satisfy their husbands' sexual needs. This concept still troubles priests and ministers and women who have been subjected to incest. Because of this, they are sometimes more accusatory toward the mother than toward the father who has committed the sexual abuse. They think that Father committed the sexual abuse because Mother failed to perform her marital duties. We observe that pastors sometimes intensify the survivor's negative feelings toward her mother, while believing that the offender had the right to a good relation, to forgiveness, and reconciliation.

A third factor that can interfere with counseling is the tendency to view family relationships primarily in terms of love and harmony, and to ignore the sources of conflict that can arise from unbalanced family power dynamics.

Another factor is that pastors sometimes feel the need to defend the church, its teachings, and God, whenever women want to talk about their traumatic experiences related to religion. Whenever a woman says that in her experience, the church fails in the real world to practice what it preaches, the response is: "But what exactly do you mean by 'the church'? The church is all of us. The church is made up of regular people, not just leaders of the clergy. You mustn't pay so much attention to the church as an institution or to the hierarchical system." This woman is given the impression that she is not suffering from oppressive teachings of the church, but from her own misconceptions about what the church actually is. When a woman says that she has difficulty with the concept of forgiveness as it is viewed by the church, she is told that she is interpreting the word "forgiveness" incorrectly. The fact that forgiveness is a much-discussed theme in churches is ignored. The pastor defends the church and what it preaches and the woman who is experiencing difficulties is implicitly told that her problems do not arise from these teachings but from her own incorrect understanding of forgiveness. When a woman says that her experience of God is as some "one" who is threatening and oppressive, a pastor typically responds: "But what you're describing isn't God! That is a false god. That is what some people have made of God." This is the image of God that is projected in Christian churches, schools, and families, that is conveniently forgotten. People often continue to have problems with this image. These problems are not solved by suggesting that they are due to the person's own misconceptions about God.

The final factor that can interfere with incest counseling is many incest survivors' attitude toward faith and church. They have been traumatized by their incest experience and by their Christian upbringing. Because of this, they often have an aversion to everything that has to do with faith and the church. They do not want to talk about it anymore or to hear anything about it. But they still have problems with their religious upbringing. Many have guilt feelings, a fear of God, and a belief that they have no rights. This fear of God arises at inopportune moments or when there are other problems. Survivors also know that most people think it ridiculous to have religious problems. In traditional therapy and in psychiatric institutions, these problems often remain unaddressed. A woman who goes to talk to a minister or priest about the religious aspects of her incest experience may not want to talk about it, but has so many problems with it that she cannot ignore it.

Recommendations from a Church Context   One of the conditions for good pastoral counseling is acknowledging one's own capabilities and incapabilities. Not every priest or minister is able to or prepared to counsel women who have experienced incest. He or she can, with the woman's cooperation, arrange for counseling by someone else.

When a priest or minister knows the family of the sexually abused woman, he or she should consider whether this will interfere with his or her ability to provide good counseling. He or she can indicate this to the woman and, with her consent, arrange for other counseling.

Child sexual abuse in families is a subject that many people find repulsive. It is difficult for them to put their feelings aside and allow the reality and the consequences of sexual abuse to register. Ministers or priests who have difficulty with this should simply say so and help the woman arrange for other counseling.

When a woman receives pastoral counseling, the problems should become clear in the first session. What does she expect to get out of these sessions? Agreements should also be made as to the length of the counseling. Usually, three or four sessions are sufficient.

During the sessions, the conversation should be devoted to the problem as stated by the woman and not to the problem as perceived by the priest or minister. For example, when a woman goes to a minister or priest because she feels afraid of God, it is frustrating for both parties when the priest or minister assumes that they must work toward repairing the woman's relationship with the offender, or must teach the woman to forgive the now deceased offender. In such situations, it is not the woman's problems that are being addressed, but the problems the minister or priest has with incest. Incest survivors have internalized the images that have been projected onto them, particularly by fathers who committed sexual abuse: for example, images of God, the Bible, women, and their own mothers. They have learned to see reality through the eyes of the offender. Through counseling, they can become aware of this, learn to let go of this way of looking at the world, and learn to look at it through their own eyes.

Counseling should concentrate on the woman's problems and feelings. She must get the room she needs to free herself from her problems with her experience and her religious upbringing. She needs to be able to express her negative feelings toward the church, her faith, and God. Counselors of incest survivors must be able to accept this. If they are unable to do this, they must be able to say so and to help the woman arrange for other counseling. When the ministers or priests are unable to understand the way the woman views God and the church, and consequently launch into a defense of both, they cannot give the woman the room she needs to let go of those aspects of religion that repress her.

Priests or ministers should only relate their own views of certain religious issues when the woman seeks their opinion. They should refrain from overwhelming her with every detail they know about the subject, and should only answer the specific question the woman asks. Furthermore, they should indicate that these are simply their own opinions and there are others who think differently. When they can also explain how they arrived at that particular standpoint, the woman feels that she is considered an equal partner in the discussion. Even when the counseling takes place on equal footing, mistakes can still occur during the conversations. These will be indicated by the woman. When the ministers or priests conduct the counseling with the attitude that they know what is good for the woman, the basic foundation for good counseling is lacking.

Methods
Two major theological issues often concern incest survivors: fear of God, and forgiveness. I explore some counseling methods, ways of handling specific Bible passages, and ways of dealing with the survivor's contempt for her mother.

Fear of God. The survivors had problems with the way they had learned to view God. They saw God as a terrifying and all-powerful ruler who always kept an eye on them and who was always looking for something for which to punish them. They were bad and had no right to a happy existence. When we become aware that a woman suffers from this oppressive image of God, we try to allow her to explain how she sees God by asking questions. We then ask her what feelings God evokes in her. We never say that she sees God in the wrong light or that what she is seeing as God is actually a false god. We do not talk about that God, nor do we try to convince her that it would be better if she looked at God in another light. First, we give her room to put her fear of God into words, to write it down, or to draw it. We encourage her to acknowledge and express her anger, her rage. We indicate that we understand her feelings of anger and rage. We ask her how she came to view God in this manner.

Then we let her give God, of whom she is afraid, a place in her life. We name the offender who sexually abused her, and one or both parents, and we ask who is on whose side. The terrifying God is always on the offender's side. We ask her whether she can imagine that God would choose her side and stand by her side. The angry feelings this evokes are then given as much space as necessary. A number of times we found that she identified God with the offender. When this became apparent, we asked, "Who are you talking about now, God or the offender?" Together we concluded that God and the offender seemed alike in many ways and that the images of God and the woman's father or the offender sometimes blur together. In this way, we overcome her fear of God and find room for another way of thinking about God. We see that, after a few sessions, God acquires a different place with regard to the offender and the abused woman. When the woman has the feeling that God is behind her or at her side across from the offender, she is no longer afraid and can muster more defenses against the offender. God is then on her side and not on that of her rapist. He no longer acts as an undermining force on her, but as a liberating and encouraging force. He helps her to doubt herself less and to believe in herself more.

Bible passages. A number of women have problems with Bible passages that keep coming back to haunt them, or remember Bible passages that oppressed them. In these instances we ask the woman to write down the passages that come to mind. First, the passage concerning the woman who was sentenced to stoning (John 8:1–11). Then, passages from Deuteronomy, in particular Deuteronomy 9:3–6, which explains that God destroys the godless; Deuteronomy 22:13–30: "But if this thing be true, and the tokens of virginity be not found for the damsel: Then they shall bring out the damsel to the door of her father's house, and the men of her city shall stone her with stones that she die: because she hath wrought folly in Israel, to play the whore in her father's house: so shalt thou put evil away from among you" (Deut. 22:20–21); and: "When men strive together one with another, and the wife of the one draweth near for to deliver her husband out of the hand of him that smiteth him, and putteth forth her hand, and taketh him by the secrets: Then thou shalt cut off her hand, thine eye shall not pity her" (Deuteronomy 25:11-12).

It is obvious that a girl who has been sexually abused by an older brother and hears such a passage is consumed by fear. We ask her how she came across this passage, when she heard it for the first time, who read the passage aloud, and what she felt when she first heard it. The more she is able to express her feelings by talking about it, writing it down, or drawing it, the more she can release her suppressed anger. Survivors feel "relieved" after such sessions, to use their own word. Only when they expressed a need to know, do we tell them a little about the way such a passage came about and its background.

Feelings toward Mother.   We found during our conversations that women had a tendency to hate and be contemptuous of their mothers more than the man who had sexually abused them. It was relatively easy for them to talk about these negative feelings. They also indicated why they had such problems with their mothers' behavior and at the same time continued to excuse their offenders. For example; "Mother was not fulfilling her sexual duties in the marriage—Father wasn't getting his due"; "Mother was sick all the time—she was of no use to Father"; "Mother was so weak, she didn't set any limits on Father's behavior. She didn't make it stop—Father needed someone to draw the line." During our conversations with priests or ministers, we saw that they intensified the sexually abused women's attitude toward their mothers and their offenders. Ministers and priests considered it particularly important that the women learn to forgive the offender, while these women often lacked the courage to blame the offender for his behavior. "I don't want to hate my father," one woman said, whose father had physically abused her and raped her repeatedly. She thought that her father's behavior was her mother's fault. Mother should have put an end to it. "I have more of a problem with my mother," this woman told us.

We find that it is easier for a woman to talk about her mother than her offender, so we primarily ask questions about the mother that keep leading us back to the offender. For example, "Why do you have such a problem with your mother?"; "You told her what your father was doing to you and she didn't make it stop?"; "Could she have stopped it then?"; "Why not?"; "What do you think she could have done?"; "Would that have helped?"; "Why not?"; "Then why do you blame her for it?"; "What do you blame your father for?"; "Didn't it bother you that he hit you and abused you?"; "Does it still bother you?"; "What is it that still bothers you?"; "Whose fault is that?"; "Could your mother have stopped it?"; "Who could have stopped it?"; "But you don't want to hate him?"; "Whom do you hate?"; "Why is that?"; "How do you feel about that?"

After a number of sessions and a long period of time following the counseling, we see that the attitude toward Mother begins to change. Sometimes this leads to more understanding for the mother's situation; other times it leads to their shared sorrow over what has happened.

Problems in Writing this Chapter As a result of the conversations we conducted with these women, I know that it is impossible to put into words the destructive impact on girls of patriarchal teachings and values. I had difficulty putting our methods on paper, because in doing so, I recalled the pain, sorrow, and rage they unleashed. I have written them down in the hope that they will help incest survivors, and many other women, to find the room to be heard.[1]

1. For additional literature on pastoral counseling, see: Mary F. Belenky, *Women's Ways of Knowing: The Development of Self, Voice, and Mind* (New York: Basic Books, 1988); Marie M. Fortune, *Sexual Violence, The Unmentionable Sin: An Ethical and Pastoral Perspective* (New York: Pilgrim Press, 1983); Emily Hancock, *The Girl Within: A Groundbreaking New Approach to Female Identity* (New York: Dutton, 1989). Imbens, J. E. L. Fransen, "It is better (not) to talk about it (*Daar kun je maar beter (niet) over praten*), Delft 1987. Imbens, J. E. L. Fransen, Hold not thy peace, my brother (*Nu dan, mijn broeder, spreek erover*) Amsterdam, 1991. Bons, M. Storm, *How are you? Pastoral Care as coming to understanding* [Hoe gaat het met jou? Pastoraat als komen tot verstaan] (Kampen, Kok 1989). Bons, M. Storm, *Feminist Pastoral Care: A Challenge to the Churches* (Vrouwenpastoraat, Kampen, Kok 1992).

Epilogue

One of the reasons we conducted this study was in order to formulate questions addressed to Christian churches. The idea was that incest survivors would be supported by feminist theologians in order to facilitate their approach to church authorities. During the study, there were times when we doubted whether we still wanted to ask questions of the Christian churches. We wondered whether churches would ever be willing to acknowledge the denial of and contempt for women that is harbored in their midst. We see this as an initial step, as a precondition for abolishing the second-class position women occupy in the church and society. In our view, the next step is that Christian churches confess their responsibility for this situation, beginning with the women who have suffered the most as a result of patriarchal theology and morality. The last step is a conversion in Christian churches from a sexist theology toward women to a liberating theology, which includes women.

We even view these questions that we address to the Christian churches as a sign of hope. In spite of all of the misery we have heard from women in the past year, and in spite of the painful experiences that we ourselves have undergone in the church anew, we do not want to give up the fight. We will keep pressing for change in the position of women in the church.

To all Christians We ask all Christian people to consider:

— What causes so many Christian men to think that they have a right to the sexuality of all of the women in their family?
— What leads so many Christian mothers and daughters to think that they are only on this earth to serve men?
— If God created man and woman in the divine image and likeness, then how can one half of that image and likeness be inferior to the other half?

To Church Leaders Church leaders have more power than ordinary Christians. They can stimulate or delay change.

Because of their powerful position, they are more responsible than lay Christians for the impact of oppressive systems. With regard to this study and to the many signals women have given in the past, we ask church leaders:

— to open their eyes to contempt for and violence against women;
— not to abuse the right to freedom of religion in order to exclude and silence women;
— to acknowledge the contempt for women in their own midst, which results in part from their policy, and to confess their responsibility for it;
— to stop silencing women and denying them their own space in the church;
— to take measures and design policies finally to put an end to the contempt for women in Christian churches in the very near future;
— to appeal to society to abolish contempt for and abuse of women through their own attitude and behavior.

To Laypeople   Church policy must be supported by the congregation. Along with church authorities, its members are responsible for practicing the policy implemented by the church. Patriarchal, hierarchical, and sexist theology and policy can be practiced as long as lay Christians raise no objections. We ask Christian laypeople the following:

— What contributions can they make to abolish the contempt for women in Christian churches?
— What response can they make to policies and statements that discriminate against women?
— How can they stimulate policies and statements that liberate women and men?
— How can they inspire women and men who work toward abolishing women's second-class position in Christian churches?
— What steps can they take right away?

To Seminaries and Graduate Schools

— What are the job prospects for women who have an education in theology?

— What measures must be taken to ensure that future theologians, priests, and ministers are not solely educated in traditional theology, which examines reality primarily from the standpoint of the experiences and insights of men?

— What contributions have been made to date by seminaries and graduate schools toward acknowledging and abolishing the existing contempt for women in Christian churches?

— What research can be stimulated in this direction?

In Closing   After deciding to pose these questions, we reformulated them several times. We did not want our questions to offend anyone unnecessarily. Nevertheless, through our talks and interviews, we know that Christian morals and theology have worked against women. We condemn this violence against women and hold those who have contributed to it responsible for their actions. This violation of women now lies exposed; if we cover it up again with "Christian" love because we lack the courage to hold someone responsible, nothing will change. When women have been able to tell us their stories, we have listened to these stories with understanding, and yet we perpetuate the subordinate position of women in the church and society because we fear the reactions of people who feel that this is directed at them or who feel accused.

After listening to these women's stories, we are prepared to deal with this fear. Their stories also give us strength to keep hoping and pressing for change in Christian churches. The encouragement and hopeful reactions we receive from people in various churches are an additional source of support in this endeavor. Some of these people told us that, upon reading the survivor's stories and contemplating them, their first reaction was to defend their own church. We hope that Christians will have the courage to let these stories touch them and will be ultimately inspired to work toward changing the position of women in society and in the church.

Appendix

Family Background
1. Date of birth, place of birth
2. Mother's profession, education
3. Father's profession, education
3a. Offender's profession, education
4. Date of parents' marriage, date of divorce (if applicable)
5. Mother's religion
6. Father's religion
6a. Offender's religion
7. Number of children: girls, boys
8. Children's educations and professions, including survivor
9. According to age, survivor is the family's ___ child.
9a. Did you have the feeling you were wanted?
10. For which political party did your mother vote?
11. For which political party did your father vote?
11a. For which political party did the offender vote?
12. What papers and magazines were read at home?
13. To which clubs did the parents and children (and offender) belong?
14. Which programs did the family watch and listen to on the television and radio?
15. Of what denomination were the schools the children attended?
16. Who visited your parents: Family, friends? Who visited you? Whom did you take home?
17. Where and how do you live now?

Incest Experience
Would you like to talk about your incest experience now or would you rather talk about it later on?
Who was the offender?
How old were you? How old was the offender?

What happened? How did you experience that?

Was violence involved?

What kind of coercion was used?

Where was your mother/father when it happened?

What made you think that it wasn't right?

How has it affected the rest of your life? Were other family members (other generations) also sexually abused? Who were they?

Why did it happen?

Were you able to talk about it? Why or why not? To whom did you try to talk?

Power Dynamics within the (Extended) Family

Can you tell a little about the relationships within your family?

— wife/husband
— mother/father
— sister/brother
— younger/older
— grandfather, uncle, etc. (if applicable)

How did your father see your mother and vice versa? How did your father and mother see the offender and vice versa (if applicable)?

How did you see your father and mother (and offender, if applicable) and vice versa?

Can you tell a little about the power dynamics in your (extended) family?

Who made decisions (examples)?

How were these decisions made?

How did your father and mother (and the offender, if applicable) get their own way?

How did you get your own way?

Did your (extended) family get outside help when there were problems?

Was faith experienced similarly or differently in the (extended) family, school, and church?

Religion in the (Extended) Family

Can you tell a little about the role religion played in your family?

What did faith mean to your father and mother (and the offender, if applicable)? What did it mean to you?

Church attendance: voluntary, taken for granted, or coerced? Who went?

When praying from whom did you learn? How did you pray (standard or own words)?

When Bible reading who read aloud? Which passages were read? From which Bible were they taken? Were they accompanied by interpretations?

Visits from church members: who visited, why did they visit? Were you present?

Positions in church: Did your mother or father (or offender, if applicable) hold a position in the church at the time? Do they now? Did you hold a position or do you now?

Religion and School

Can you tell a little about the religious atmosphere at the school(s) you attended?

What did teachers talk about at school regarding religion (for example, good and evil, the Bible, unbelievers, Christians and the world, politics and history)?

What role did the Bible play in religion at school?

What images of women did you get from these stories (Bible, saints, martyrs, and so on)?

Who taught the religion lessons (lay teacher, nun, priest, minister)?

Religion and Church

Can you tell a little about the religious atmosphere in the church you and your family attended?

What was the image of the ideal woman and the ideal man in the church? What was the image of the ideal mother and the ideal father?

How did they see motherhood and fatherhood? Did your parents read Christian literature about parenthood (for example, magazines such as "Mother" [Dutch Reformed]) or "Marriage and Family" (Catholic)?

What image of people in general did you get from the church (for example, good, salvation through baptism, bad, original sin; we [churchgoers] good, they [outside the church] bad)?

Do you remember passages, stories, or figures from the Bible (Old Testament, New Testament, Paul's writings)?

Were they inspiring, exciting, awful?
How do you feel about religion now?

Attitudes toward Sexuality
Were messages about sexuality similar or different at home, at school, and at church?
Can you tell a little about how nudity, menstruation, pregnancy, tenderness, and cuddling were handled at home?
What was the response to questions on these subjects?
What was the reaction when someone had to get married?
What kind of sex education did you receive (at home, at school, at church, or elsewhere)?
Who gave it?
What was your reaction?
About what or whom were you warned? Why?
How was sexuality supposed to be? How did you learn that? What was your family model?
Was sexuality beautiful, dirty, scary? How did you know that?
Was sexuality for women as well as men?
Who got pleasure from it?
Who was responsible for it? For what exactly?
Who had to have respect for whom?
Who took the initiative? How was that supposed to be done?

Incest Experience
Would you like to talk about your incest experience now?
Who was the offender?
How old were you? How old was the offender?
What happened? How did you experience that (nature of the abuse)?
Was violence involved?
What kind of coercion was used?
Where was your mother/father when it happened?
What made you think that it wasn't right?
How has it affected the rest of your life?
Were other family members (and other generations) also sexually abused? Who were they?
Why did it happen?
Were you able to talk about it? Why or why not? To whom did you try to talk?

Survivor's Views

What connection do you think religion had with the way physicality and sexuality were handled in your house (correlation)?

What connection do you see between your religious upbringing and your incest experience?

What does your faith have to do with your incest experience?

What aspects of religion did you experience as liberating?

What aspects of religion did you experience as oppressive?

What do you associate with these words?

  good
  evil
  guilt
  responsibility
  forgiveness (when to forgive)
  love thy neighbor (as thyself?)
  injustice
  sexuality
  incest/sexual abuse
  obedience
  love
  trust

Why did it happen and why did you keep silent about it at the time? Do you see a connection with your religious upbringing?

What is the most important aspect you see in this context?

How were you able to stop it, or how did it stop?

Do you see a connection between your resistance, breaking your silence, and your faith?

Did you have inspiring role models in your surroundings or in your faith?

What do you believe in? Where do you get your courage and strength?

Bibliography

Achterhuis, H., *The Market of Well-being and Happiness* [De markt van welzijn en geluk]. Baarn 1980.

Acker, H., and M. Rawie, *Sexual Violence Against Women and Girls* (Seksueel Geweld tegen vrouwen en meisjes). Ministry for Social Affairs and Employment, The Hague, 1982.

Amnesty International, *Torture: Manmade* [Martelen is mensenwerk]. Amsterdam, 1984.

Armstrong, K., *The Gospel According to Women, Christianity's Creation of the Sex War in the West.* New York, 1987.

Association Against Child Sexual Abuse Within the Family, *The Sentence for Silence is Life* [De straf op zwijgen is levenslang]. Amsterdam, 1983.

Badinter, E., *L'Amour En Plus: Histoire de l'amour maternel XVII–XX Siècle* [De mythe van de moederliefde]. Trans. Utrecht, 1983.

Belenky, M. Field, *Women's Ways of Knowing: The Development of Self, Voice and Mind.* U.S.A., 1986.

Beurmanjer, R., and M. de Groot, *Two Jars of Water* [Twee emmers water halen]. Haarlem, 1982.

Bible, *The Authorized (King James) Version of the Holy Bible.* Trinitarian Bible Society, London, various editions.

Bible, *The Holy Bible with Analysis, Explanatory Notes, Evengelical Reflections, Etc. by the Late Rev. John Brown,* Minister of the Gospel at Haddington (East Lothian, Scotland), printed and published by Brightly and Childs at Bungay, 1813.

Bible, *The Jerusalem Bible,* Reader's Edition. Doubleday, New York and Darton, Longman and Todd, London, 1971.

Bible, *New World Translation of the Holy Scriptures,* Revised. Watchtower Bible and Tract Society (Jehovah's Witnesses), Brooklyn, New York, 1984.

Bible, *The Revised Standard Version of the Holy Bible.* William Collins Sons & Co, Glasgow and New York, 1946, 1952, 1971.

Bible, *The Thompson Chain Reference Bible*, 5th Improved Edition. B. B. Kirkbridge Bible Co., Indianapolis, Indiana, 1988.

Bloem, M., *Problems in Caring Services* [Knelpunten in de hulpverlening]. Social sciences thesis, Utrecht, 1983.

Bons, M. Storm., *How are you? Pastoral Care as coming to understanding* [Hoe gaat het met jou? Pastoraat als komen tot verstaan]. Kampen, 1989.

Bons, M. Storm., *Feminist Pastoral Care: A Challenge to the Churches*. Vrouwenpastoraat, Kampen, 1992.

Bots, M., and M. Noorman, *The Balm of Motherhood* [Moederschap als balsem]. Amsterdam, 1981.

Bots, M., and C. Verheijen, *Motherhood, A Report on Scientific Research Conducted on Motherhood* [Moederschap. Trendrapport over wetenschappelijk onderzoek op het gebied van moederschap]. The Hague, 1983.

Bouwman, G., *Feminine Values in the Theology of Paul* [De vrouwelijke waarden in de theologie van Paulus]. Averbode, 1981.

Brownmiller, S., *Against Our Will: Men, Women and Rape*. New York, 1976.

Bullinga, M., *The Army Makes A Man of You* [Het leger maakt een man van je]. Nijmegen, 1984.

Carter Heyward, I., *Touching Our Strength: The Erotic as Power of the Erotic and the Love of God* [Lecture on book of the same title]. University of Grongingen, Grongingen (Netherlands), 1989.

Chodorow, N., *The Reproduction of Mothering, Psychoanalysis and the Sociology of Gender*, Berkeley, 1978 [Waarcom vrouwen moederen]. Translation, Amsterdam, 1980.

Christ, C. P., *Diving Deep and Surfacing, Women Writers on Spiritual Quest*. Boston, 1980.

Clanton, Jann Aldredge, *In Whose Image? God and Gender*. New York, 1990.

Coles, R., *The Spiritual Life of Children*. Boston, 1990.

Daly, M., *Beyond God the Father, Toward a Philosophy of Women's Liberation*. Boston, 1973.

Daly, M., *Gyn/Ecology, The Metaethics of Radical Feminism*. London, 1979.

De Neef, C. E. J., and S. J. De Ruiter, *Report on Sexual Violence against Women Refugees: Report on the nature and impact of sexual violence undergone by these women elsewhere* [Rapport sexueel geweld tegen vrouwelijke vluchtelingen]. Ministry for Social

Affairs and Employment, The Hague, 1984.

Draijer, N., *The World in Reverse, Preliminary Study Commissioned by the Ministry for Social Affairs and Employment* [De omgekeerde wereld. Vooronderzoek in opdracht van het ministerie van Sociale Zaken en Werkgelegenheid]. The Hague, 1985.

Draijer, N., "Sexual Contacts between Children and Adults or Elders" in *Sexual Violence and Heterosexuality: Research Developments Since 1968* ["Sexsuele kontakten tussen kinderen en volwassenen of ouderen"]. Ministry of Social Affairs and Employment, The Hague, 1984.

Draijer, N., *Sexual Abuse of Girls by Relatives: A National Study of the Magnitude, Nature, Family Backgrounds, and Emotional, Psychological and Psychosomatic Impact* [Seksueel misbruik van meisjes door verwanten. Een landelijk onderzoek naar de omvang, de aard, de gezinsachtergronden, de emotionele betekenis en de psychische en psychosomatische gevolgen]. Amsterdam, 1988.

Dresen, G., and A. Van Heyst (ed.), *A Virtuous Woman* [Een sterke vrouw]. Amersfoort, 1984.

Dutch Reformed Churches, *Marriage Services of the Dutch Reformed Churches* [Huwelijksformulier van de Gereformeerde Kerken]. New edition, 1982.

Ensink, B. and F. Albach, *Fear of Sexual Violence* [Angst voor seksueel geweld]. Leiden, 1983.

Eversen, M., *Instructing Caring Services Professionals on Intrafamilial Child Sexual Abuse: Does it help?* [Voorlichting aan hulpverlenenden over seksuele kindermishandeling binnen het gezin: helpt dat?]. Thesis (MBO-sd), Leeuwarden, 1984.

Finkelhor, D., *Sexually Victimized Children.* New York, 1979.

Fiorenza, E. Schüssler, *In Memory of Her, A Feminist Theological Reconstruction of Christian Origins.* New York and London, 1983.

Fortune, M. M., *Sexual Violence, The Unmentionable Sin.* New York, 1984.

Foucault, M., *The History of Absurdity* [Geschiedenis van de waanzin]. Translation, Meppel, 1982.

Freire, P., *Pedagogy of the Oppressed.* New York and London, 1970; Harmondsworth, 1972.

Frenken, J., and J. Doomen, *Criminal Sexuality* [Strafbare seksualiteit]. Deventer, 1984.

Frenken, J. and C. Van Lichtenburcht, *Incest, Facts, Background and Caring Services: A Symposium* [Incest, feiten, achtergronden en hulpverlening – een symposium]. NISSO Studies, Zeist, 1984.

General Synod of Dutch Reformed Churches, *Order of Services for Reformed Churches in the Netherlands* [Orden van Dienst voor de Gereformeerde Kerken in Nederland]. Leusden, 1981.

Hacohen, Rabbi Shmoeël Avidor, *Touching Heaven, Touching Earth, Hassidic Humor & Wit* [Met één been op de grond, Chassidische humor en Wijsheid]. Tel Aviv (Israel), 1976; Dutch translation Amstelveen, 1976.

Hancock, E., *The Girl Within. A Groundbreaking New Approach to Female Identity.* New York, 1989.

Hendriks, J., *Emancipation* [Emancipatie]. Alphen a. d. Rijn, 1981.

Henderson, H., *Sexual Behavior in Practice: Fertile Days in Marriage* [Het seksueel Gedrag in de Praktijk; Vruchtbare dagen in het huwelijk]. General Netherlands Publishers, Rotterdam/ Antwerp, after 1954.

Herman, J. L., *Father-Daughter Incest.* Cambridge, Mass., 1981.

Hugolina, Sister, and G. J. Ten Dam, *The Carillon: Readings for Older Girls in our Catholic Grade Schools* [Het Klokkenspel; Leesstof voor oudere meisjes van onze katholieke scholen]. Helmond, 1952.

Imbens, J. E. L. Fransen, "Learning to Deal with the Fear of Rape, Lesson Models for Boys and Girls 14 years old and up" [Omgaan met angst voor verkrachting, Lesmodellen voor jongens en meisjes vanaf 14 jaar] in *Berichten en Belangen, Catechism Teachers Association Bulletin*, 1983 and 1984.

Imbens, J. E. L. Fransen, *Thecla and the Church* [Thekla en de kerk]. Voorburg, 1984.

Imbens, J. E. L. Fransen, "Women are Tired of Waiting" ["Vrouwen zijn het wachten beu"] in *De Bazuin* 64 1981, no. 37.

Imbens, J. E. L. Fransen, "It is better (not) to talk about it (*Daar kun je maar beter (niet) over praten*), Delft 1987.

Imbens, J. E. L. Fransen, Hold not thy peace, my brother (*Nu dan, mijn broeder, spreek erover*) Amsterdam, 1991.

Jeansonne, S. Pace, *The Women of Genesis, From Sarah to Potiphar's Wife.* Minneapolis, 1990.

John Paul II, *Male and Female in the Image of God.* Antwerp, 1981.

Kelly, L., *Surviving Sexual Violence.* Cambridge, England, 1988.

Kempe, R. S., and H. Kempe, "Child Abuse and Neglect", in *The International Journal*, 1984, no. 2.

Leonard, L., *The Wounded Woman* [Gekwetste Vrouw]. Rotterdam, 1983.

Man-u-script, no. 10, Eindhoven, May 1984.

Masson, J. M., *The Assault on Truth: Freud's Suppression of the Seduction Theory*. New York, 1984.

McGuire, L. S. and N. N. Wagner, "Sexual Dysfunction in Women who were molested as Children: One Response Pattern and Suggestions for Treatment" in *Journal of Sex and Marital Therapy* 4, 1978, no. 1.

Mernissi, F., *Beyond the Veil*, New York/London/Sydney/Toronto, 1975.

Meyer, J., *Gender as an Organization Principle* [Sekse als organisatieprincipe]. Amsterdam, 1983.

Mijlof, B. "The Association Against Child Sexual Abuse Within the Family" in J. Moors and H. Wemekamp, *Hands Off* [Handen thuis]. Deventer, 1984.

Miller, A., *Prisoners of Childhood: The Drama of the Gifted Child and the Search for the True Self*. Basic Books, New York, 1981.

National Liturgy Council, *Marriage* [Het Huwelijk]. Hilversum, 1981.

Neeskens, B., and A. Klein Herenbrink, *What's Incest?* [Wat heet incest]. Psychology thesis, Nijmegen, 1984.

Nelson, S. *Incest, facts and myths*, translation, Deventer, 1984.

New Directions in Language: New Language Method for Roman Catholic Elementary Schools Fifth Grade. [Taal in nieuwe banen: Nieuwe taalmethode voor het R. K. Lager ondermijs, vijfde klas]. J. F. Duwaer & Zonen, Amsterdam, 1957.

PSVG pamphlet no. 18, "Incest", 1983.

Rijnaarts, J., "Was Noreen Winchester an Exception? Fathers Who Rape Their Daughters" in *Socialist Feminist Readings*, 1979, no. 3, pp. 73–79.

Rijnaarts, J., "Thoughts on Intrafamilial Sexual Child Abuse (incest) in *Sexuality Theme Book*, University of Nijmegen's Women's Studies Winter Session, Nijmegen, 1983.

Roelofs, G. T., "Providing Help in Cases of Intrafamilial Child Sexual Abuse (exploitative incest)" [Hulpverlening bij sexueel misbruik van kinderen binnen het gezin (uitbuitingsincest)] in *Sextant*, 1983, no. 3, pp. 3–4.

Roelofs, G. T., "Sexuality Within the Family" [Seksualiteit binnen het gezin] in *Sexual Caring Services Handbook*, Deventer, 1984.

Ruether, R. Radford, *Mary – The Feminine Face of the Church*. Philadelphia, 1979.

Rush, F., *The Best Kept Secret: Sexual Abuse of Children*. New York, 1980.

Schillebeeckx, E., *God is New Every Moment: Conversations with Edward Schillebeeckx* [God is ieder ogenblik nieuw: Gesprekken met Edward Schillebeeckx]. Baarn, 1982.

Sgrogi, S., *Handbook of Clinical Intervention in Child Sexual Abuse.* Lexington, Mass. 1982.

Shepher, J., *Incest. A Biosocial View.* New York, 1983.

Simonis, A. J., *Thoughts on the Women's Place in Society and the Church* [Gedachten over de plaats van de vrouw in samenleving en kerk]. Lecture to the Catholic Women's Guild 1981 and for the KRO radio network ("Reflections", Sunday 11 May, 1980).

Sölle, D., *Suffering* [Lijden]. Translation, Baarn, 1979.

Sölle, D., *Fantasy and obedience: The Future and Christian Ethics* [Fantasie en gehoorzaamheid; toekomst en christelijke ethiek]. Translation, Baarn, 1979.

Sölle, D., *Choose Life* [Kies het leven]. Translation, Baarn, 1980.

Staa, M. and H. Woelinga, *If Your Father Owns You . . .* [Als je vader je bezit . . .]. Developmental Psychology thesis, Amsterdam, 1983.

Trible, Ph., "Eve and Adam: Genesis 3 – 3 Reread" in *Womanspirit Rising: A Feminist Reader in Religion.* Ed. C. P. Christ and J. Plaskow, New York, 1979.

Universal Declaration of Human Rights. UNO, New York, 1948.

Van Den Bosch, D., *You're Left Standing There . . . Alone* [Daar sta je dan . . . alleen]. Eindhoven, 1984.

Van Deun, G., *Missal Containing All Masses from the Missale Romanum* [Missaal bevattende alle missen van het missale Romanum]. Mosmans, Den Bosch, 1947.

Van Dijk, F., "Who Can Find A Virtuous Woman?" in *Teach Me About Women* (ed. H. Lam and S. Strikwerda) ["Een Sterke vrouw, wie zal haar vinden?"]. The Hague, 1981.

Van Dijk, F., "Reading the Bible from a Feminist Perspective" [Bijbellezen in feministisch perspectif] in *Woman and the Word* 2, 1982, no. 6.

Van Maris, B., and J. Rijnaarts, "Daughter and Sister Rape" [Dochter- en zusterverkrachting] in *Opzij*, 1983, no. 2, pp. 8–14.

Weinberg, S. K., *Incest Behaviour.* New York, 1955.

Welfare Weekly [Welzijnsweekblad], 1982, no. 34 (various authors).

Woolf, V., *A Room of One's Own.* New York, 1957.